To Teachers and School Officers.

Any school book published by the AMERICAN BOOK COMPANY will be sent to any address on receipt of the published list-price. Teachers and School Officers are cordially invited to correspond with the Company upon any matter pertaining to school books.

Descriptive and classified Price-lists, Bulletins of New Books, and other circulars of information will be sent free to any address on application to the Publishers:

AMERICAN BOOK COMPANY,

NEW YORK,   CINCINNATI,   CHICAGO.

THE NATIONAL STANDARD.

...

The Leading Series of School Books published in this Country are based
upon **WEBSTER**, the acknowledged Standard of the English Language

THE

ELEMENTARY
SPELLINGBOOK,

BEING

AN IMPROVEMENT

ON THE

AMERICAN SPELLING BOOK.

BY NOAH WEBSTER, LL.D.

THE LATEST REVISED EDITION.

NEW YORK ·:· CINCINNATI ·:· CHICAGO
AMERICAN BOOK COMPANY.

Sold by all the principal Booksellers throughout the
United States of America and its Territories.

STANDARD SCHOOL BOOKS.

The AMERICAN BOOK COMPANY invites the attention of Teachers and School Officers to its large and varied list of school and college text-books, which have been prepared by leading educators and represent the most approved methods of instruction.

Its list embraces standard books in every department of study and for every grade of schools.

The large number and great variety of its publications offer to school boards, principals, and teachers an exceptional opportunity to make a judicious selection of text-books suitable for the different subjects of study and for all grades of instruction. Catalogues, price-lists, and other circulars of information will be sent free on application to the Publishers:

AMERICAN BOOK COMPANY,

NEW YORK,   CINCINNATI,   CHICAGO.

PREFACE.

IN this revision of the Elementary Spelling Book, the chief object aimed at is to bring its notation into a correspondence with that of the recently issued Quarto Dictionary, in which a more extended system of orthoëpical marks has been adopted for the purpose of exhibiting the nicer discriminations of vowel sounds. A few of the Tables, however, and a few single columns of words, are left without diacritical signs as exercises in notation, a familiarity with which is important to all who consult the dictionary. A little attention to the *Key to the Sounds of the marked Letters* will aid both teacher and pupil in this interesting exercise. As it has been found inconvenient to insert the whole Key at the top of the page, as heretofore, frequent reference to the full explanation of the pointed letters on page 14 may be desirable.

In Syllabication it has been thought best not to give the etymological division of the Quarto Dictionary, but to retain the old mode of Dr. Webster as best calculated to teach *young* scholars the true pronunciation of words.

The plan of classification here executed is extended so as to comprehend every important variety of English words, and the classes are so arranged, with suitable directions for the pronunciation, that any pupil, who shall be master of these *Elementary Tables*, will find little difficulty in learning to form and pronounce any words that properly belong to our vernacular language.

The Tables intended for *Exercises* in Spelling and forming words, contain the original words, with the terminations only of their derivatives. These Tables will answer the important purposes of teaching the *manner* of forming the various derivatives, and the distinctions of the parts of speech, and thus anticipate, in some degree, the knowledge of grammar; at the same time, they bring into a small compass a much greater number of words than could be otherwise comprised in so small a book.

The pronunciation here given is that which is sanctioned by the most general usage of educated people, both in the United States and in England. There are a few words in both countries whose pronunciation is not settled beyond dispute. In cases of this kind, the Editor has leaned to regular analogies as furnishing the best rule of decision.

In orthography there are some classes of words in which usage is not uniform. No two English writers agree on this subject; and what is worse, no lexicographer is consistent with himself. In this book, as in Dr. Webster's dictionaries, that mode of spelling has been adopted which is the most simple and best authorized. The Editor has followed the rules that are held to be legitimate, and has rendered uniform all classes of words falling within them. If established rules and analogies will not control the practice of writers, there is no authority by which uniformity can be produced.

The reading lessons are adapted, as far as possible, to the capacities of children, and to their gradual progress in knowledge. These lessons will serve to substitute variety for the dull monotony of spelling, show the practical use of words in significant sentences, and thus enable the learner the better to understand them. The consideration of diversifying the studies of the pupil has also had its influence in the arrangement of the lessons for spelling. It is useful to teach children the signification of words, as soon as they can comprehend them; but the understanding can hardly keep pace with the memory, and the minds of children may well be employed in learning to spell and pronounce words whose signification is not within the reach of their capacities; for what they do not clearly comprehend at first, they will understand as their capacities are enlarged.

The objects of a work of this kind being chiefly to teach *orthography* and *pronunciation*, it is judged most proper to adapt the various Tables to these specific objects, and omit extraneous matter. In short, this little book is so constructed as to condense into the smallest compass a complete SYSTEM of ELEMENTS for teaching the language; and however small such a book may appear, it may be considered as the most important class book, not of a religious character, which the youth of our country are destined to use.

W. G. W.

NEW YORK, 1866.

PREFACE TO THE LATEST EDITION.

THE modifications in this revision are not of a character to embarrass those teachers who use the previous editions in the same class. The principal changes which have been made are :

In many instances an improved form of type ;

The substitution of living words in the place of those words which have become obsolete ;

The omission of orthoëpical marks where they are clearly unnecessary, as explained below ;

The correction of a few errors in pronunciation, etc., etc. ;

The addition, at the end of the book, of four new pages of common words difficult to spell.

The repetition of the orthoëpical mark has been omitted as needless in a succession of two or more words having the same vowel letter and sound. In such cases only the first word is marked—the marked syllable of this leading word being the key to the corresponding unmarked syllables in the words which follow. But whenever there is a liability to mispronunciation, the right way is indicated by marking the doubtful syllable.

ANALYSIS OF SOUNDS

IN THE ENGLISH LANGUAGE.

The Elementary Sounds of the English language are divided into two classes, ***vowels*** and ***consonants.***

A *vowel* is a clear sound made through an open position of the mouth-channel, which molds or shapes the voice without obstructing its utterance; as *a* (in *far*, in *fate*, etc.), *e*, *o*.

A *consonant* is a sound formed by a closer position of the articulating organs than any position by which a vowel is formed, as *b*, *d*, *t*, *g*, *sh*. In forming a consonant the voice is compressed or stopped.

A *diphthong* is the union of two simple vowel sounds, as *ou* (äŏŏ) in *out*, *oi* (aĭ) in *noise*.

The English Alphabet consists of twenty-six letters, or single characters, which represent vowel, consonant, and diphthongal sounds—a, b, c, d, e, f, g, h, i, j, k, l, m, n, o, p, q, r, s, t, u, v, w, x, y, z. The combinations *ch*, *sh*, *th*, and *ng* are also used to represent elementary sounds; and another sound is expressed by *s*, or *z*; as, in *measure*, *azure*, pronounced *mĕzh'ŏŏr*, *ăzh'ŭr*.

Of the foregoing letters, *a*, *e*, *o*, are always simple vowels; *i* and *u* are vowels (as in *in*, *us*), or diphthongs (as in *time*, *tune*); and *y* is either a vowel (as in *any*), a diphthong (as in *my*), or a consonant (as in *ye*).

Each of the vowels has its regular long and short sounds which are most used; and also certain *occasional* sounds, as that of *a* in *last*, *far*, *care*, *fall*, *what*; *e* in *term*, *there*, *prey*; *i* in *firm*, *marine*; *o* in *dove*, *for*, *wolf*, *prove*; and *u* in *furl*, *rude*, and *pull*. These will now be considered separately.

A. The regular long sound of *a* is denoted by a horizontal mark over it; as, ān'cient, pro-fāne'; and the regular short sound by a curve over it; as, căt, păr'ry.

Occasional sounds.—The Italian sound is indicated by two dots over it; as, bär, fä'ther;—the short sound of the Italian *a*, by a single dot over it; as, fȧst, lȧst; —the broad sound, by two dots below it; as, b̤all, st̤all;—the short sound of broad *a*, by a single dot under it; as, what, quạd'rant;—the sound of *a* before *r* in certain words like *care*, *fair*, etc., is represented by a sharp or pointed circumflex over the *a*, as, câre, hâir, fâir, etc.

E. The regular long sound of *e* is indicated by a horizontal mark over it; as, mēte, se-rēne'; the regular short sound, by a curve over it; as, mĕt, re-bĕl'.

Occasional sounds.—The sound of *e* like *a* in *care* is indicated by a pointed circumflex over the *e*, as in thêir, whêre; and of short *e* before *r* in cases where it verges toward short *u*, by a rounded circumflex, or wavy line, over it; as, hẽr, pre-fẽr'.

I, O, U. The regular long and short sounds of *i*, *o*, and *u* are indicated like those of *a* and *e* by a horizontal mark and by a curve; as, bīnd, bĭn; dōle, dŏll; tūne, tŭn.

Occasional sounds.—When *i* has the sound of long *e* it is marked by two dots over it; as, fä-tïgue', ma-rïne';—when *o* has the sound of short *u*, it is marked by a single dot over it; as, dȯve, sȯn;—when it has the sound of ōō, it is marked with two dots under it; as, mo̤ve, pro̤ve;—when it has the sound of ŏŏ, it is marked with a single dot under it; as, woḷf, wo'man;— when it has the sound of broad *a*, this is indicated by a pointed circumflex over the vowel; as, nôrth, sôrt; —the two letters *oo*, with a horizontal mark over them, have the sound heard in the words bōōm, lōōm;—with a curve mark, they have a shorter form of the same sound; as, bŏŏk, gŏŏd;—when *u* is sounded like short *oo*, it has a single dot under it; as, fụll, pụll; while its lengthened sound, as when preceded by *r*, is indicated by two dots; as in rṳde, rṳ'ral, rṳ'by.

Note.—The long *u* in unaccented syllables has, to a great extent, the sound of *oo*, preceded by *y*, as in *educate*, pronounced ĕd'yoo-kāte: *nature*, pronounced năt'yoor.

The long sound of *a* in *late*, when shortened, coincides nearly with that of *e* in *let*; as, *adequate, disconsolate, inveterate.*

The long *e*, when shortened, coincides nearly with the short *i* in *pit* (compare *feet* and *fit*). This short sound of *i* is that of *y* unaccented, at the end of words; as, in *glory*.

The short sound of broad *a* in *hall*, is that of the short *o* in *holly*, and of *a* in *what*.

The short sound of long *oo* in *pool*, is that of *u* in *pull*, and *oo* in *wool*.

The short sound of *o* in *not*, is somewhat lengthened before *s, th,* and *ng*; as in *cross, broth, belong.*

The pronunciation of the diphthongs *oi* and *oy* is the same and uniform; as, in *join, joy*.

The pronunciation of the diphthongs *ou* and *ow* is the same and uniform; as, in *sound, now*. But in the termination *ous, ou* is not a diphthong, and the pronunciation is *us*; as, in *pious, glorious.*

A combination of two letters used to express a single sound is called a digraph; as, *ea* in *head*, or *th* in *bath*.

The digraphs *ai* and *ay*, in words of one syllable, and in accented syllables, have the sound of *a* long. In the unaccented syllables of a few words, the sound of *a* is nearly or quite lost; as, in *certain, curtain*. The digraphs *au* and *aw*, have the sound of broad *a* (*a* in *fall*); *ew*, that of *u* long, as in *new*; and *ey*, in unaccented syllables, that of *y* or *i* short, as in *valley*.

When one vowel of a digraph is marked, the other has no sound; as, in *court, road, slow.*

The digraphs *ea, ee, ei, ie,* when not marked, have, in this book, the sound of *e* long; as, in *near, meet, seize, grieve.*

The digraph *oa*, when unmarked, has the sound of *o* long.

Vowels, in words of one syllable, followed by a single consonant and *e* final, are long; as, in *fate, mete, mite, note, mute,* unless marked, as in *dove, give.*

The articulations or sounds represented by the consonants are best apprehended by placing a vowel before them in pronunciation, and prolonging the second of the two elements; thus, eb, ed, ef, eg, ek, el, em, en, ep, er, es, et, ev, ez.

Those articulations which wholly stop the passage of the breath from the mouth, are called *close*, or *mute*, as b, d, g, k, p, t.

Those articulations which are formed either wholly or in part by the lips, are called *labials*; as, b, f, m, p, v.

Those which are formed by the tip of the tongue and the teeth, or the gum covering the roots of the teeth, are called *dentals*; as, d, t, th (as in *thin, this*).

Those which are formed by the flat surface of the tongue and the palate, are called *palatals*; as, g, k, ng, sh, j, y.

The letters *s* and *z* are called also *sibilants*, or hissing letters.

W (as in *we*) and **y** (as in *ye*) are sometimes called *semi-vowels*, as being intermediate between vowels and consonants, or partaking of the nature of both.

B and **p** represent one and the same position of the articulating organs; but *p* differs from *b* in being an utterance of the breath instead of the voice.

D and **t** stand for one and the same articulation, which is a pressure of the tongue against the gum at the root of the upper front teeth; but *t* stands for a whispered, and *d* for a vocal sound.

F and **v** stand for one and the same articulation, the upper teeth placed on the under lip; but *f* indicates an expulsion of voiceless breath; *v*, of vocalized breath, or tone.

Th in **thin** and **th** in **this** represent one and the same articulation, the former with breath, the latter with voice.

S and **z** stand for one and the same articulation; *s* being a hissing or whispered sound, and *z* a buzzing and vocal sound.

Sh and **zh** have the same distinction as *s* and *z*, whispered and vocal; but *zh* not occurring in English words, the sound is represented by *si* or by other letters; as, in *fusion, osier, azure*.

G and **k** are cognate letters, also **j** and **ch**, the first of each couplet being vocal, the second aspirate or uttered with breath alone.

Ng represents a nasal sound.

B has one sound only, as in *bite*. After *m*, or before *t*, it is generally mute; as in *dumb, doubt*.

C has the sound of *k* before *a, o, u, l* and *r*, as in *cat, cot, cup, clock*, and *crop;* and of *s* before *e, i*, and *y*, as in *cell, cit, cycle*. It may be considered as mute before *k;* as, in *sick, thick*. C, when followed by *e* or *i* before another vowel, unites with *e* or *i* to form the sound of *sh*. Thus, *cetaceous, gracious, conscience*, are pronounced *ce ta'shus, gra'shus, con'shense*.

D has its proper sound, as in *day, bid;* when preceded in the same syllable by a whispered or non-vocal consonant, it uniformly takes the sound of *t*, as in *hissed* (hist).

F has one sound only; as, in *life, fever*, except in *of*, in which it has the sound of *v*.

G before *a, o*, and *u*, is a close palatal articulation; as, in *gave, go, gun;* before *e, i*, and *y*, it sometimes represents the same articulation, but generally indicates a compound sound, like that of *j;* as in *gem, gin, gyves*. Before *n* in the same syllable it is silent; as, in *gnaw*.

H is a mark of mere breathing or aspiration. After *r* it is silent; as, in *rhetoric*.

I in certain words has the use of *y* consonant; as, in *million*, pronounced *mill'yun*. Before *r* it has a sound nearly resembling that of short *u*, but more open; as, in *bird, flirt*.

J represents a compound sound, pretty nearly equivalent to that represented by *dzh*; as, in *joy*.

K has one sound only; as, in *king*. It is silent before *n* in the same syllable; as, in *knave*.

L has one sound only; as, in *lame, mill*. It is silent in many words, especially before a final consonant; as, in *walk, calm, calf, should*.

M has one sound only; as, in *man, flame*. It is silent before *n* in the same syllable; as, in *mnemonics*.

N has one sound only; as, in *not, son*. It is silent after *l* and *m*; as, in *kiln, hymn, solemn*.

P has one sound only; as, in *pit, lap*. At the beginning of words, it is silent before *n, s,* and *t*; as, in *pneumatics, psalm, pshaw, ptarmigan*.

Q has the sound of *k*, but it is always followed by *u*, and these two letters are generally sounded like *kw*; as, in *question*.

R is sounded as in *rip, trip, form, carol, mire*.

S has its proper sound, as in *send, less;* or the sound of *z*, as in *rose*. Followed by *i* preceding a vowel, it unites with the vowel in forming the sound of *sh*; as in *mission,* pronounced *mish'un;*—or of its vocal correspondent *zh*; as in *osier*, pronounced *o'zher*.

T has its proper sound, as in *turn*, at the beginning of words and at the end of syllables. Before *i*, followed by another vowel, it unites with *i* to form the sound of *sh*, as in *nation, partial, patience,* pronounced *na'shun, par'shal, pa'shense*. But when *s* or *x* precedes *t*, this letter and the *i* following it preserve their own sounds; as in *bastion, Christian, mixtion,* pronounced *bast'yun, krist'yan, mikst'yun*. T is silent in the terminations *ten* and *tle* after *s;* as in *fasten, gristle;* also in the words *often, chestnut, Christmas,* etc.

V has one sound only; as, in *voice, live*, and is never silent.

W before *r* in the same syllable is silent, as in *wring, wrong*. In most words beginning with **wh**, the *h* precedes the *w* in utterance, that is, *wh* is simply an aspirated *w*; thus *when* is pronounced *hwen*. But if *o* follows this combination, the *w* is silent, as in *whole,* pronounced *hole*.

X represents *ks*, as in *wax;* but it is sometimes pronounced like *gz;* as, in *exact*. At the beginning of words, it is pronounced like *z;* as, in *Xenophon*.

Z has its proper sound, which is that of the vocal *s;* as, in *maze*.

Ch has very nearly the sound of *tsh;* as, in *church;* or the sound of *k;* as, in *character;* or of *sh*, as in *machine*.

Gh is mute in every English word, both in the middle and at the end of words, except in the following: *cough, chough, clough, enough, laugh, rough, slough, tough, trough,* in which it has the sound of *f*; *hough, lough, shough*, in which it has the sound of *k*; and *hiccough*, in which it has the sound of *p*. At the beginning of a word, it is pronounced like *g* hard; as in *ghastly, ghost, gherkin*, etc.; hence this combination may be said not to have a proper or regular sound in any English word.

Ph has the sound of *f*, as in *philosophy*; except in *Stephen*, pronounced *Ste'rn*.

Sh has one sound only; as. in *shall*.

Th has two sounds; whispered, as in *think, both*; and vocal, as in *thou, this*. When vocal, the *th* is marked thus, (th) as in thou.

Sc has the sound of *sk*, before *a, o, u*, and *r*; as. in *scale. scoff, sculpture, scroll*; and the sound of *s* alone before *e, i*, and *y*; as, in *scene, scepter, science, Scythian*.

ACCENT.

Accent is a forcible stress or effort of voice on a syllable, distinguishing it from others in the same word, by a greater distinctness of sound.

The accented syllable is designated by the mark (').

The general principle by which accent is regulated, is, that the stress of voice falls on that syllable of a word, which renders the articulations most easy to the speaker, and most agreeable to the hearer. By this rule has the accent of most words been imperceptibly established by a long and universal consent.

When a word consists of three or more syllables, ease of speaking requires usually a secondary accent, of less forcible utterance than the primary, but clearly distinguishable from the pronunciation of unaccented syllables; as in *su'perflu'ity, lit'era'ry*.

KEY TO THE PRONUNCIATION.
VOWELS.
REGULAR LONG AND SHORT SOUNDS.

LONG.—ā, as in *fame*; ē, as in *mete*; ī, as in *fine*; ō, as in *note*; ū, as in *mute*; ȳ, as in *fly*.

SHORT.—ă, as in *fat*; ĕ, as in *met*; ĭ, as in *fin*; ŏ, as in *not*; ŭ, as in *but*; y̆, as in *nymph*.

See over.

VOWELS.—Occasional Sounds.

EXAMPLES.

â, as in *care*, ... âir, shâre, pâir, beâr.

ä *Italian*, as in . . . . fäther, fär, bälm, päth.

a̤, as in *last*, ... a̤sk, gra̤ss, da̤nce, bra̤nch.

a̤ *broad*, as in *all*, . . . ca̤ll, ta̤lk, ha̤ul, swa̤rm.

a̤, as in *what* (like short *o*) wa̤n, wa̤nton, wa̤llow.

ê like â, as in . . . . thêre, hêir, whêre, êre.

ē, as in *term*, ... ērmine, vērge, prefēr.

e̜ like long *a*, as in . . pre̜y, the̜y, e̜ight.

ï like long *e*, as in . . pïque, machïne, mïen.

ĭ, as in *bird*, ... fĭrm, vĭrgin, dĭrt.

ȯ like short *u*, as in . . dȯve, sȯn, dȯne, wȯn.

o̤ like long *oo*, as in . . pro̤ve, do̤, mo̤ve, to̤mb.

o̤ like short *oo*, as in . . bo̤som, wo̤lf, wo̤man.

ô like broad *a*, as in . . ôrder, fôrm, stôrk.

ōō (long *oo*), as in . . . mōōn, fōōd, bōōty.

ŏŏ (short *oo*), as in . . fŏŏt, bŏŏk, wŏŏl, gŏŏd.

u long, preceded by *r*, as in ru̜de, ru̜mor, ru̜ral.

ṳ like ŏŏ, as in . . . . pṳt, pṳsh, pṳll, fṳll.

e, i, o (italic) are silent . tok*e*n, cous*i*n, mas*o*n.

Regular Diphthongal Sounds.

oi, or oy (unmarked), as in . oil, join, toy.

ou, or ow (unmarked), as in out, owl, vowel.

CONSONANTS. EXAMPLES.

ç *soft*, like *s sharp*, as in . çede, merçy.

e *hard*, like *k*, as in . . . call, concur.

ch (unmarked), as in . . child, choose, much.

çh *soft*, like *sh*, as in . . . machine, çhaise.

eh *hard*, like *k*, as in . . chorus, epoch.

ḡ *hard*, as in . . . . ḡet, beḡin, foḡḡy.

ġ *soft*, like *j*, as in . . . ġentle, ġinġer, eleġy.

s *sharp* (unmarked), as in . same, gas, dense.

s̤ *soft*, or *vocal*, like *z*, as in . ha̤s, amṳse, prison.

th *sharp* (unmarked), as in . thing, path, truth.

t̲h *flat*, or *vocal*, as in . . t̲hine, t̲heir, wit̲her.

ng (unmarked), as in . . . sing, single.

n̲ (much like *ng*), as in . . lin̲ger, lin̲k, un̲cle.

x̲, like *gz*, as in . . . . ex̲ist, aux̲iliary.

ph (unmarked), like *f*, as in sylph. qu (unmarked), like *kw*, as in queen.
wh (unmarked), like *hw*, as in what, when, awhile.

14

THE ALPHABET.

ROMAN LETTERS.		ITALIC.		NAMES OF LETTERS.
a	A	*a*	*A*	a
b	B	*b*	*B*	be
c	C	*c*	*C*	ce
d	D	*d*	*D*	de
e	E	*e*	*E*	e
f	F	*f*	*F*	ef
g	G	*g*	*G*	je
h	H	*h*	*H*	aytch
i	I	*i*	*I*	i
j	J	*j*	*J*	ja
k	K	*k*	*K*	ka
l	L	*l*	*L*	el
m	M	*m*	*M*	em
n	N	*n*	*N*	en
o	O	*o*	*O*	o
p	P	*p*	*P*	pe
q	Q	*q*	*Q*	cu
r	R	*r*	*R*	ar
s	S	*s*	*S*	es
t	T	*t*	*T*	te
u	U	*u*	*U*	u
v	V	*v*	*V*	ve
w	W	*w*	*W*	double u
x	X	*x*	*X*	eks
y	Y	*y*	*Y*	wi
z	Z	*z*	*Z*	ze
&*		*&**		and

— ◆◆ —

DOUBLE LETTERS.

ff, ffl, fi, fl, ffi, æ, œ.

* This is not a letter, but a character standing for *and*.

OLD ENGLISH.

𝕬 𝕭 𝕮 𝕯 𝕰 𝕱 𝕲 𝕳 𝕴 𝕵 𝕶 𝕷 𝕸 𝕹
𝕺 𝕻 𝕼 𝕽 𝕾 𝕿 𝖀 𝖁 𝖂 𝖃 𝖄 𝖅 &

𝖆 𝖇 𝖈 𝖉 𝖊 𝖋 𝖌 𝖍 𝖎 𝖏 𝖐 𝖑 𝖒 𝖓 𝖔 𝖕 𝖖 𝖗 𝖘
𝖙 𝖚 𝖛 𝖜 𝖝 𝖞 𝖟

SCRIPT.

A B C D E F G H
I J K L M N O
P Q R S T U V
W X Y Z

a b c d e f g h i j k l m n o p q
r s t u v w x y z

1 2 3 4 5 6 7 8 9 0

No. 1.—I.

ba	be	bi	bo	bu	by
ça	çe	çi	ço	çu	çy
da	de	di	do	du	dy
fa	fe	fi	fo	fu	fy
ga	ge	gi	go	gu	gy

go on.	by me.	it is.	is he?
go in.	we go.	to me.	he is.
go up.	to us.	to be.	I am.
an ox.	do go.	on it.	on us.

No. 2.—II.

hā	hē	hī	hō	hū	hȳ
ja	je	ji	jo	ju	jy
ka	ke	ki	ko	ku	ky
la	le	li	lo	lu	ly
ma	me	mi	mo	mu	my
na	ne	ni	no	nu	ny

is he in?	do go on.	is it on?
he is in.	I do go on.	it is on.
is he up?	is it so?	is it in?
he is up.	it is so.	it is in.

No. 3.—III.

pā	pē	pī	pō	pū	pȳ
ra	re	ri	ro	ru	ry
sa	se	si	so	sū	sy
ta	te	ti	to	tu	ty
va	ve	vi	vo	vu	vy
wa	we	wi	wo	wu	wy

is he to go?	is it by us?	we go to it.
he is to go.	it is by us.	he is by me.
am I to go?	if he is in.	so he is up.
I am to go.	go up to it.	so I am up.

No. 4.—IV.

ăb	ĕb	ĭb	ŏb	ŭb
ae	ee	ie	oe	ue
ad	ed	id	od	ud
af	ef	if	of	uf
ag	eg	ig	og	ug

am I to go in?   so he is to go up.
I am to go in.   is he to be by me?
is he to go in?   he is to be by me.
he is to go in.   I am to be by it.

No. 5.—V.

ăj	ĕj	ĭj	ŏj	ŭj
ak	ek	ik	ok	uk
al	el	il	ol	ul
am	em	im	om	um
an	en	in	on	un
ap	ep	ip	op	up

No. 6.—VI.

är	ẽr	îr	ôr	ûr
ăs	ĕs	ĭs	ŏs	ŭs
at	et	it	ot	ut
av	ev	iv	ov	uv
ax	ex	ix	ox	ux
az	ez	iz	oz	uz

is he to do so by me?   it is to be by me.
he is to do so by me.   by me it is to be.
so I am to be in.   I am to be as he is.
he is to go up by it.   he is to be as I am.

No. 7.—VII.

blā	blē	blī	blō	blū	blȳ
ela	ele	eli	elo	elu	ely
fla	fle	fli	flo	flu	fly
gla	gle	gli	glo	glu	gly
pla	ple	pli	plo	plu	ply
sla	sle	sli	slo	slu	sly

No. 8.—VIII.

brā	brē	brī	brō	brụ	brȳ
era	ere	eri	ero	erụ	ery
dra	dre	dri	dro	drụ	dry.

MQVE, SÓN, WQLF, FÓOT, MÓON, ÔR ; RULF, PULL ; EXIST ; €=K ; Ġ= J ; Ș= Z ; ÇH= SH.

frā	frē	frī	frō	frų	frȳ
gra	gre	gri	gro	grü	gry

No. 9.—IX.

prā	prē	prī	prō	prų	prȳ
tra	tre	tri	tro	trų	try
wra	wre	wri	wro	wrų	wry
cha	che	chi	cho	chū	chy
sha	she	shi	sho	shu	shy
ska	ske	ski	sko	sku	sky

She fed the old hen.
The hen was fed by her.
See how the hen can run.
I met him in the lot.
The cow was in the lot.
See how hot the sun is.
It is hot to-day.
See the dog run to me.
She has a new hat.

She put her hat on the bed.
Did you get my hat?
I did not get the hat.
My hat is on the peg.
She may go and get my hat.
I will go and see the man.
He sits on a tin box.

No. 10.—X.

phā	phē	phī	phō	phū	phȳ
qua	que	qui	quo	quy	qu
spa	spe	spi	spo	spu	spy
sta	ste	sti	sto	stu	sty
sea	sçe	sçi	seo	seu	sçy
swa	swe	swi	swo	swu	swy

No. 11.—XI.

splā	splē	splī	splō	splū	splȳ
spra	spre	spri	spro	sprų	spry
stra	stre	stri	stro	strų	stry
shra	shre	shri	shro	shrų	shry

BÄR, LÄST, CÂRE, FALL, WHĄT: HẼR, PRẸY, THÉRE; G̃ET; BĪRD, MARĪNE; LIŊK;

| serā | serē | serī | serō | seru̧ | serȳ |
| sela | selc | seli | selo | selū | sely |

No. 12.—XII.

eăb	fĭb	hŏb	eūb	săp	lăd	bĭd	gŏd
dab	jib	job	dub	rĭp	mad	hid	hod
nab	nib	lob	sub	nip	pad	did	sod
tab	rib	mob	hub	sŏp	sad	lid	nod
nĕb	bŏb	rob	rub	băd	lĕd	rid	odd
web	cob	sob	tub	gad	red	kid	pod
bĭb	fob	bŭb	lăp	had	wed	mid	rod

A new cap.

A cob-web.

He has got a new tub.

He is not a bad boy.

The lad had a new pen.

He saw a mad dog.

She led him to bed.

I hid it in the box.

Put on his new bib.

Do not go to the tub.

She can rub off the dust.

She put my cap in the tub.

He had a new red cap.

I can do as I am bid.

No. 13.—XIII.

lŏg	cūd	făg	tăg	pĭg	dŭg	păg	kăm
dog	mud	hag	rag	fig	hug	rug	lam
bog	băg	jag	wag	rig	jug	dăm	jam
bŭd	cag	lag	lĕg	wig	tug	ham	ram
rud	sag	nag	keg	bŭg	mug	jam	yam

She has a new bag for me.

I can tag the boy.

A big dog can run.

He has fed the pig.

The man can put on his wig.

My nag can run in the lot.

Do not let a bug get on the bed.

I put the mug in my new tin box.

I can rub the ink off my pen on a rag.

He may put the red jug in my new tin box.

No. 14.—X I V.

hĕm	gŭm	dăn	rĕn	mĕn	fĭn	wĭn	gŭn
ġem	hum	fan	ben	pen	hin	€ŏn	pun
dĭm	mum	man	den	ten	kin	don	run
him	rum	pan	fen	wen	pin	bŭn	sun
rim	sum	ran	hen	bĭn	sin	dun	tun
dŭm	băn	tan	ken	din	tin	fun	nun

No. 15.—X V.

hăp	găp	pĭp	mŏp	fär	făt	văt	nĕt
rap	dĭp	sip	top	tar	rat	bĕt	wet
map	hip	kip	pop	jar	hat	jet	pet
lap	rip	nip	sop	mar	mat	ġet	set
pap	tip	fŏp	lop	par	sat	let	yet
tap	lip	hop	bär	băt	pat	met	hăş

No. 16.—X V I.

bĭt	pĭt	jŏt	gŏt	nŭt	vĕx	fŏx	eăn
çit	sit	lot	wot	rut	fĭx	wạd	eap
fit	wit	not	bŭt	lăx	mix	wạn	eat
lit	bŏt	pot	€ut	tax	pix	wạr	sap
mit	€ot	ro⁺	hut	wax	six	wạş	ġĭn
nit	dot	sot	jut	sĕx	bŏx	wạt	chit

Ann can hem my cap.
She has a new fan.
He hid in his den.
The pig is in his pen.
I see ten men.
He had a gun.
I saw him run.
The map is wet.
She will sit by me.
He has €ut my pen.
I had a nut to eat.
€an you get my hat?

It is in my lap.
I will get a new map.
A bat can fly.
A €at can eat a rat.
I met the boy.
He sat on my box.
Now the sun is set.
I met six men to-day
Ten men sat by me.
I put the pin on my tin box.
Let him get the wax.

BÄR, LÀST, ÇÂRE, FALL, WHAT; HÉR, PREY, THÉRE; ĞET; BÎRD, MARÎNE; LIŊK;

No. 17.—XVII.

bābe	hīde	mōde	āçe	bīçe	eāğe	lāke
ċade	ride	lode	dace	dice	gaġe	take
fade	side	node	face	lice	paġe	make
jade	tide	rode	lace	mice	raġe	rake
lade	wide	lobe	pace	nice	saġe	sake
made	ōde	robe	race	rice	dōġe	hake
wade	bode	eābe	mace	vice	hūġe	wake
bīde	ċode	tube	īce	āġe	bāke	ċake

No. 18.—XVIII.

dīke	yōke	dāle	mīle	dōle	eāme	
like	dūke	male	nile	hole	dame	
pike	Luke	hale	pile	mole	fame	
tike	fluke	pale	tile	pole	game	
ċōke	āle	sale	vile	sole	lame	
joke	bale	tale	wile	tole	name	
poke	eale	bīle	bōle	mūle	same	
woke	gale	file	eole	rüle	tame	

No. 19.—XIX.

āpe	rīpe	mōpe	ōre	mōre	wōve	
eāpe	wipe	hope	bore	sore	gāze	
tape	tȳpe	rope	eore	tore	haze	
nape	ċōpe	mēre	fore	yore	maze	
rape	pope	here	gore	eove	raze	
pīpe	lope	sere	lore	rove	eraze	

No. 20.—XX.

ċūre	kīne	lāne	āte	bīte	dōse	
lure	nine	mane	date	çite	bone	
pure	pine	pane	gate	kite	eone	
dīne	sine	sane	fate	mite	zone	
fine	wine	eane	hate	rite	hone	
line	vine	wane	late	site	tone	
mine	bāne	base	mate	dive	Jūne	

MOVE, SÒN, WOLF, FŎOT, MŌON, ÔR; RŬLE, PULL; EXIST; ç=K; ḡ=J, ṣ=Z; ÇH=SH.

tīne	vāne	eāse	pāte	hīve	tūne
fāne	vase	rate	rīve	fāme	sāne

No. 21.—XXI.

tōrn	ălps	eămp	ĭmp	bŭmp	rŭmp
worn	sealp	lamp	ḡimp	dump	erump
sworn	hĕlp	elamp	limp	chump	pump
ûrn	kelp	ramp	pimp	jump	trump
burn	yelp	eramp	erimp	lump	eärp
churn	ḡŭlp	stamp	shrimp	elump	searp
spurn	pulp	vamp	pŏmp	plump	harp
turn	dămp	hĕmp	romp	mump	sharp

No. 22.—XXII.

ȧsp	erĭsp	chŏps	pīet	rȧft	wĕft
gasp	wisp	ăet	striet	eraft	ḡĭft
hasp	drĕgṣ	faet	dŭet	draft	shift
elasp	tŏngṣ	paet	ȧft	graft	lift
rasp	lŭngṣ	taet	baft	waft	rift
grasp	lĕnṣ	traet	haft	hĕft	drift
lĭsp	ḡŭlf	sĕet	shaft	left	sift

No. 23.—XXIII.

ŏft	pĕlt	eōlt	ȧnt	pĕnt	dĭnt
loft	welt	dolt	chant	çent	lint
soft	ḡĭlt	jolt	grant	spent	flint
tŭft	hilt	hold	slant	rent	splint
bĕlt	milt	eănt	pant	sent	mint
felt	spilt	seant	bĕnt	tent	print
melt	tilt	plant	dent	vent	tint
smelt	bōlt	rant	lent	went	stint

No. 24.—XXIV.

brŭnt	wĕpt	smärt	snôrt	lȧst	zèst
grunt	swept	part	sort	blast	hest
runt	ärt	tart	tort	mast	chest

ăpt	eärt	stärt	hûrt	påst	jĕst
chapt	dart	pĕrt	shīrt	vast	lest
kĕpt	hart	vert	flirt	dĭdst	blest
slept	chart	wert	eàst	midst	nest
erept	mart	shôrt	fast	bĕst	pest

No. 25.—XXV.

rĕst	quĕst	mĭst	eŏst	thĭrst	lŭst
erest	west	grist	fîrst	bŭst	must
drest	zest	wrist	bûrst	dust	rust
test	fĭst	wist	eurst	gust	erust
vest	list	lŏst	durst	just	trust

Fire will burn wood and coal.
Coal and wood will make a fire.
The world turns round in a day.
Will you help me pin my frock?
Do not sit on the damp ground.
We burn oil in tin and glass lamps.
The lame man limps on his lame leg.
We make ropes of hemp and flax.
A rude girl will romp in the street.
The good girl may jump the rope.
A duck is a plump fowl.
The horse drinks at the pump.
A pin has a sharp point.
We take up a brand of fire with the tongs.
Good boys and girls will act well.
How can you test the speed of your horse?
He came in haste, and left his book.
Men grind corn and sift the meal.
We love just and wise men.
The wind will drive the dust in our eyes.
Bad boys love to rob the nests of birds.
Let us rest on the bed, and sleep, if we can.
Tin and brass will rust when the air is damp.

MǪVE, SǑN, WǪLF, FŎŎT, MŎŎN, ǑR; RỤLE, PỤLL; EXIST; €=K; ĝ=J; S̲=Z; ÇH=SH.

No. 26.—XXVI.

WORDS OF TWO SYLLABLES, ACCENTED ON THE FIRST.

bā´ ker	trō ver	sō lar	wō fụl	pā pal
sha dy	elo ver	po lar	po em	eō pal
la dy	do nor	lū nar	fo rụm	vī al
tī dy	vā por	sō ber	Sā tan	pē nal
hō ly	fa vor	pā çer	fū eĭ	ve nal
lī my	fla vor	ra çer	du el	fī nal
sli my	sa vor	grō çer	erụ el	ō ral
bō ny	ha lo	çī der	grụ el	ho ral
po ny	sō lo	spi der	pū pĭl	mū ral
po ker	hē ro	wā fer	lā bel	nā sal
tī ler	ne gro	ea per	lī bel	fa tal
eā per	tȳ ro	tī ĝer	lō eal	na tal
pa per	out go	mā ker	fo eal	rụ ral
ta per	sā go	ta ker	vo eal	vī tal
vī per	tū lip	ra ker	lē gal	tō tal
bi ter	çē dar	sē ton	re gal	o val
fē ver	brī er	rụ in	dī al	plī ant
ō ver	fri ar	hȳ men	tri al	ĝi ant

Bakers bake bread and cakes.
I like to play in the shady grove.
Some fishes are very bony.
I love the young lady that shows me how to read.
A pony is a very little horse.
We poke the fire with the poker.
The best paper is made of linen rags.
Vipers are bad snakes, and they bite men.
An ox loves to eat clover.
The tulip is very pretty, growing in the garden.
A dial shows the hour of the day.
Cedar trees grow in the woods.
The blackberry grows on a brier.

BÄR, LÅST, CÁRE, FALL, WHAT; HÊR, PREY, THÉRE; ĜET; BÎRD, MARÏNE; LIŊK;

Cider is made of apples.
A tiger will kill and eat a man.
A raker can rake hay.
A vial is a little bottle.
A giant is a very stout, tall man.
The Holy Bible is the book of God.

No. 27.—XXVII.

scăb	erĭb	grŭb	blĕd	plŏd	stăg
stab	drib	shrub	bred	trod	serag
blab	squib	stub	sped	seŭd	snag
slab	chŭb	shăd	shred	stud	drag
crab	club	clad	shed	slug	swag
drab	snub	glad	sled	brag	flag
glĭb	scrub	brad	shŏd	crag	sham
snib	drub	flĕd	clod	shag	cram

No. 28.—XXVIII.

clăm	prĭm	scăn	spĭn	trăp	slĭp
dram	trim	clan	grin	serap	grip
slam	swim	plan	twin	strap	serip
swam	frŏm	span	chăp	chĭp	drip
stĕm	seŭm	bran	clap	ship	trip
skĭm	plum	glĕn	flap	skip	strip
brim	grum	chĭn	slap	clip	frit
grim	drum	skin	snap	flip	split

No. 29.—XXIX.

chŏp	chär	flăt	slĭt	blŏt	slŭt
shop	spar	plat	smit	clot	smut
slop	star	spat	spit	plot	glut
crop	stĭr	brat	split	spot	strut
stop	blûr	frĕt	grit	grot	flăx
prop	slur	whet	seŏt	trot	flŭx
scär	spur	tret	shot	shŭt	flŏss

MOVE, SÓN, WQLF, FŎŎT, MŌŌN, ÔR; RŪLE, PŲLL; EXIST; Є=K; Ġ=J; S̩=Z; ÇH=SH.

Ann can spin flax.
A shad can swim.
He was glad to see me.
The boy can ride on a sled.
A plum will hang by a stem.
The boy had a drum.

He must not drink a dram.
He set a trap for a rat.
Ships go to sea.
The boy can chop.
The man shot a ball.
I saw her skim the milk in a pan.

No. 30.—X X X.

bŭlb	bōld	bănd	brănd	wĕnd	fŏnd
bärb	eold	hand	ĕnd	blend	pond
garb	gold	land	bend	bīnd	fŭnd
ħērb	ḟeld	rand	fend	find	bärd
verb	hold	bland	lend	hind	eard
eûrb	mold	grand	mend	kind	hard
chīld	sold	gland	rend	mind	lard
mild	told	sand	send	rind	pard
wild	seold	stand	tend	wind	searf
ōld	ănd	strand	vend	bŏnd	bīrd

No. 31.—X X X I.

hērd	sûrf	sŭch	lănch	bŭnch	lătch
eûrd	seurf	fĭlch	blanch	hunch	match
surd	rĭch	milch	branch	lunch	patch
turf	mŭch	pătch	stanch	punch	snatch
ärch	pouch	erŏtch	dĭtch	swĭtch	erŭtch
march	erouch	botch	hitch	twitch	Dutch
starch	tôrch	blotch	pitch	skĕtch	plush
harsh	chûrch	ĭtch	stitch	stretch	flush
marsh	lurch	bitch	witch	elŭtch	erush

To filch is to steal. We must not filch.
A bird sits on a branch to sing.

No. 32.--XXXII.

WORDS OF TWO SYLLABLES, ACCENTED ON THE SECOND.

a bāse′	re elāim′	un sāy′	ben zoin′
de base	pro elaim	as say	a void
in ease	dis elaim	a way	a droit
a bate	ex elaim	o bey	ex ploit
de bate	de mēan	eon vey	de eoy
se date	be mōan	pur vey	en joy
ere ate	re tāin	sur vey	al loy
ob late	re main	de fȳ	em ploy
re late	en grōss	af fȳ	an noy
in flate	dis ereet	de nȳ	de stroy
eol late	al lāy	de erȳ	eon voy
trans late	de lay	re boil	es pouse
mis state	re lay	de spoil	ea rouse
re plēte	in lay	em broil	de vour
eom plete	mis lay	re eoil	re dound
se erete	dis play	sub join	de vout
re çīte	de eay	ad join	a mount
in çite	dis may	re join	sur mount
po lite	de fray	en join	dis mount
ig nite	ar ray	eon join	re eount
re deem	be tray	dis join	re nown
es teem	ˋpōr tray	mis join	en dow
de elāim	a stray	pur loin	a vow

Strong drink will debase a man.

Hard shells incase clams and oysters.

Men inflate balloons with gas, which is lighter than common air.

Teachers like to see their pupils polite to each other.

Idle men often delay till to-morrow things that should be done to-day.

MOVE, SÔN, WOLF, FOOT, MOÔN, ÔR ; RULE, PULL ; EXIST ; €=K ; Ġ=J ; S=Z ; ÇH=SH.

Good men obey the laws of God.

I love to survey the starry heavens.

Careless girls mislay their things.

The fowler decoys the birds into his net.

Cats devour rats and mice.

The adroit ropedancer can leap and jump and perform as many exploits as a monkey.

Wise men employ their time in doing good to all around them.

In the time of war, merchant vessels sometimes have a convoy of ships of war.

Kings are men of high renown,

Who fight and strive, to wear a crown.

God created the heavens and the earth in six days, and all that was made was very good.

To purloin is to steal.

No. 33.—XXXIII.

deed	breed	glee	steel	green	sleek
feed	seed	free	deem	seen	meek
heed	weed	tree	seem	teen	reek
bleed	bee	eel	teem	steen	creek
meed	fee	feel	sheen	queen	Greek
need	see	heel	keen	ween	seek
speed	lee	peel	spleen	leek	week
reed	flee	reel	sereen	cheek	beef

No. 34.—XXXIV.

deep	weep	leer	lees	meet	brood
sheep	sweep	fleer	bees	greet	geese
keep	beer	sneer	beet	street	fleece
sleep	deer	peer	feet	sweet	sleeve
peep	cheer	seer	sheet	food	reeve
creep	sheer	steer	fleet	mood	breeze
steep	jeer	queer	sleet	rood	freeze

BÄR, LÀST, €ÂRE, F̧ALL, WḨĄT: HȨR, PRȨY, THȨRE; ĠET; B̈IRD, MARÌNE; LIN̦K;

No. 35.--XXXV.

boom	groom	loo	troop	boose	rook
€oom	boon	€oo	stoop	choose	brook
doom	loon	two	swoop	noose	€rook
loom	moon	€oop	boor	€ook	took
bloom	noon	scoop	moor	hook	wool
gloom	spoon	loop	poor	look	wood
room	soon	sloop	loose	stook	good
broom	swoon	droop	goose	nook	stood
fool	spool	boot	root	proof	són
pool	stool	€oot	roof	blóod	wón
tool	roost	moot	woof	flóod	tón

Plants grow in the ground from seeds.
The man cuts down trees with his ax.
Eels swim in the brook.
Sharp tools are made of steel.
The sun seems to rise and set each day.
The ax has a keen edge and cuts well.
In the spring the grass looks green and fresh.
I have seen the full moon.
A king and queen may wear crowns of gold.
I will kiss the babe on his cheek.
We go to church on the first day of the week.
The man put a curb round our deep well.
Wool makes the sheep warm.
Men keep their pigs in pens.
We lie down and sleep in beds.
The new broom sweeps clean.
The wild deer runs in the woods.
The red beet is good to eat.
If I meet him in the street. I will greet him with
    a kind look, and show him my new book.

MOVE, SŎN, WOLF, FŎOT, MOŌN, ŎR; RULE, PULL; EXIST; €=K; Ġ=J; Ş=Z; ÇH=SH.

No. 36.-- XXXVI.

băck	păck	quăck	quĭck	rĭck	wĭck
hack	rack	bĕck	chick	brick	€lŏck
jack	€rack	deck	€lick	€rick	lock
lack	track	chĕck	kick	trick	block
black	sack	neck	lick	sick	hock
slack	tack	pĕck	nick	tick	shock
smack	stack	speck	pick	stick	flock

No. 37.—XXXVII.

pŏck	chŭck	stŭck	bŭlk	€lănk	prănk
rock	luck	ĕlk	hulk	flank	tank
brock	€luck	welk	skulk	plank	ĭnk
€rock	pluck	yelk	bănk	slank	link
frock	muck	ĭlk	dank	rank	blink
mock	truck	bilk	hank	€rank	€link
sock	struck	silk	shank	drank	slink
bŭck	suck	milk	lank	frank	sink
duck	tuck	kilt	blank	shrank	brink

No. 38.—XXXVIII.

prĭnk	drŭnk	märk	īrk	ȧsk	dĭsk
shrink	trunk	park	dirk	bask	risk
mink	sunk	spark	kirk	€ask	brisk
wink	slunk	stark	quirk	hask	frisk
drink	ärk	jĕrk	€ôrk	flask	bŭsk
pink	lark	€lerk	fork	mask	dusk
spŭnk	dark	perk	stork	task	husk
junk	hark	smĭrk	lûrk	dĕsk	bŏss
skunk	shark	shīrk	Turk	whĭsk	tŭft

The smell of the pink is sweet.
I can play when my task is done.

BÄR, LÁST, CÂRE, FALL, WHĂT; HÊR, PREY, THÈRE; ĞET; BÎRD, MAFÎNE; LIŊK;

No. 39.—XXXIX.

bŭsk	snärl	chûrl	bärm	bärn	bŏrn
musk	twĭrl	purl	farm	tarn	eorn
rusk	whirl	ĕlm	harm	yaru	seorn
tusk	eûrl	helm	charm	kĕrn	morn
dusk	furl	fĭlm	spĕrm	fern	lorn
märl	hurl	ärm	term	stern	horn

No. 40.—XL.

ḡăff	seŏff	pŭff	eall	wąll	quĕll
staff	doff	ruff	fall	thrall	well
quaff	bŭff	stuff	gall	small	dwell
skĭff	euff	ădd	hall	squall	swell
eliff	huff	ŏdd	mall	smĕll	ĭll
tiff	luff	ĕgg	pall	spell	bill
stiff	bluff	ąll	tall	sell	quill
ŏff	muff	ball	stall	tell	ebb

No. 41.—XLI

ḡĭll	kĭll	stĭll	rōll	dŭll	ĭnn
ḡąll	skill	quill	seroll	gull	bin
hill	shrill	squill	droll	hull	wrĕn
mill	spill	will	troll	skull	bûrr
rill	trill	swill	stroll	lull	purr
drill	sill	bōll	toll	mull	bụsh
frill	fill	poll	eŭll	trull	pụsh

No. 42.—XLII.

ăss	trăss	ḡŭĕss	kĭss	mŏss	trŭss
bass	brass	less	bliss	eross	bust
lass	grass	bless	miss	dross	bûr
glass	çĕss	mess	Swiss	eost	bụll
elass	dress	eress	bŏss	bŭss	fụll
mass	press	chess	loss	fuss	pụss
pass	stress	tress	gloss	muss	hûrt

MOVE, SÒN, WOLF, FŎŎT, MOÒN, ÔR; RULE, PULL; EXIST; €=K; Ġ=J; Ş=Z; CH=SH.

No. 43.—XLIII.

SINGULAR.	PLURAL.	SINGULAR.	PLURAL.	SINGULAR.	PLURAL.
stāve	stāveş	ĕgg	ĕggş	quĭll	quĭllş
clĭff	clĭffs	hạll	hạllş	pōll	pōllş
mill	millş	wall	wallş	skŭll	skŭllş
pill	pillş	bĭll	bĭllş	ĭnn	ĭnnş
bạll	bạlls	sill	sillş	bĕll	bĕllş

A skiff is a small rowboat.

A cliff is a high steep rock.

Leave off your bad tricks.

A tarn is a small lake among the mountains.

A ship has a tall mast.

I like to see a good stone wall round a farm.

A pear tree grows from the seed of a pear.

A good boy will try to spell and read well.

Do not lose or sell your books.

A good son will help his father.

I dwell in a new brick house.

If you boil dry beans and peas they will swell.

A duck has a wide flat bill.

One quart of milk will fill two pint cups.

One pint cup will hold four gills.

I saw a rill run down the hill.

A brook will turn a mill.

A bull has a stiff neck.

The frost will kill the leaves on the trees.

When the cock crows, he makes a shrill loud
 noise.

A cat will kill and eat rats and mice.

Hogs feed on swill and corn.

The skull is the bony case that encloses the brain.

Puss likes to sit on your lap and purr.

A gull is a large sea fowl that feeds on fish.

Some sea bass are as large as shad.

BÄR, LȦST, CÁRE, FẠLL, WHẠT; HẼR, PRẸY, THĒRE; ĜET; BÏRD, MARÏNE; LIƝK;

Brass is made of zinc and copper.
The rain will make the grass grow.
You must keep your dress neat and clean.
The moon is much smaller than the sun.
I will try to get a mess of peas for dinner.
Let me go and kiss that sweet young babe.
Moss grows on trees in the woods.
Fire will melt ores, and the metal will run off
    and leave the dross.
God will bless those who do his will.

No. 44.—XLIV.

WORDS OF TWO SYLLABLES, ACCENTED ON THE FIRST.

băn' quet	pŏt' ash	pĭtch' er	băn' dy
gŭs set	fĭl lip	butch er	ean dy
rus set	gŏs sip	ŭsh er	hand y
cŏs set	bĭsh op	wĭtch erȧft	stûr dy
çĭv et	găl lop	tăn ġent	stŭd y
riv et	shal lop	pun ġent	lăck ey
vĕl vet	trŏl lop	co ġent	jŏck ey
hăb it	tûr ġid	ûr ġent	mŏn key
rab bit	bĕg gar	tăl ent	tûrn kēy
ôr bit	vŭl gar	frag ment	mĕd ley
eóm fit	çĕl lar	sĕg ment	ăl ley
prŏf it	pĭl lar	fĭg ment	gal ley
lĭm it	eŏl lar	pig ment	val ley
sŭm mit	dol lar	păr rot	vŏl ley
vŏm it	pop lar	pĭv ot	pul ley
hĕr mit	grăm mar	băl lot	bär ley
ärm pit	nĕe tar	mär mot	pars ley
mĕr it	tär tar	răm pärt	mŏt ley
spĭr it	môr tar	mŏd est	kĭd ney
eŭl prit	jab ber	tĕm pest	dŏn key
vĭṣ it	rŏb ber	fŏr est	chĭm ney

MǪVE, SǑN, WǪLF, FǑOT, MOǑN, ÒR; RỤLE, PỤLL; EXIST; Ç=K; Ǵ=J; Ş=Z; ÇH=SH.

trăn′sit	lŭb′ber	ĭn′quest	hŏn′ey
ean to	blub ber	eŏn quest	mŏn ey
shĭv er	ăm ber	här vest	joûr ney
sil ver	mĕm ber	ĭn mōst	eŭm frey
eòv er	lĭm ber	ŭt mōst	lăm prey
sŭl phur	tim ber	ĭm pōst	jēr şey
mûr mur	ŭm ber	chĕst nut	ker şey
mŭf fler	eum ber	eŏn test	eler ġy
săm pler	lum ber	jăck daw	tăn şy
mĕl on	num ber	mĭl dew	ral ly
sēr mon	bär ber	eûr few	sal ly
drăg on	mēr çer	ĕd dy	tal ly
eǫu pŏn	wòn der	ḡĭd dy	jēl ly
grănd sòn	yŏn der	mŭd dy	sĭl ly
lack er	ġĭn ġer	rud dy	fŏl ly
grŏt to	chär ġer	ġĕn try	jol ly
kĭd năp	trench er	sŭl try	ōn ly

Cotton velvet is very soft to the feel.

Rabbits have large ears and eyes, that they may hear quick, and see well in the dark.

We like to have our friends visit us.

Visitors should not make their visits too long.

Silver spoons are not apt to rust.

Beggars will beg rather than work.

Cents are made of copper, and dollars, of silver.

One hundred cents are worth a dollar.

A dollar is worth a hundred cents.

Dollars are our largest silver coins.

Silver and copper ores are dug out of the ground, and melted in a very hot fire.

A mercer is one who deals in silks and woolen cloths.

A grotto is a cavern or cave.

BÄR, LÀST, CÀRE, FẠLL, WHẠT; HẼR, PRẸY, THĒRE; ĜET; BĪRE, MARĪNE; LIŊK;

No. 45.—X L V.

bădġe	slĕdġe	bŭdġe	swĭnġe	gôrġe	pärse
fadġe	wedġe	judġe	twinġe	ûrġe	ẽrse
ĕdġe	mĭdġe	grudġe	lounġe	gurġe	terse
hedġe	ridġe	hĭnġe	plŭnġe	purġe	verse
ledġe	brĭdġe	crinġe	sẽrġe	surġe	côrse
pledġe	lŏdġe	frinġe	verġe	ġẽrm	gorse
fledġe	podġe	sinġe	dîrġe	cŏpse	morse

No. 46. —X L V I.

house	rĭch	quĕnch	mŭnch	kĕtch
louse	bĕlch	stench	gulch	retch
mouse	bĭrch	wench	bătch	flītch
souse	bĕnch	ĭnch	hatch	nŏtch
cûrse	blench	clinch	catch	potch
purse	drench	fĭnch	snatch	hutch
pärch	French	flinch	scratch	sȳlph
pērch	tench	pinch	ĕtch	lymph
seôrch	trench	winch	fetch	nymph

The razor has a sharp edge.

A ledge is a ridge of rocks.

The farmer splits rails with a wedge.

A judge must not be a bad man.

Doors are hung on hinges.

Birch wood will make a hot fire.

If you go too near a hot fire it may singe or scorch your frock.

The troops march to the sound of the drum.

Six boys can sit on one long bench.

The birds fly from branch to branch on the trees and clinch their claws fast to the limbs.

The first joint of a man's thumb is one inch long.

I wish I had a bunch of sweet grapes.

MOVE, SÓN, WOLF, FŌŌT, MOON, ÔR; RŪLE, PÛLL; EXIST; Ç—K; Ġ—J; S—Z; ÇH—SH.

A cat can catch rats and mice; and a trap will
 catch a fox.
A hen will sit on a nest of eggs and hatch
 chickens.
The latch holds the door shut.
We can light the lamp with a match.
Never snatch a book from any one.
A cross cat will scratch with her sharp nails.

No. 47.—XLVII.

rīṣe	clōṣe	ūṣe	ḡuīde	thȳme
wiṣe	noṣe	fuṣe	ḡuile	shrīne
ḡuiṣe	roṣe	muṣe	quite	sphēre
chōṣe	proṣe	phraṣe	quote	grīme

The sun will set at the close of the day.
Good boys will use their books with care.
A man can guide a horse with a bridle.
The earth is not quite round. It is not so long
 from north to south as it is from east to west.
A sphere is a round body or globe.
In the nose are the organs of smell.
We love to hear a chime of bells.
A shrine is a case or box; a hallowed place.
A great heat will fuse tin.
His prose is written in a good style.
A phrase is a short form of speech, or a part
 of a sentence.

No. 48.—XLVIII.

void	spoil	point	noiṣe	hoist	pound
oil	broil	coin	poiṣe	joist	round
boil	soil	loin	coif	moist	ground
coil	toil	join	quoif	bound	sound
foil	oint	groin	quoit	found	wound
roil	joint	quoin	foist	hound	mound

No. 49.--XLIX.

loud	trout	pouch	flour	mount	clout
proud	chouse	foul	sour	out	flout
cloud	grouse	owl	count	bout	snout
shroud	spouse	cowl	fount	scout	pout
ounce	rouse	prowl	fowl	gout	spout
bounce	browse	scowl	howl	shout	sprout
flounce	touse	stout	growl	lout	choice
pounce	crown	brown	rout	our	voice
grout	frown	clown	couch	scour	poise
crout	town	gown	slouch	hour	noise

We can burn fish oil in lamps.

We boil beets with meat in a pot.

Pears are choice fruit.

When you can choose for yourself, try to make
    a good choice.

The cat and mouse live in the house.

The owl has large eyes and can see in the night.

One hand of a watch goes round once in an
    hour.

Wheat flour will make good bread.

Limes are sour fruit.

A hog has a long snout to root up the ground.

A trout is a good fish to eat.

An ox is a stout, tame beast.

Fowls have wings to fly in the air.

Wolves howl in the woods in the night.

A dog will growl and bark.

The cold frost turns the leaves of the trees
    brown, and makes them fall to the ground.

Rain will make the ground moist.

You can broil a beefsteak over the coals of fire.

We move our limbs at the joints.

Land that has a rich soil will bear large crops
  of grain and grass.

A pin has a head and a point.

A dime is a small coin worth ten cents.

Men play on the bass viol.

A great gun makes a loud noise.

Men hoist goods from the hold of a ship with
  ropes.

The beams of a wooden house are held up by
  posts and joists; these are parts of the frame.

God makes the ground bring forth fruit for
  man and beast.

The globe is nearly round like a ball.

The dark cloud will shed its rain on the ground
  and make the grass grow.

No. 50.—L.

sēa	rēad	āid	gōurd	pēaçe	hēave
pea	gōad	laid	sourçe	lease	weave
flea	load	maid	€ourse	prāişe	leave
plea	road	staid	erēase	€ōarse	blūe
bead	toad	bōard	grease	hoarse	flue
mead	woad	hoard	çe.se	brēve	glue

No. 51.—L I.

bȳe	bāize	lōaf	ēach	tēach	blēak
lye	raişe	fiēf	beach	€ōach	fleak
eye	maize	chief	bleach	roach	speak
ēaşe	shēaf	liēf	peach	broach	peak
teaşe	leaf	brief	reach	lēash	sneak
sēize	neaf	grief	breach	beak	€reak
cheeşe	ōaf	wāif	preach	leak	freak

Few men can afford to keep a coach.

BĂR, LĂST, CÂRE, FALL, WHẠT; HĒR, PREY, THÊRE; ĞET; BÎRD, MARÎNE; LIŊK;

No. 52.—LII.

break	ōak	pēal	shōal	nāil	tāil
steāk	croak	seal	āil	snail	vail
strēak	soak	veal	bail	pail	quail
sereak	bēal	weal	fail	rail	wail
squeak	deal	zeal	hail	frail	bōwl
weak	heal	cōal	jail	grail	sōul
shriēk	meal	foal	flail	trail	bēam
twēak	neal	goal	mail	sail	dream

No. 53.—LIII.

flēam	stēam	bēan	miēn	grāin	plāin
gleam	fōam	dean	mōan	brain	slain
ream	loam	lean	loan	strain	main
bream	roam	elean	roan	sprain	pain
eream	āim	glean	groan	chain	rain
seream	elaim	mean	fāin	lain	drain
team	maim	wean	gain	blain	train

When the wind blows hard the sea roars, and its waves run high.

We have green peas in the month of June.

No man can make a good plea for a dram.

Girls are fond of fine beads to wear round their necks.

Girls and boys must learn to read and spell.

Men load hay with a pitchfork.

A load of oak wood is worth more than a load of pine wood.

A toad will jump like a frog.

A saw mill will saw logs into boards.

A gourd grows on a vine, like a squash.

You can not teach a deaf and dumb boy to speak.

The man who drinks rum may soon want a loaf of bread.

MOVE, SÓN, WOLF, FÒÒT, MOÒN, ÒR; RÙLE, PÙLL; EXIST; Ç=K; Ġ=J; S=Z; ÇH=SH.

The waves of the sea beat upon the beach.
Bleachers bleach linen and thus make it white.
The miller grinds corn into meal.
The flesh of calves is called veal.
Apples are more plentiful than peaches.
The preacher is to preach the gospel.
Teachers teach their pupils, and pupils learn.
A roach is a short, thick, flat fish.
Men get their growth before they are thirty.
The beak of a bird is its bill, or the end of its bill.
Greenland is a bleak, cold place.

No. 54.—LIV.

WORDS OF THREE SYLLABLES, ACCENTED ON THE FIRST, AND
LEFT UNMARKED AS AN EXERCISE IN NOTATION.

bot' a ny	fel' o ny	sor' cer y
el e gy	col o ny	im age ry
prod i gy	har mo ny	witch er y
ef fi gy	cot ton y	butch er y
eb o ny	glut ton y	fish er y
en er gy	can o py	quack er y
lit ur gy	oc cu py	crock er y
in fa my	quan ti ty	mock er y
big a my	sal a ry	cook er y
blas phe my	reg is try	cut ler y
en e my	beg gar y	gal ler y
am i ty	bur gla ry	rar i ty
vil lain y	gran a ry	em er y
com pa ny	gloss a ry	nun ner y
lit a ny	lac ta ry	frip per y
lar ce ny	her ald ry	fop per y
des ti ny	hus band ry	or re ry
cal um ny	rob ber y	ar ter y
tyr an ny	chan ce ry	mas ter y

BÄR, LÅST, ÇÅRE, FALL, WHAT; HĔR, PRĘY, THÉRE; ĜET; BÎRD, MARÎNE; LIŅK;

mys' ter y	liv' er y	fac' to ry
bat ter y	cav al ry	vic to ry
flat ter y	rev el ry	his to ry
lot ter y	bot tom ry	black ber ry
but ter y	pil lo ry	bar ber ry
ev er y	mem o ry	sym me try
rev er y	arm o ry	rib ald ry

Botany is the science of plants.

An elegy is a funeral song.

A prodigy is something very wonderful.

An effigy is an image or likeness of a person.

Blasphemy is contemptuous treatment of God.

Litany is a solemn service of prayer to God.

Larceny is theft, and liable to be punished.

Felony is a crime that may be punished with death.

Salary is a stated allowance for services.

Husbandry is the tillage of the earth.

We are delighted with the harmony of sounds.

A glossary is used to explain obscure words.

History is an account of past events. A great part of history is an account of men's crimes and wickedness.

No. 55.—L V.

blāde	chīde	glōbe	spāçe	trīçe	brāke
shade	glide	probe	braçe	twiçe	drake
glade	slide	glēbe	graçe	stāĝe	slake
spade	bride	ĝïbe	traçe	shake	quake
grade	pride	bribe	slīçe	flake	strīke
trade	stride	seribe	miçe	stake	spike
braid	erude	tribe	spiçe	snake	chōke
jade	prude	plāçe	priçe	spake	poke

MỌVE, SÔN, WỌLF, FŎŎT, MŌŌN, ÔR; RỤLE, PỤLL; EXIST; ꞓ=K; Ġ=J; Ṣ=Z; ÇH=SH.

brōke	smīle	shāme	slīme	spūme
spoke	stile	blame	prime	chīne
smoke	spile	ꞓlīme	ꞓrime	swine
stroke	frāme	chime	plūme	twine

A blade of grass is a single stalk. The leaves of corn are also called blades.

The shade of the earth makes the darkness of night.

A glade is an opening among trees.

A grade is a degree in rank. An officer may enjoy the grade of a captain or lieutenant.

Trade is the purchase and sale, or the exchange of goods.

Smoke rises, because it is lighter than the air.

A globe is a round body, like a ball.

A bribe is given to corrupt the judgment.

A smile shows that we are pleased.

We have heard the chime of church bells.

No. 56.—LVI.

WORDS OF TWO SYLLABLES, ACCENTED ON THE FIRST.

băn′ ter	măt′ ter	lĭꞓ′ tor	tăn′ ner
ꞓan ter	tat ter	vĭꞓ tor	ĭn ner
çĕn ter	lĕt ter	dŏꞓ tor	din ner
en ter	fet ter	tĭn der	tin ner
wĭn ter	el der	pĕd dler	sin ner
fĕs ter	nev er	tĭl ler	ꞓôr ner
pes ter	ev er	sŭt ler	hăm per
tes ter	sev er	hăm mer	pam per
sĭs ter	lĭv er	ram mer	tam per
fŏs ter	riv er	sŭm mer	tĕm per
băt ter	măn or	lĭm ner	ten ter
hat ter	tĕn or	băn ner	sĭm per

BĂR, LĂST, CÂRE, FĄLL, WHĄT; HẼR, PRĘY, THÈRE; ĞET; BĪRD, MARĪNE; LIŊK;

elăp′ per	tŭn′ nel	hŏv′ el	ăn′ vil
pĕp per	fun nel	nov el	bĕz el
dĭp per	kĕr nel	mär vel	eŏr al
eŏp per	gŏs pel	pĕn çil	bär ter
hop per	bär rel	măn fụl	ear ter
ŭp per	sŏr rel	sĭn fụl	măs ter
sup per	dŏr sal	aw fụl	eas tor
vĕs per	mor sel	pĕr il	pas tor
reb el	vĕs sel	tŏn sil	pär lor
eăn çel	tĭn sel	dos sil	gar ner
eam el	grăv el	fos sil	fär del
pan nel	bĕv el	lĕn til	art fụl
kĕn nel	lev el	eăv il	dar nel
fen nel	rev el	çĭv il	harp er

We have snow and ice in the cold winter.

The little sister can knit a pair of garters.

Never pester the little boys.

Hatters make hats of fur and lambs' wool.

Peaches may be better than apples.

The rivers run into the great sea.

The doctor tries to cure the sick.

The new table stands in the parlor.

A tin peddler will sell tin vessels as he travels.

The little boys can crack nuts with a hammer.

The farmer eats his dinner at noon.

I can dip the milk with a tin dipper.

We eat bread and milk for supper.

The farmer puts his cider into barrels.

Vessels sail on the large rivers.

My good little sister may have a slate and pen-
cil; and she may make letters on her slate.

That idle boy is a very lazy fellow.

The farmer puts his bridle and saddle upon his
horse.

MOVE, SÓN, WOLF, FOOT, MOÒN, ÒR ; RULE, PULL ; EXIST ; €=K ; G̣=J ; S̱=Z ; ÇH=SH.

Paper is made of linen and cotton rags.
Spiders spin webs to catch flies.

No. 57.—LVII.

mōurn	grōwn	hēap	fēar	spēar	ōar
borne	vāin	cheap	year	rear	hoar
shorn	wain	leap	hear	drear	roar
ōwn	swain	neap	shea_	sear	soar
shown	twain	reap	blear	tēar	boar
blown	train	sōap	elear	weâr	piēr
flown	stain	ēar	smear	sweâr	tier
sown	lane	dear	near	teâr	bier

No. 58.—LVIII.

àir	yoūr	stīlts	pēat	mōat	wāit
fair	tọur	chintz	treat	groạt	bruit
hair	ēaves̱	ēat	seat	eight	fruit
chair	leaves̱	beat	grēat	freight	sūit
lair	greaves̱	feat	ōat	weight	mīlt
pair	pāins̱	heat	bloat	bāit	built
stair	shēars̱	bleat	eoat	gait	g̣uilt
hêir	g̣uĕss	meat	goat	plait	eōurt
fōur	g̣uest	neat	float	trait	sāint

No. 59.—LIX.

ēast	wāist	elew	spew	yew	mōw
beast	dew	flew	erew *	bōw	row
least	few	brew *	serew *	show	snow
feast	hew	slew	drew *	low	erow
yeast	chew *	mew	grew *	blow	grow
bōast	Jew	new	shrew *	flow	strow
roast	view	views̱	strew *	glow	sōw
toast	blew	pew	stew	slow	stow

* **ew.** in the starred words, is pronounced like **o͞o** ; in the other
words, like **u͞**.

We do not like to see our own sins.
I like to see a full blown rose.
A vain girl is fond of fine things.
The moon is in the wane from full to new moon.
A dog can leap over a fence.
Much grain will make bread cheap.
I like to see men reap grain.
God made the ear, and He can hear.
Men shear the wool from sheep.
Flint glass is white and clear.
Fowls like to live near the house and barn.
Can a boy cry and not shed a tear?
Twelve months make one year.
I love to eat a good ripe pear.
The good boy will not tear his book.
A wild boar lives in the woods.
The lark will soar up in the sky to look at the
    sun.
The rain runs from the eaves of the house.
The sun heats the air, and makes it hot.
The old sheep bleats, and calls her lamb to her.
I wish you to treat me with a new hat.
A chair is a better seat than a stool.
I will wear my greatcoat in a cold wet day.
I have seen the ice float down the stream.
Boys and girls are fond of fruit.
The sun will rise in the east, and set in the west.
A beast can not talk and think, as we do.
We roast a piece of beef or a goose.
A girl can toast a piece of bread.
We chew our meat with our teeth.
Live coals of fire glow with heat.
A moat is a deep trench round a castle or other
    fortified place.

MǪVE, SǑN, WǪLF, FŎŎT, MŎŎN, ǑR ; RŲLE, PŲLL ; EXIST ; Ç=K ; Ġ=J ; Ş=Z ; ÇH = SH.

däunt	täunt	slänt	bärġe
haunt	vaunt	lärġe	sä*lv*e
flaunt	gränt	charġe	searf

No. 60.—L X.

fraud	squash	awl	yawl	yawn
broad	wash	bawl	dawn	dwarf
sauçe	swash	sprawl	fawn	watch
eauşe	quash	brawl	lawn	vault
gauze	gawk	erawl	pawn	fault
elauşe	hawk	drawl	spawn	aught
pauşe	haul	trawl	brawn	naught
paunch	maul	waul	drawn	eaught

No. 61.—L X I

brīne	serāpe	seōpe	shāve	drīve
tine	drape	trope	slave	drōve
shōne	shape	snore	plate	strove
erone	erape	slāte	prate	grove
drone	grape	state	quīte	elove
prone	snīpe	grate	smite	gloze
stone	gripe	grave	spite	froze
prune	stripe	brave	sprite	prīze
drupe	tripe	erave	trite	smōte

Forks have two, three, or four tines.
We keep salt meat in brine.
Grapes grow on vines, in clusters.
Smoke goes through the pipe of a stove.
The boy loves ripe grapes.
Bedcords are long ropes.
Nut wood and coal will make a warm fire.
Shut the gate and keep the hogs out of the yard.
Slates are stone, and used to cover roofs of houses.

BÄR, LÅST, CÂRE, FALL, WHAT; HÊR, PREY, THÊRE; GET; BIRD, MARÏNE; LIŊK;

We burn coal in a grate.
I had some green corn in July, on a plate.
Dig up the weeds and let the corn grow.
Bees live in hives and collect honey.
He was dull, and made trite remarks.

No. 62.—LXII.

WORDS OF THREE SYLLABLES, ACCENTED ON THE FIRST.

ăm′ i ty	ŏb′ lo quy	dȳ′ nas ty
jŏl li ty	sĭn ew y	gāy e ty
nŭl li ty	găl ax y	loy al ty
ĕn mi ty	pĕd ant ry	roy al ty
săn i ty	ĭn fant ry	ū ṣu ry (ā′zhoo-)
van i ty	găl lant ry	rā pi er
bal eo ny	bĭg ot ry	nau ti lus
lĕn i ty	ăn çes try	pau çi ty
dĭg ni ty	tap es try	moi e ty
dĕp ū ty	mĭn is try	prĕl a çy
trĭn i ty	in dus try	ăl i quot
păr i ty	çĕnt ū ry	man i fest
eōm i ty	mēr eu ry	ŭp per mōst
vĕr i ty	ĭn ju ry	ut ter mōst
den si ty	pēr ju ry	eŏn tra ry
en ti ty	pĕn ū ry	çĕl e ry
eăv i ty	lŭx ū ry	plē na ry
lĕv i ty	hĕr e sy	sā li ent
lăx i ty	em bas sy	lē ni ent
pĕn al ty	dē i ty	ve he ment
nŏv el ty	fe al ty	brī er y
făe ul ty	pī e ty	boun te oŭs
mŏd est y	pō e sy	moun tain oŭs
prŏb i ty	eru el ty	eoun ter feĭt
ăm nes ty	pū ri ty	fraud ū lent
bŏt a ny	nu di ty	wạ ter y

MŎVE, SŎN, WŎLF, FŎŎT, MŎŎN, ŎR; ETLE, PULL; EXIST; Є=K; Ġ=J; S=Z; ℭH=SH.

No. 63.—LXIII.

WORDS OF THREE SYLLABLES, ACCENTED ON THE SECOND.

a bāse′ ment	dis bûrse′ ment	au tŭm′ nal
al lūre ment	in dôrse ment	how ĕv er
de bāse ment	ärch bĭsh op	em bär rass
in çīte ment	ad vĕnt ūre	in stall ment
ex çite ment	dis frăn chĭṣe	in thrall ment
en slāve ment	en fran chĭṣe	hy draul ies
a maze ment	mis eŏn strue	en joy ment
in quī ry	de poṣ it	em ploy ment
un ēa ṣy	re poṣ it	a mass ment
eon vey ançe	at trĭb ūte	em bär go
pur vey or	im mŏd est	im prove ment
sur vey or	un lŭck y	at tor ney
sur vey ing	ap pĕn dix	an noy ançe

No. 64.—LXIV.

WORDS OF TWO SYLLABLES, ACCENTED ON THE FIRST.

blăn′ dish	blĕm′ ish	bûr′ nish	noŭr′ ish
bran dish	skīr mish	pŭn ish	skĭt tish
fûr bish	văn ish	elown ish	slŭt tish
rŭb bish	fĭn ish	snăp pish	lăv ish
sĕlf ish	gär nish	par ish	rav ish
ch ûrl ish	tar nish	chĕr ish	pŭb lish
fur nish	var nish	floŭr ish	pŏt ash

Vain persons are fond of the allurements of dress.

Strong drink leads to the debasement both of the mind and the body.

We look with amazement on the evils of stror · drink.

The gambler wishes to get money without earning it.

An indorser indorses his name on the back of a note; and his indorsement makes him liable to pay the note.

An archbishop is a chief dignitary of the church.

Merchants often deposit money in the bank for safe keeping.

BÄR, LÄST, CÂRE, FALL, WHAT; HÊR, PREY, THÊRE; ĜET; BÏRD, MARÏNE; LIᴎK;

Autumnal fruits are the fruits that ripen in autumn.
The wicked know not the enjoyment of a good conscience.
Parents should provide useful employment for their children.
Men devoted to mere amusement misemploy their time.

No. 65.—L X V.

THE UNMARKED VOWELS (EXCEPT e FINAL) IN THIS LESSON
HAVE A SOUND APPROACHING THAT OF SHORT **u.**

hôrse' băck	hĕm' lŏck	joûr' nal
lămp black	fĕt lŏck	răs cal
băr rack	măt tock	spī nal
răn săck	hŏŏd wĭᴎk	cŏn trīte
hăm mock	bul wark	trĭb ūte
hăd dock	pĭtch fôrk	stăt ūte
păd lŏck	dăm ask	cŏn cāve
wĕd lŏck	sy̆m bol	cŏn clāve
fīre lŏck	vẽr bal	ŏe tāve
hĭll ock	mĕd al	rĕs cue
bull ock	vẽr nal	văl ue

No. 66.—L X V I.

a IN **ate,** UNMARKED, DOES NOT HAVE THE FULL SOUND OF
LONG **a.**

sĕn' ate	stăg' nāte	elī' mate	fī' nīte
ĭn grāte	fĭl trāte	prĕl ate	pōst age
păl ate	prŏs trāte	vī brāte	plū mage
stĕl lāte	frŭs trāte	pi rate	trī umph
ĭn māte	dīe tāte	eū rate	stāte ment
mĕss māte	tĕs tāte	prī vate	rāi ment

When an old house is pulled down, it is no small job to re-
move the rubbish.
Washington was not a selfish man.   He labored for the good
of his country more than for himself.
Exercise will give us a relish for our food.
In China, thousands sometimes famish with hunger.
Riding on horseback is good exercise.

MOVE, SON, WOLF, FOOT, MOON, ÔR; RULE, PULL; EXIST; €=K; Ġ=J; S=Z; CH=SH.

Lampblack is a fine soot formed from the smoke of tar, pitch, or pine wood.

The Indians traffic with our people, and give furs for blankets.

Granite is a kind of stone which is very strong, handsome, and useful in building.

The Senate of the United States is called the Upper House of Congress.

Water will stagnate, and then it is not good.

Heavy winds sometimes prostrate trees.

Norway has a cold climate.

Medals are sometimes given as a reward at school.

We punish bad men to prevent crimes.

We pity the slavish drinkers of rum.

The drunkard's face will publish his vice and his disgrace.

No. 67.—LXVII.

WORDS OF FOUR SYLLABLES, THE PRIMARY ACCENT ON THE FIRST; THE LAST COLUMN LEFT UNMARKED.

lū′ mi na ry	ĭg′ no min y	mer′ ce na ry
eū li na ry	çêr e mo ny	mil li ner y
mō ment a ry	ăl i mo ny	or di na ry
nū ga to ry	mat ri mo ny	sem i na ry
nu mer a ry	pat ri mo ny	pul mo na ry
brē vi a ry	pär si mo ny	sub lu na ry
ĕf fi ea çy	ăn ti mo ny	lit er a ry
del i ea çy	tĕs ti mo ny	form u la ry
ĭn tri ea çy	drŏm e da ry	ar bi tra ry
eŏn tu ma çy	prĕb end a ry	ad ver sa ry
ob sti na çy	see ond a ry	em is sa ry
ăe eu ra çy	eẍ em pla ry	com mis sa ry
ĕẍ i ġen çy	ăn ti qua ry	cem e ter y
ex çel len çy	tĭt ū la ry	see re ta ry
eŏm pe ten çy	eŭs tom a ry	mil i ta ry
ĭm po ten çy	ħŏn or a ry	sol i ta ry
mis çel la ny	pär çe na ry	sed en ta ry
nĕç es sa ry	mĕd ul la ry	vol un ta ry

BÄR, LÀST, CÀRE, FALL, WHAT; HER, PREY, THÈRE; GET; BĪRD, MARĪNE; LIƝK;

trĭb'ū ta ry   dŷs'en ter y   man'da to ry
săl ū ta ry   prĕs by ter y   pur ga to ry
an çil la ry   prŏm is so ry   dil a to ry
cap il la ry   prĕd a to ry   or a to ry
ax il la ry   pref'a to ry   dor mi to ry
eŏr ol la ry   pŭl sa to ry   mon i to ry
măx il la ry   mĭn a to ry   ter ri to ry
ad ver sa ry   aud it o ry   tran si to ry
al a bas ter   ĕx ere to ry   in ven to ry
plan et a ry   jăn i za ry   con tro ver sy
stat ū a ry   mŏn as ter y   leg is la tive
sanct ū a ry   ăl le go ry   leg is lat ure
sŭmpt ū a ry   dĕs ul to ry   leg is la tor

The sun is the brightest luminary.

The moon is the luminary of the night.

The streets, houses, and shops in New York are illuminated by gas lights.

Potatoes and turnips are common culinary roots used in our kitchens.

We admire the rose for the delicacy of its colors and its sweet fragrance.

There is a near intimacy between drunkenness, poverty, and ruin.

The obstinate will should be subdued.

Wedlock is the old Anglo-Saxon term for matrimony.

Antimony is a hard mineral, and is used in making types for printing.

A witness must give true testimony.

A dromedary is a large quadruped.

Worldly men make it their primary object to please themselves; duty holds but a secondary place in their esteem.

It is customary for tipplers to visit taverns.

Grammar is a difficult but ordinary study.

A seminary means a place of instruction.

Napoleon was an arbitrary emperor. He disposed of kingdoms as he chose.

The devil is the great adversary of man.

MOVE, SÒN, WOLF, FŌŌT, MŌŌN, ÒR; RŪLE, PŪLL; EXIST; Ç͟ K; Ġ J; S̩=Z; CH SH.

Food is necessary to animal life.

Alabaster is a kind of marble or limestone.

An emissary is a secret agent employed to give information to an enemy, or to act as a spy.

The planetary worlds are those stars which go round the sun.

A secretary is a writer, or a scribe.

Our actions are voluntary, proceeding from free will.

The Ohio River has many large tributary streams which contribute to increase its waters.

Pure water and good air are salutary.

A church is called a sanctuary or holy place.

The dysentery is a painful disease.

A promissory note is a note by which a man promises to pay a sum of money.

The remarks at the beginning of a discourse are called prefatory remarks.

Dilatory people are such as delay doing their work.

An orator makes orations; and oratory is the art of public speaking.

The auditory is the company who attend as hearers of a discourse.

They could not agree and had a bitter controversy.

No. 68.—LXVIII.

WORDS OF THREE SYLLABLES, ACCENTED ON THE SECOND.

im môr′ tal	in fẽr′ nal	re plĕv′ in
pa rĕnt al	ma ter nal	a băn don
ae quĭt tal	pa ter nal	pĭ as ter
en ăm el	e ter nal	pĭ las ter
im pan el	in ter nal	as sĕv er
ap păr el	dī ûr nal	dis sev er
ū tĕn sil	noe tur nal	de lĭv er
un çĭv il	pro eŏn sul	e lix ir
trī ŭmph al	un çẽr tain	pre çĕp tor
in fôrm al	in elĕm ent	eom pŏs̩ ĭte
bap tĭs̩ mal	de tēr mine	en ăm or
hī bẽr nal	as săs sin	to bae eo

BÄR, LĂST, CÂRE, FALL, WHĂT; HÊR, PREY, THÊRE; ĜET; BÏRD, MARÏNE; LIŊK;

sī rŏe' eo   sur rĕn' der   a pŏs' tāte

me mĕn to   diş ôr der   pro mŭl gate

pĭ men to   när çis sus   in eär nate

mu lăt to   eo lŏs sus   vol eā no

pal mĕt to   im pēr fect   Oe tō ber

en vel op   in ter pret   in elo şūre

de vel op   in hăb it   dis elo şure

De çem ber   eo hab it   eom po şure

Sep tem ber   pro hĭb it   ex po şure

No vem ber   dis erĕd it   fore elo şure

en eŭm ber   de erep it   dis eŏv er

eon sĭd er   in hĕr it   dis col or

be wil der   de mer it   re eov er

mis fôrt ūne   pŏme grăn ate   dis com fit

me ăn der   ex am ple   diş ăs ter

en ĝĕn der   in tĕs tāte   re pàss ing

The soul is immortal; it will never die.

Our bodies are mortal; they will soon die.

Utensils are tools to work with. Plows, axes, and hoes are utensils for farming; needles and scissors are utensils for making garments.

A formal meeting is one where the forms of ceremony are observed; when people meet without attending to these formalities it is called an informal meeting.

Children are sometimes bewildered and lost in the woods.

Sons and daughters inherit the estate and sometimes the infirmities of their parents.

The diurnal motion of the earth is its daily motion, and this gives us day and night.

Tobacco is a native plant of America.

Pimento is the plant whose berries we call allspice.

Savage nations inhabit huts and wigwams.

Paternal care and maternal love are great blessings to children, and should be repaid with their duty and affection.

The blowing up of the steamship was a terrible disaster to us.

Pomegranate is a fruit of about the size of an orange.

MOVE, SÓN, WOLF, FÓOT, MOON, ÔR ; RULE, PULL ; EXIST ; €=K ; Ġ=J ; Ş=Z ; ÇH SH.

No. 69.—LXIX.

bāy	jāy	slāy	drāy	trāy	swāy
day	lay	may	fray	stray	splay
fay	elay	nay	gray	say	prey
gay	flay	pay	pray	stay	dey
hay	play	ray	spray	way	bey

No. 70.—LXX.

bey	joy	toy	haw	elaw	raw	saw
eoy	eloy	eaw	jaw	flaw	eraw	law
hoy	troy	daw	draw	maw	straw	paw

No. 71.—LXXI.

swamp	smalt	swart	pōrt	lĭve	glŏve
wasp	spalt	quart	most	eóme	work*
waş	salt	pōrk	dŏll	some	worst*
halt	want	fort	loll	dove	shóve
malt	wart	sport	ġĭve	love	monk

No. 72.—LXXII.

bow	mow	sow	worm*	dīrt	squīrt
eow	now	vow	frónt	flirt	first
how	brow	kēy	wont	shirt	ward
plow	plow	ley	wort*	skirt	warm

The farmer cuts his grass to make hay.
Bricks are made of clay baked in a kiln.
You may play on a mow of hay.
A dray is a kind of low cart.
When we eat we move the under jaw; but the upper jaw of most animals is fixed.
Little boys are fond of toys.
The sting of a wasp is very painful.
A swamp is wet, spongy land.
A monk lives in retirement from the world.

* o like û (wûrk, wûrst, wûrm, wûrt).

BĀR, LĀST, €ÂRE, FĄLL, WHĄT; HĒR, PRĘY, THÉRE; ĜET; BĪRD, MARÏNE; LIŊK;

Smalt is a blue glass of cobalt.

Malt is barley steeped in water, fermented and dried in a kiln; of this are made ale and beer.

No. 73. -LXXIII.

WORDS OF TWO SYLLABLES, ACCENTED ON THE FIRST.

lăd' der	shĕl' ter	chärt' er	chär' nel
blad der	fĭl ter	lŏb ster	bär ren
mad der	mil ler	lĭt ter	flŏr in
fŏd der	chăp ter	mŏn ster	rob in
ŭl çer	sŭf fer	glĭs ter	eof fin
eăn çer	pĭl fer	chăt ter	mŭf fin
ŭd der	bădĝ er	shat ter	bŏd kin
shud der	lĕdĝ er	elŭt ter	wĕl kin
rud der	bănk er	flut ter	năp kin
pud der	eank er	plăt ter	pĭp kin
găn der	hank er	smat ter	bŭs kin
pan der	tŭm bler	spat ter	ĝŏb lin
ĝĕn der	săd dler	shĭv er	mŭs lin
slen der	aut ler	slĭv er	lū çid
ren der	skĭm mer	quiv er	bär on
ten der	glim mer	eŭl ver	flag on
çĭn der	prŏp er	tôr por	wag on
hin der	€lăp per	ĕr ror	fĕl on
pŏn der	skĭp per	ter ror	găl lon
ŭn der	slip per	mĭr ror	lĕm on
blun der	crŏp per	hŏr ror	găm mon
plun der	ăs per	çĕn sor	mam mon
thun der	prŏs per	spŏn sor	€om mon
sun der	lĕss er	sēe tor	eăn non
ôr der	dress er	săch el	çĭt ron
bor der	äft er	flan nel	tĕn on
mûr der	räft er	chap el	eăn ton
dĭf fer	rănt er	grav el	pĭs ton

MOVE, SÒN, WOLF, FOOT, MOON, ÒR; RULE, PULL; EXIST; €=K; Ġ=J; S=Z; ÇH=SH.

ŏf′ fer	prŏe′ tor	trăv′ el	sĕx′ ton
€of fer	chăn nel	pŏm mel	kĭm bo
s€of fer	€ūd ġel	bush el	stū€ €o
prof fer	hătch el	chăn çel	dĭt to

The farmer hatchels flax; he sells corn by the bushel, and
butter by the firkin.

Little boys and girls love to ride in a wagon.

Four quarts make a gallon. A barrel is thirty gallons, more
or less.

Lemons grow on trees in warm climates.

The robin is a pretty singing-bird.

A napkin is a kind of towel.

Brass is a compound of copper and zinc.

The channel of a river is where the main current flows.

Firemen have ladders to climb upon houses.

The farmer fodders his cattle in winter.

The sailor steers a vessel with a rudder.

A gander is white and a goose gray.

Broom corn grows with a long slender stalk.

The eye is a very tender organ, and one of the most useful
members of the body.

No. 74.—LXXIV.

WORDS OF TWO SYLLABLES, ACCENTED ON THE FIRST.

brāçe′ let	drī′ ver	tū′ mor	erī′ sis
dī et	mā jor	lā bor	grā ter
qui et	mī nor	ta bor	fō eus
sē eret	stū por	ō dor	mū eus
pō et	ju ror	€o lon	bō lus
to phet	prē tor	dē mon	flā grant
eȳe let	tū tor	ī ron (*i′urn*)	va grant
tū mult	prī or	ā pron	tȳ rant
bōl ster	rā zor	dew lăp	dē çent
hōl ster	trē mor	eru et	re cent
grā ver	hū mor	bā sis	nō cent
qua ver	ru mor	ū′ nit	lū cent

BÄR, LÀST, ÇÂRE, F̣ALL, WHḀT: HȆR, PRĘY, THȆRE; ĠET; BĪRD, MARĪNE; LIꞐK;

---

trī' dent	vā' cant	need' y	hā' zy
prụ dent	flū ent	erō ny	la zy
stū dent	frē quent	pū ny	dō zy
ā ġent	se quent	vā ry	slēa zy
rē ġent	rī ot	dū ty	jăs per
eō ġent	pi lot	nā vy	bär gain
sī lent	bâre fŏŏt	gra vy	eăp tain
ēase ment	prē çept	safe ty	çĕr tain
pave ment	pōst script	sụre ty	mŭr rain
move ment	o vert	glō ry	vĭl lain
mō ment	rụ by	sto ry	vī sor
cī pher	spī çy	erā zy	slăn der

Ladies sometimes wear bracelets on their arms.

Watts was a very good poet; he wrote good songs.

Rabbits hide themselves in secret places.

A bolster is put at the head of a bed.

Men in old age love a quiet life.

A graver is a tool for engraving.

A holster is a case for carrying a pistol.

The driver is one who drives a team.

A minor is a young person not twenty-one years old.

Miners work in mines under ground.

A juror is one who sits to try causes and give a verdict according to the evidence.

The rose emits a pleasant flavor.

Labor makes us strong and healthy.

A colon is one of the stops in reading.

A pastor does not like to see vacant seats in his church.

Girls wear aprons to keep their frocks clean.

Nero was a wicked tyrant at Rome.

Every person should wear a decent dress.

A major is an officer next above a captain.

A vagrant is a wandering, lazy fellow.

Cedar is the most durable species of wood.

A postscript is something added to a letter.

The streets of cities are covered with pavements.

MOVE, SÒN, WOLF, FOOT, MOON, OR; RULE, PULL; EXIST; ε=K; Ġ=J; S̬=Z; ÇH=SH.

No. 75.—LXXV.

WORDS OF THREE SYLLABLES, ACCENTED ON THE SECOND.

ar rī′ val	die tā′ tor	dis fĭg′ ūre
ap prŏv al	tes ta tor	trans fig ūre
eo ē val	en vī ron	eon jĕet ūre
re fū ṣal	pa gō da	de bent ūre
re prī ṣal	tor pē do	in dent ūre
pe ru ṣal	bra vā do	en răpt ūre
de erē tal	tor na do	eon tĕxt ūre
re çī tal	lum ba go	eom mĭxt ure
re qui tal	vī ra go	eon tin ūe
prī mē val	far ra go	for bid ding
un e qual	pro vī ṣo	un ĕr ring
eo e qual	po tā to	pro çeed ing
re new al	oe ta vo	ex çeed ing
ī dē al	sub serī ber	sub al tern
il le gal	re vi val	es pou ṣal
de nī al	en dān ġer	en eoun ter
de eri al	de çī pher	ren eoun ter
tri bū nal	ma neū ver	a vow al
a eu men	hī ā tus	ad vow ṣon
le gu men	quī ē tus	dis loy al
dis sēi ziu	eon fĕss or	dis eoŭr aġe
in çī ṣor	ag gress or	en eoŭr aġe
ere ā tor	sue çess or	mo làs sĕṣ
speε ta tor	pre fĭg ūre	de pärt ūre

We often wait for the arrival of the mail.
Coeval signifies of the same age.
Reprisal is seizing anything from an enemy in retaliation.
An incisor is a fore tooth.
Our blood is often chilled at the recital of acts of cruelty.
Requital is a recompense for some act.
Primeval denotes what was first or original.

BÄR, LÁST, €ÄRE, FALL, WE̩AT; HẼR, PRE̩Y, THȨRE; ĠET; BĨRD, MARĨNE; LIŊK;

A tribunal is a court for deciding causes.

Acumen denotes quickness of perception.

Illegal is the same as unlawful. It is illegal to steal fruit from another's orchard or garden.

A virago is a turbulent, masculine woman.

Molasses is the syrup which drains from sugar when it is cooling.

The potato is a native plant of America.

No. 76.—LXXVI.

WORDS OF THREE SYLLABLES, ACCENTED ON THE LAST.

ap per tāin′	pre €on çēive′	dis af fēet′
su per vēne	o ver drīve	o ver whelm
in ter vene	dis ap prọve	mis in fòrm
im por tūne	o ver rēach	€oun ter äet
op por tune	o ver lo͝ok	in di rēet
in se eure	dis in thrạll	in €or reet
in ter fēre	re in stall	in ter seet
pre ma tūre	dis es teem	€on tra dĭet
im ma ture	mis de mēan	o ver sĕt
ad ver tīṣe	un fōre seen	in ter mĭt
re €om pōṣe	fōre or dain	rep re ṣĕnt
de €om poṣe	o ver strain	dis €on tent
in ter poṣe	as çer tain	çĩr eum vent
pre dis poṣe	en ter tain	un der went
re in stāte	re ap pēar	o ver sho͞ot
im po līte	dis in tẽr	in ter çĕpt
re ū nite	in ter spẽrse	in ter rŭpt
dis ū nite	re im bûrse	o ver tŏp
dis re pūte	çĩr eum vŏlve	re ap point
in ter lēave	o ver hăng	un der gō
in ter weave	o ver match	o ver lēap
mis be hāve	dis em bärk	o ver sleep
un de çēive	un der sĕll	dis ap pēar

MOVE, SON, WOLF, FOOT, MOON, OR; RULE, PULL; EXIST; Ç=K; Ġ=J; Ṣ=Z; ÇH=SH.

moun tain eer'	fin an çier'	o ver east'
en ġin eer	brig a dier	re in vĕst
dom i neer	gren a dier	eo ex ĭst
mu ti neer	bom bar dier	prē ex ist
pī o neer	deb o nâir	in ter mix
aue tion eer	reṣ er voir	o ver thrōw
o ver seer	o ver joy	o ver flōw
prī va teer	mis em ploy	o ver lāy
vol un teer	es pla nāde	dis o bey
gaz et teer	in ex pērt	dis al low

No. 77.—LXXVII.
WORDS OF TWO SYLLABLES, ACCENTED ON THE FIRST.

ăt' las	eŏp' y	hŭr' ry	flăb' by
sūe eor	hăp py	flŭr ry	shab by
hŏn or	pŏp py	här py	tab by
răn eor	pŭp py	ĕn try	lŏb by
ean dor	sun dry	sen try	grĭt ty
splĕn dor	bĕl fry	dŭsk y	pŭt tv
rĭg or	fel ly	pal try	lĕv y
vĭg or	eăr ry	vĕs try	bev y
văl or	măr ry	pĭt y	prĭv y
fĕr vor	păr ry	seăn ty	ĕn vy
seŭlp tor	bĕr ry	plĕn ty	dŏx y
elăm or	fer ry	tes ty	prox y
tĕn nis	cher ry	bet ty	eŏl or
elăs sic	mer ry	pet ty	wŏr ry
ax is	per ry	jet ty	păr ty
fan çy	sŏr ry	dīt ty	ar bor
pĕn ny	eŭr ry	wit ty	har bor

An atlas is a book of maps.
You must be good, or you can not be happy.
When you make letters, look at your copy.
The poppy is a large flower.
The puppy barks, as well as the dog.

BÄR, LÀST, ÇÂRE, FĄLL, WHĄT; HĒR, PRĘY, THÉRE; ĜET; BĪRD, MARĪNE; LIŊK;

The place where the bell hangs in the steeple is called the
    belfry.

Horses carry men on their backs.

We cross the ferry in a boat.

The cherry is an acid fruit.

We are sorry when a good man dies.

Never do your work in a hurry.

Boys like a warm fire in a wintery day.

The farmer likes to have plenty of hay for his cattle, and
    oats for his horses.

The lily is a very pretty flower.

Glass is made fast in the window with putty.

No. 78,—LXXVIII.

WORDS OF THREE SYLLABLES, ACCENTED ON THE FIRST.

băn´ish ment	pŏl´y glot	tĕn´den çy
blan dish ment	bēr ga mot	pŭn ġen çy
pŭn ish ment	ăn te pàst	elĕm en çy
răv ish ment	ĭn ter est	eûr ren çy
pĕd i ment	pĕn te eost	sŏl ven çy
sed i ment	hạl i but	bäŋk rupt çy
ăl i ment	fûr be lōw	sŭm ma ry
eŏm pli ment	bĕd fel lōw	länd la dy
lĭn i ment	çĭe a trix	rĕm e dy
mĕr ri ment	pär a dox	eŏm e dy
det ri ment	sär do nўx	pĕr fi dy
sen ti ment	Săt ur day	mél o dy
dŏe ū ment	hŏl i day	mŏn o dy
tĕg ū ment	rŭn a wāy	pär o dy
mŏn ū ment	eăr a way	prŏs o dy
ĭn stru ment	eàst a way	eûs to dy
eŏn ti nent	lĕg a çy	erŭ çi fix
eăl a mint	făl la çy	dī a leet
ĭd i ot	pŏl i çy	ō ri ent
găl i ot	ĭn fan çy	ā pri eot
chăr i ot	eŏn stan çy	vā ean çy

MOVE, SŎN, WQLF, FŎOT, MŌON. ÔR; RULE, PULL; EXIST; €=K; Ġ=J; S=Z; ÇH.=SH.

vā′ gran çy	prī′ va çy	ob′ lo quy
lū na cy	pō ten cy	dī a ry
dē cen cy	plī an cy	rō ṣa ry
pā pa cy	flū en cy	no ta ry
rē ġen cy	mu ti ny	vo ta ry
pī ra çy	serụ ti ny	gro çer y
eō ġen cy	pē o ny	drā per y
sē ere cy	ī ron y	ī vo ry

No. 79.—LXXIX.

WORDS OF FOUR SYLLABLES, ACCENTED ON THE SECOND.

a ē′ ri al	no tā′ ri al	in tē′ ri or
an nū i ty	ma tē ri al	pos te ri or
me mō ri al	im pe ri al	ex te ri or
de mo ni æ	ar te ri al	pro prī e tor
am mo ni æ	är mō ri al	ex trā ne oŭs
ad jū di eāte	mer eū ri al	spon ta ne ous
e lu çi dāte	em pō ri um	eu ta ne ous
im mē di ate	sen so ri um	er rō ne ous
re pū di āte	tra pē zi um	tĕr rā que ous
eol lē ġi ate	erī te ri on	tär ta re ous
ex fō li āte	çen tū ri on	eom mō di ous
in ē bri āte, v.	al lō di al	fe lo ni ous
ex eō ri āte	al lo di um	här mo ni ous
ap pro pri āte	en eo mi um	gra tū i tous
in fū ri āte	tra ġē di an	for tu i tous
al lē vi āte	eom e di an	luẋ u ri ant
ab bre vi āte	eol le ġi an	e lu so ry
an nī hi lāte	çe rụ le an	il lu so ry
æ eū mu lāte	bar bā ri an	eol lu so ry
il lu mi nāte	gram ma ri an	so çī e ty
e nu mer āte	in fē ri or	im pū ri ty
re mu ner āte	su pe ri or	se eu ri ty
in eôr po rāte	an te ri or	ob seu ri ty

All clouds float in the aërial regions.

The aërial songsters are birds of the air.

Gravestones are placed by graves, as memorials of the dead. They call to our remembrance our friends who are buried under them or near them.

The blossoms of spring send forth an agreeable smell.

There is an immediate communication between the heart and the brain.

Men who have been instructed in colleges are said to have a collegiate education.

Laudanum is given to alleviate pain.

The sun illuminates our world.

Our bodies are material, and will return to dust; but our souls are immaterial, and will not die.

Arterial blood is that which flows from the heart through the arteries.

An actor of a tragedy upon the stage is called a tragedian.

A collegian is a student at college.

God has made two great lights for our world—the sun and the moon; the sun is the superior light, and the moon is the inferior, or lesser light.

The exterior part of a house, is the outside; the interior is that within.

No. 80.—LXXX.

WORDS OF TWO SYLLABLES, ACCENTED ON THE FIRST.

mŭş' lin	eôr' ban	eŏn' gress	ăb' jeet
lĭnch pĭn	kĭtch en	prog ress	ŏb ject
rĕş in	chick en	fôr tress	sŭb ject
rŏş in	mär tin	mĭs tress	vĕr dict
măt in	slŏv en	bŭt tress	rĕl ict
sat in	grĭf fin	rĭck ets	dĭs trict
spav in	ûr chin	spĭr its	in stinct
sav in	dŏl phin	nŏn plus	prē çinct
wĕl kin	pĭp pin	grăm pus	ġib bet
ten don	här ness	mўs tie	shĕr bet
Làt in	wĭt ness	brick băt	dŭl çet
eôr don	in gress	pĕr feet	lăn cet

MŎVE, SŎN, WQLF, FŎŎT, MŌŌN, ÔR ; RŪLE, PULL ; EXIST ; €=K ; Ġ=J ; S=Z ; CH=SH.

bŭf′fet	bŭck′et	bĭl′let	€ôr′net
fĭdġ et	blănk et	fil let	hor net
bŭdġ et	mär ket	skil let	bûr net
răck et	bàs ket	mil let	trŭm pet
latch et	€às ket	€ŏl let	lăp pet
frĕsh et	brĭs ket	gŭl let	tĭp pet
jăck et	mŭs ket	mul let	€är pet
plack et	văl et	€ăm let	€lär et
brack et	tab let	ham let	gar ret
tĭck et	trĭp let	ḡĭm let	fĕr ret
€rick et	gŏb let	in let	tŭr ret
wick et	€ôrse let	bŏn net	ŏff set
dŏck et	măl let	sŏn net	on set
pock et	pal let	rŭn net	€ôr set
sock et	wal let	gär ment	bul let

The old Romans used to write in the Latin language.
The linchpin secures the cart wheel to the axletree.
Satin is a rich glossy silk.
The falcon is a bird of the hawk kind.
Ladies should know how to manage a kitchen.
The little chickens follow the hen.
The martin builds its nest near the house.
A witness must tell all the truth in court.
Our Congress meets once a year to make laws.
The sloven seldom keeps his hands clean.
The dolphin is a sea fish.
A boy can harness a horse and hitch him to a wagon.
We harness horses for the coach or gig.
A good mistress will keep her house in order.
The grampus is a large fish living in the sea.
A relict is a woman whose husband is dead.
Boys love to make a great racket.
Brickbats are pieces of broken bricks.
The doctor sometimes bleeds his patients with a lancet.
When large hailstones fall on the house they make a great
    racket.
The little boy likes to have a new jacket.

BÄR, LÅST, €ÂRE, FALL, WHĄT; HÊR, PREY, THÊRE; ĜET; BÏRD, MARÏNE; LIŊK;

No. 81.—LXXXI.

WORDS OF THREE SYLLABLES, ACCENTED ON THE SECOND.
THE LAST COLUMN IS LEFT UNMARKED.

re vĕnge′ fụl	in vĕnt′ ĭve	in ac′ tive
for ḡet ful	per çep tive	de fect ive
e vent ful	prc sŭmp tive	ef fect ive
neg leet ful	eon sump tive	ob ject ive
dis gŭst ful	de çĕp tive	e lect ive
dis trust ful	as sêrt ive	ad he sive
sue çĕss ful	a bòr tive	co he sive
un skïll ful	dĭ ĝĕst ive	de ci sive
eol lée̯t ĭve	ex pŭl sive	cor ro sive
pros peet ive	eom pul sive	a bu sive
per speet ive	im pul sive	con clu sive
eor reet ive	re pul sive	ex clu sive
in vee tive	de fēn sive	in clu sive
vin dïe tive	of fen sive	e lu sive
af fliet ive	sub vēr sive	de lu sive
at trăet ive	dis eûr sive	al lu sive
dis tīnet ive	ex eur sive	il lu sive
sub jūne tive	in eur sive	eol lu sive
eon jupe tive	sue çĕss ive	ob tru sive
in duet ive	ex çess ive	in tru sive
pro duet ive	pro gress ive	pro tru sive
de strue tive	op press ive	e va sive
eon struet ive	ex press ive	per sua sive
in çĕn tive	im press ive	as sua sive
re ten tive	sub mĭs sive	dis sua sive
at ten tive	per mis sive	un fad ing
pre vent ive	trans mis sive	un feel ing

We are apt to live forgetful of our continual dependence on
   the will of God.

We should not trust our lives to unskillful doctors or drunken
   sailors.

Washington was a successful general.

MOVE, SÒN, WOLF, FÒOT, MÒON, ÔR ; RŲLE, PŲLL ; EXIST ; €=K ; Ġ=J ; S̡=Z ; ÇH=SH.

A prospective view, means a view before us.

Perspective glasses are such as we look through, to see things at a distance.   Telescopes are perspective glasses.

Rum, gin, brandy, and whisky are destructive enemies to mankind.   They destroy more lives than wars, famine, and pestilence.

An attentive boy will improve in learning.

Putrid bodies emit an offensive smell.

The drunkard's course is progressive; he begins by drinking a little, and shortens his life by drinking to excess.

The slōth is an inactive, slow animal.

The President of the United States is elected once every four years.   He is chosen by electors who are elected by people of the different States.

No. 82.—LXXXII.

WORDS OF FOUR SYLLABLES, ACCENTED ON THE FIRST.

jū′ di ea tūre	spĭr′ it ū oŭs	eăr′ i ea tūre
ĕx pli ea tĭve	spir it ū al	tĕm per a ture
păl li a tive	lin e a ment	lĭt er a ture
spĕe ū la tive	vĭs̡ ion a ry	ăg ri eul ture
eŏp ū la tive	mis sion a ry	hòr ti eul ture
nom i na tive	die tion a ry	prĕs by ter y
op er a tive	stā tion a ry	des ul to ry
fĭg ū ra tive	ĕst ū a ry	prŏm on to ry
vĕg e tā tive	mẽr çe na ry	pĕr emp to ry
ĭm i tā tive	mĕs en ter y	eăs̡ ū is try

No. 83.—LXXXIII.

WORDS OF THREE SYLLABLES, ACCENTED ON THE FIRST.

rĕl′ a tĭve	prĭm′ i tĭve	ăd′ jee tĭve
ăb la tive	pûr ga tive	ŏb vi oŭs
năr ra tive	lĕn i tive	ĕn vi ous
lax a tive	trăn si tive	pēr vi ous
ĕx ple tive	sĕn si tive	păt ū lous
neg a tive	sŭb stan tive	pĕr il ous

BÄR, LÀST, €ÂRE, ₣ALL, WH₡T; HẼR, PE₡Y, THÊRE; ĞET; BĪRD, MARĪNE; LIŊK;

seŭr' ril oŭs	sĕd' ū loŭs	pŏp' ū loŭs
mär vel ous	glănd ū lous	quĕr ụ lous
₣rĭv o lous	gran ū lous	ĭn fạ mous
făb ū lous	pĕnd ū lous	blăs phe mous
nĕb ū lous	serŏf ū lous	dē vi ous
glŏb ū lous	ĕm ū lous	pre vi ous
erēd ū lous	trem ū lous	lī bel ous

No. 84. — LXXXIV.

WORDS OF TWO SYLLABLES, ACCENTED ON THE FIRST.

bŏn' fīre	spĕnd' thrift	eạl' dron	wor' ship
săm phire	sûr ₣eit	chăl dron	(wûr' ship)
săp phire*	dĕs €ant, n.	saf fron	stär līght
quăg mire	ped ant	mŏd ern	mid night
ĕm pire	pend ant	bĭck ern	ŭp right
ŭm pire	vēr dant	lăn tern	ĭn sight
wĕl fāre	sŏl emn	çĭs tern	fŏr ₣eit
härd ware	€ol umn	păt tern	nŏn sūit
wĭnd pīpe	vol ūme	slat tern	prĭṣ on
băg pipe	ăn s₩er	bĭt tern	gär den
hŏrn pipe	€ŏṇ quer	tăv ern	mēr chant
brĭm stōne	€ôr sâir	gŏv ern	doŭb let
săṇ guĭne	grănd eūr	stŭb born	fŏre head
prĭs tĭne	phȳṣ ies	chĕck er	vīne yard
trib ūne	tăe ties	vĭe ar	€uck ōō
fôrt une	ŏp ties	hĕ*i*f er	€ŏŏp er
lănd seāpe	eăl endṣ	chăm fer	wạ ter
pam phlet	fŏr ward	pärs ley	mawk ish
prŏph et	rĭch eṣ	friĕnd ship	awk ward
eon traet	ăsh eṣ	härd ship	dwarf ish

Brimstone is a mineral which is dug from the earth.

Children should answer questions politely.

When the sun shines with clearness, it is the most splendid
object that we can see.

* Pronounced *săf' fīre.*

MOVE, SÓN, WOLF, FÓOT, MŌON, ÒR; RULE, PULL; EXIST; €=K; Ġ=J; S=Z; CH=SH.

Potashes and pearlashes are made from common ashes.

Thirty-six bushels of coal make one chaldron.

Saffron is a well-known garden plant.

To keep the wind from blowing out the candle, we put it into a lantern.

A wooden cistern is not very durable.

Many persons spend too much time at taverns.

Mules are sometimes very stubborn animals.

The cuckoo visits us early in the spring.

Carrots have long tapering roots.

Twelve o'clock at night is midnight.

A merchant is one who exports and imports goods, or who buys and sells goods, especially by wholesale.

Water flows along a descent by the force of gravity.

God governs the world in infinite wisdom; the Bible teaches us that it is our duty to worship Him.

It is a solemn thing to die and appear before God.

No. 85.—LXXXV.

WORDS OF THREE SYLLABLES, ACCENTED ON THE FIRST.

chĕr′ u bim	pôr′ eu pīne	seôr′ pi on
sĕr a phim	ŏr i ġin	băr ris ter
mär tyr dom	jăv e lin	dŭl çi mer
ĭd i om	rav e lin	măr i ner
draw ing-rōom	här le quin	eŏr o ner
eăt a plaṣm	myr mi don*	eăn is ter
ŏs tra çiṣ n	lĕx i eon	mĭn is ter
găl li çiṣm	dee a gon	sin is ter
skĕp ti çiṣm	ŏe ta gon	prĕs by ter
sўl lo ġiṣm	pĕn ta gon	quĭck sil ver
hĕr o iṣm	hep ta gon	mĕt a phor
băr ba riṣm	hex a gon	băch e lor
ăs ter iṣm	pŏl y gon	chan çel lor
aph o riṣm	chăm pi on	ĕm per or
mag net iṣm	• pòm pi on	eŏn quer or

* Pronounced *mĕr′ mĭ-don*.

sĕn′ a tor   eā′ pi as   pow′ er fụl

ŏr a tor   ea ri ĕş   eā ve at

€oun sel or   a ri ēş   bāy o net

ĕd it or   ū ni €orn   rōşe ma ry

€red it or   pōr ti €o   fruit er y

mŏn i tor   ạu dit or   fōōl er y

ăn çes tor   ạl ma nae   drōll er y

pär a mọur   wạ ter fạll   straw ber ry

€ŏp per as   quạd ra tūre   quạl i ty

pol i ties   €ȯv ert ūre   lạu re ate

hĕm or rhoidş   wạ ter man   house wïfe ry

ăs ter oidş   salt-çel lar   buọy an çy

rē qui em   ē qui nox   dĕnt ist ry

dī a phraɡm   €oun ter poişe   sŏph ist ry

chām ber lɑin   €oun ter märch   pôr phy ry

ĭn ter im   €oun ter sïɡn   prŏph e çy

mē te or   boun ti fụl   ŏff seour ing

Cherubim is a Hebrew word in the plural number.

True heroism may sometimes be shown in everyday employment.

We ought to pity the mistakes of the ignorant, and try to
correct them.

The porcupine can raise his sharp quills, in the same manner
as a hog erects his bristles.

All mankind have their origin from Adam.

A lexicon is a dictionary explaining words.

Goliath was the champion of the Philistines.

Pompions are now commonly called *pumpkins.*

The sting of a scorpion is poisonous and fatal.

Mariners are sailors who navigate ships on the high seas.

We put tea into a canister to keep its flavor.

Quicksilver is heavier than lead; and it flows like a liquid,
but without moisture.

Abraham was the great ancestor of the Hebrews.

Cicero was the most celebrated of the Roman orators.

If John sells goods to James on credit, John is the creditor,
and James is the debtor.

MOVE, SÒN, WOLF, FOOT, MOÒN, ÒR; RULE, PULL; EXIST; €=K; Ġ=J; Ş=Z; ÇH=SH.

No. 86.—LXXXVI.

WORDS OF TWO SYLLABLES, ACCENTED ON THE SECOND.

€om pĕl′	be ḡĕt′	pro jĕet′, *v.*	ex tĭnet′
dis pel	for ḡet	tra ject, *v.*	de fŭnct
ex pel	re gret	ob ject, *v.*	de eŏct
re pel	be set	sub ject, *v.*	de dŭct
im pel	un fĭt	de ject	in duct
pro pel	sub mit	de fect	€on duct, *v.*
fŏre tell	ad mit	af fect	ob struct
ful fĭll	e mit	ef fect	in struct
dis till	re mit	in fect	€on struct
in still	trans mit	e lect	re plănt
ex till	€om mit	se lect	im plant
ex tŏl	per mit	re flect	sup plant
ja păn	re fit	in flect	dis plant
tre pan	ae quit	neg lect	trans plant
rat tan	out wit	€ol lect	le vant
dĭ van	re ăet	€on nect	de sçent
be ḡĭn	en act	re spect	la ment
with in	€om pact	sus pect	aug ment, *v.*
un pin	re fract	e rect	af fĭx, *v.*
hēre in	in fract	€or rect	pre fix, *v.*
a nŏn	sub tract	di rect	in fix
up on	de tract	de tect	trans fix
per hăps	re tract	pro tect	pro lix
re vōlt	€on tract, *v.*	ad dict	€om mix
a dŭlt	pro tract	pre dict	çe mĕnt, *v.*
re şult	ab stract, *v.*	af flict	€on sent
in sult, *v.*	dis tract	in flict	fo ment
€on sult	ex tract, *v.*	€on flict, *v.*	fer ment
de €ănt	trans act	de pict	dis sent
re €ant	re jĕct	re strict	in tent
a bĕt	e ject	sue einct	€on tent
ea det	in ject	dis tinct	ex tent

BÄR, LÂST, €ÂRE, F̣ALL, WHA̧T; HÊR, PRE̤Y, THÉRE; ĜET; B̄ĪRD, MAᴇĪNE; LIN̄K;

e vĕnt′	ᴇom plāint′	æ ᴇount′	be lōw′
re prĭnt	re straint	al low	be stōw
pre tĕxt	ᴇon straint	en dow	af frŏnt
re lăx	dis traint	ba shạw	ᴇon frŏnt
per plĕx	æ quaint	be dew	re prọve
an nex	ap point	es chew	dis prọve
de vour	dis joint	re new	im prọve
a loud	a noint	fōre shōw	re plỹ

Heavy clouds foretell a shower of rain.
The rattan is a long slender reed that grows in Java.
Good children will submit to the will of their parents.
Let all your precepts be succinct and clear.
We elect men to make our laws for us.
Idle children neglect their books when young, and thus reject their advantages.
The little busy bees collect honey from flowers; they never neglect their employment.
The neck connects the head with the body.
Children should respect and obey their parents.
Parents protect and instruct their children.
Satan afflicted Job with sore boils.
The lady instructs her pupils how to spell and read.
Teachers should try to implant good ideas in the minds of their pupils.
The kind mother laments the death of a dear infant.
A bashaw is a title of honor among the Turks; a governor. The word is now commonly spelled *pasha*.
"If sinners entice thee, consent thou not," but withdraw from their company.

No. 87.--LXXXVII.
WORDS OF TWO SYLLABLES, ACCENTED ON THE FIRST.

fĭs′ ᴇal	pĭt′ ᴇōal	mĕn′ tal	tĭm′ brel
ŏf fal	mŏr al	mŏr tal	mŏn̲ grel
fŏrm al	çĕn tral	vĕs tal	quạr rel
dĭs mal	văs sal	rev el	squir rel
chär ᴇōal	dĕn tal	găm brel	mĭn strel

MOVE, SÓN, WOLF, FÓOT, MOON, ÔR; RULE, PÚLL; EXIST; €=K; Ġ=J; S=Z; ÇH=SH.

hănd′ sel	hûrt′ fụl	eŭs′ tom	kĭng′ man
chĭṣ el	wĭst ful	bŏt tom	hŭnts man
dăm ṣel	lŭst ful	plăt fôrm	fŏot man
trav ail	măd am	sär €aṣm	grŏg ram
tĕn dril	mĭll dăm	mī aṣm	eăp stan
stĕr ĭle	bĕd lam	făn taṣm	sĭl van
nŏs tril	bŭck ram	sŏph iṣm	tûr ban
trăn quil	bạl sam	băp tiṣm	făm ĭne
hand bill	ĕm blem	ăl um	sär dĭne
wĭnd mill	prŏb lem	vĕl lum	ĕn ġĭne
găm bol	sỹs tem	mĭn im	mär lĭne
sỹm bol	pĭl grim	nŏs trum	ĕr mĭne
fŏot stōol	king dom	frŭs trum	ver min
pĭs tol	sĕl dom	tûr ban	jăs mĭne
hănd fụl	€arl dom	ôr gan	rap ĭne
vĕnġe ful	wĭṣ dom	or phan	dŏ€ trĭne
wĭsh ful	vĕn om	horse man	dĕs tĭne
băsh ful	mŭsh rōom	eär man	phăl anx
skĭll ful	trăn som	pĕn man	sī ren
hĕlp ful	blŏs som	ġēr man	ĭn grāin
blĭss ful	phăn tom	chûrch man	pär boil
frĕt ful	sỹmp tom	work man	breech ing
			[brĭch′ĭng]

Charcoal is wood charred, or burned to a coal.
Pit coal is dug from the earth for fuel.
Never quarrel with your playmates.
A squirrel will climb a tree quicker than a boy.
A ship is a vessel with three masts.
The nose has two nostrils through which we breathe and smell.
We sit in chairs and put our feet on a footstool.
The farmer sows his grain by handfuls.
Children may be helpful to their parents.
Try to be a skiliful workman (wûrk′man).
An artist is one who is skiliful in some art.
The fox is said to be an artful animal.
Little boys and girls must not be fretful.

A kingdom is a country ruled by a king.
A wise man will make a good use of his knowledge.
A chill is a symptom of fever.
The chewing of tobacco is a useless habit.

No. 88.—LXXXVIII.

WORDS OF TWO SYLLABLES, ACCENTED ON THE FIRST.

bōat' swain	fōre' tŏp	rē' gress
chiēf tain	main tŏp	çȳ press
neū ter	chăm ber	fā moŭs
pew ter	shōul der	spī nous
bēa ver	mōld er	vi nous
cleav er	rān ġer	sē rous
weav er	mān ġer	pō rous
sew er	strān ġer	nī trous
lāy er	dān ġer	griēv ous
prâyer fụl	çī pher	trēat ment
māy or	twī līght	wāin seot
ō yer	mōon light	main mast
eōl ter	dāy light	hīnd mōst
mō hâir	skȳ light	fōre most
trāi tor	fōre sight	sīgn post
hōme ward	pōr trait	bȳ law
out ward	bōw sprit	rāin bōw
wā ġeṣ	tī dingṣ	flȳ blow
breech eṣ	dọ ingṣ	eā lix
[brich'ĕz]	mōor ingṣ	phē nix
erāy on	fīre ärmṣ	rē flux
ā corn	twee zerṣ	week dāy
hōme spun	heed less	Frī day
snōw drŏp	ē gress	pāy dāy

The boatswain takes care of the ship's rigging.
Pewter is made chiefly of tin and lead.
The fur of the beaver makes the best hats.
The weaver weaves yarn into cloth.

MŎVE, SŎN, WOLF, FŎŎT, MŎŎN, ÔR; RŲLE, PŲLL; EXĮST; €=K; Ġ=J; Ş=Z; ÇH=SH.

Oak trees produce acorns, and little animals eat them.

Spring is the first season of the year.

The planet Saturn has a bright ring around it.

The mason puts a layer of mortar between bricks.

The mayor of a city is the chief magistrate.

Judas was a traitor: he betrayed his master; that is, he gave him up to his enemies.

The hair that is over the forehead is called a foretop.

The farmer feeds his horse in a manger.

We should be attentive and helpful to strangers.

Firearms were not known a few hundred years ago.

Intemperance is a grievous sin of our country.

Parents deserve the kind treatment of children.

The United States have a large extent of seacoast.

The rainbow is a token that the world will not be drowned again, but that the regular seasons will continue.

A portrait is a picture bearing the likeness of a person.

Mohair is made of camels' hair.

Pay the laborer his wages when he has done his work.

Prayer is a duty, but it is in vain to pray without a sincere desire of heart to obtain what we pray for; to repeat the words of a prayer, without such desire, is solemn mockery.

No. 89.—LXXXIX.

WORDS OF TWO SYLLABLES, ACCENTED ON THE SECOND.

du rĕss′	ea rĕss′	dis trĕss′	ro bŭst′
a màss	ad dress	as sess	ad just
re pàss	re dress	pos sess	un just
sur pàss	ag gress	a mĭss	in trust
eui răss	trans gress	re miss	dis trust
mo răss	de press	dis miss	mis trust
ae çess	re press	em bŏss	un mĭxt
re çess	im press	a eross	be twixt
ex çess	op press	dis eŭss	a vērt
eon fess	sup press	ae eŏst	sub vert
un less	ex press	ex haust	re vert

BÄR, LÀST, CÂRE, FALL, WHĄT; HĒR, PRĘY, THÊRE; ĜET; BÎRD, MARÏNE; LIŊK;

dĭ vẽrt'	im pōrt', v.	eon trȧst', v.	dĭ vĕst'
eon vert, v.	eom port	a mĭdst	in vest
per vert, v.	sup port	in fĕst	be quest
a lert	trans port, v.	sug ġest	re quest
in ert	re sôrt	dĭ ġest, v.	sub sĭst
ex pert	as sort	be hest	de sist
de ṣert	de tort	mo lest	in sist
in sert	re tort	ar rest	eon sist
as sert	eon tort	de test	per sist
es eôrt, v	dis tort	eon test, v.	as sist
de pôrt	ex tort, v.	pro test, v.	un twist
re port	un hûrt	at test	re ṣist

The miser amasses riches, and keeps his money where it will
do no good.
Confess your sins and forsake them.
Unless you study you will not learn.
The fond mother loves to caress her babe.
Paul addressed Felix upon the subject of a future judgment.
Bridges are made across rivers.
An unjust judge may give a false judgment.
William Tell was an expert archer.
The fearful man will desert his post in battle.
Wolves infest new countries and destroy the sheep.
We detest robbers and pirates.
The wicked transgress the laws of God.

No. 90. XC.

WORDS OF FOUR SYLLABLES. ACCENTED ON THE SECOND.
a, IN A FINAL SYLLABLE ENDING IN **ate,** IF UNMARKED,
HAS NOT ITS FULL LONG SOUND.

trī ĕn'ni al	sep tĕn'ni al	lix ĭv'i um
lĭx ĭv i al	sex ten ni al	e quĕs tri an
mil lĕn ni al	ter res tri al	il lĭt er ate
quȧd ren ni al	eol lāt er al	a dŭl ter āte
per en ni al	de lĭr i um	as sĕv er āte

MOVE, SÓN, WOLF, FÓOT, MÖON, ÓR; RULE, PULL; EXIST; €=K; Ġ=J; Ş Z; ÇH=SH

de çĕm'vi rate	e răd' i €ate	æ eŏm' mo dāte
e lăb o rate	çer tĭf i ate	€om men su rate*
€or rŏb o rāte	in dĕl i €ate	in ves ti gāte
in vīg or āte	pre văr i €ate	re tăl i āte
de lin e āte	au thĕn ti €ate	€on çĭl i āte
e văp o rāte	do mes ti €ate	€a lŭm ni āte
in æ €u rate	prog nŏs ti €ate	de mŏn stra tĭve
€a paç i tāte	in tox i €ate	de rĭv a tĭve
re sŭs çi tāte	re çĭp ro €ate	€on sĕrv a tĭve
de bĭl i tāte	e quiv o €ate	de fĭn i tĭve
fa çil i tāte	in văl i dāte	in fin i tĭve
de eăp i tāte	€on sŏl i dāte	re trib ū tĭve
pre çĭp i tāte	in tĭm i dāte	€on sĕ€ ū tĭve
in dĕf i nĭte	di lăp i dāte	ex e€ ū tĭve

A triennial assembly is one which continues three years, or is
  held once in three years.
The Parliament of Great Britain is septennial, that is, formed
  once in seven years.
The sun will evaporate water on the ground.
It is difficult to eradicate vicious habits.
Never retaliate an injury, even on an enemy.
Never equivocate or prevaricate, but tell the plain truth.
A definitive sentence is one that is final.
Liquors that intoxicate are to be avoided as poison.
Love and friendship conciliate favor and esteem.

No. 91.—X C I.

WORDS OF TWO SYLLABLES, ACCENTED ON THE SECOND.

æ quīre'	per spīre'	re quīre'	ex plōre'
ad mire	sus pire	in quire	re store
as pire	ex pire	es quire	se €ūre
re spire	de şire	a dōre	pro €ure
trans pire	re tire	be fore	ob s€ure
in spire	en tire	de plore	en dure
€on spire	at tire	im plore	ab jure

* Pronounced *€om mĕn' shoo rate*.

BÄR, LÁST, €ÂRE, FĄLL, WHĄT; HÊR, PRĘY, THÈRE; ĞET; BĬRD, MARĪNE; LIŊK;

ad jūre′	pro mōte′	re çēive′	im pēach′
al lure	de note	per çeive	ap prōach
de mure	re fūte	de rīve	en €roach
im mure	€on fute	de prive	re proach
ma nure	sa lute	ar rive	be seech
in ure	dĭ lute	€on trive	€on ġēal
im pure	pol lute	re vive	re peal
as sure (-shur)	vo lute	sur vive	ap peal
ma tūre	per mute	un glūe	re veal
de çēase	€om pute	al lŭde	ġen teel
de €rease	de pute	re būte	as sāil
re lease	dis pute	un trųe	out sail
in €rease	be hāve	re move	de tail, v.
pre çīse	en slave	be hoove	re tail, v.
€on çise	for gave	ap prove	en tail
mo rōse	en grave	a€ €rųe	€ur tail
jo €ose	de prave	dis sēize	a vail
im brųe	sub dūe	ap prīse	pre vail
dis €ōurse	in due	as size	be wail
ū nīte	a chiēve	re liēf	€on trōl
iġ nite	aġ grieve	be hoof	en roll
in vite	re prieve	a loof	pa trol
re mōte	re trieve	re proof	ob līġe

People admire the beautiful flowers of spring.

The rainbow excites our admiration.

Men acquire property by industry and economy; but it is more easy to acquire property than to keep it.

Farmers put manure on their fields to enrich the land and obtain good crops.

The light on this side of the moon, increases all the time from new to full moon; and then it decreases till it becomes new moon again; and so it continues increasing and decreasing.

Wise farmers contrive to procure a good living, by honest labor, and commonly succeed.

It is not honorable to dispute about trifles.

MOVE, SÓN, WOLF, FŎŎT, MOON, ÓR ; RULE, PULL ; EXIST ; ℮=K ; Ġ=J ; S=Z ; ÇH=SH.

A field requires a good fence to secure the crops.

The clouds often obscure the sky in the night, and deprive us of the light of the moon and stars.

You must not try to deceive your parents.

The buds of the trees survive the winter; and when the warm sun shines, in the spring, the leaves and blossoms come forth upon the trees, the grass revives, and springs up from the ground.

Before you rise in the morning or retire at night, give thanks to God for his mercies, and implore the continuance of his protection.

No. 92.—XCII.

WORDS OF TWO SYLLABLES, ACCENTED ON THE SECOND.

be tween'	sus tāin'	en twīne'	re vēre'
ea reen	ea jōle	pōst pōne	se vere
eam pāign	eon sole	de throne	eom peer
ar raign	pis tole	en throne	ea reer
or dain	mis rule	a tone	bre vier
dis dain	hu māne	je jūne	bab ōon
re gain	in sane	trī une	buf foon
eom plain	ob sçēne	eom mune	dra goon
ex plain	gan grene	at tune	rae eoon
a main	ter rene	es eāpe	doub loon
ab stain	eon vene	e lōpe	bal loon
do main	eom bīne	de elâre	gal loon
re frain	de fine	in snare	shal loon
re strain	re fine	de spair	plat oon
dis train	eon fine	pre pare	lam poon
eon strain	sa line	re pair	här poon
eon tain	de eline	eom pare	mon soon
ob tain	ea nine	im pair	bas soon
de tain	re pine	sin çēre	fes toon
per tain	su pine	ad here	pol troon
at tain	en shrine	eo here	dis ōwn
dis tain	dĭ vine	aus tere	un *known*

un sōwn	a līght	a wāit	eon tour
a dọ	de līght	de çēit	be sīdes
out dọ	a right	eon çeit	re çēipt
a gō	af fright	a mọur	re liēve

When the moon passes between the earth and the sun, we call it new; but you must not think that it is more new at that time, than it was when it was full: we mean, that it begins anew to show us the side on which the sun shines. God ordained the sun to rule the day; and the moon and stars to give light by night.

The laws of nature are sustained by the immediate presence and agency of God.

The heavens declare an Almighty power that made them.

The science of astronomy explains the causes of day and night, and why the sun, and moon, and stars appear to change their places in the heavens.

Air contains the vapors that rise from the earth; and it sustains them, till they fall in dews, and in showers of rain, or in snow or hail.

Grapevines entwine their tendrils round the branches of trees.

Laws are made to restrain the bad, and protect the good.

Glue will make pieces of wood adhere.

The careful ant prepares food for winter.

We often compare childhood to the morning: morning is the first part of the day, and childhood is the first stage of human life.

Do not postpone till to-morrow what you should do to-day.

A harpoon is an instrument for striking whales.

Monsoon is a wind in the East Indies, that blows six months from one quarter, and then six months from another.

Be careful to keep your house in good repair.

Refrain from all evil; keep no company with immoral men.

Never complain of unavoidable calamities.

Let all your words be sincere, and never deceive.

A poltroon is an arrant coward, and deserves the contempt of all brave men.

Never practice deceit, for this is sinful.

To revere a father, is to regard him with fear mingled with respect and affection.

Brevier is a small kind of printing letter.

MOVE, SÓN, WOLF, FOOT, MOON, ÔR; RULE, PULL; EXIST; €=K; Ġ—J; Ş—Z; CH=SH.

No. 93.—XCIII.
WORDS OF FOUR SYLLABLES, THE FULL ACCENT ON THE THIRD,
AND A WEAK ACCENT ON THE FIRST.

an te çed' ent
dis a gree ment
çir eum jā çent
re en fōrçe ment
pre en gāge ment
en ter tāin ment
in €o hēr ent
in de çī sĭve
su per vi şor
€on ser vā tor
des pe ra do
bas ti na do
brag ga dō ci o (-shĭ-o)
mis de mēan or
ap pa rā tus
af fi da vit
ex ul ta tion
ad a măn tĭne
man ū faet ūre
su per strŭet ure
per ad vĕnt ure
met a môr phōse
in nu ĕn do
su per €är go
in ter nŭn ci o (-shĭ-o)
är ma dĭl lo
man i fĕs to
laz a ret to
dis en €ŭm ber
pred e çĕs sor
in ter çes sor

mal e fãe' tor
ben e fae tor
met a phȳş ies
math e măt ies
dis in hĕr it
ev a nĕs çent
€on va les çent
ef flo res çent
€or res pŏnd ent
in de pĕnd ent
re im bûrse ment
dis €on tĕnt ment
om ni prĕş ent
in ad vērt ent
pre ex ĭst ent
€o ex ist ent
in ter mit tent
in ter măr ry
ō ver shad ōw
ae çi dĕnt al
in çi dent al
o ri ent al
fun da ment al
or na ment al
sae ra ment al
reġ i ment al
det ri ment al
mon ū ment al
in stru ment al
hor i zŏn tal
dis a vow al

BÄR, LÅST, CÂRE, FĄLL, WHĄT; HËR, PRĘY, THÉRE; ĠET; BÏRD, MARÏNE; LIŊK;

Gage is a French word, and signifies to pledge.

The banks engage to redeem their notes with specie, and they are obliged to fulfill their engagements.

To preëngage means to engage beforehand.

I am not at liberty to purchase goods which are preëngaged to another person.

To disengage, is to free from a previous engagement.

A mediator is a third person who interposes to adjust a dispute between parties at variance.

How can a young man cleanse his way?

Oh, how love I Thy law!

No. 94.—XCIV.

WORDS OF THREE SYLLABLES, ACCENTED ON THE FIRST,
LEFT UNMARKED FOR EXERCISE IN NOTATION.

NOUNS.	NOUNS.	ADJECTIVES.
cin′ na mon	por′ rin ger	du′ te ous
et y mon	stom a cher	a que ous
grid i ron	ob se quies	du bi ous
and i ron	prom i ses	te di ous
skel e ton	com pass es	o di ous
sim ple ton	in dex es	stu di ous
buf fa lo	am ber gris	co pi ous
cap ri corn	em pha sis	ca ri ous
cal i co	di o cese	se ri ous
in di go	o li o	glo ri ous
ver ti go	o ver plus	cu ri ous
cal i ber	pu is sance	fu ri ous
bed cham ber	nu cle us	spu ri ous
cin na bar	ra di us	lu mi nous
of fi cer	ter mi nus	glu ti nous
col an der	blun der buss	mu ti nous
lav en der	syl la bus	ru in ous
prov en der	in cu bus	lu di crous
cyl in der	ver bi age	dan ger ous
in te ger	Sir i us	hid e ous
scav en ger	cal a mus	in fa mous
har bin ger	mit ti mus	ster to rous

MŎVE, SŎN, WŎLF, FŎOT, MŎON, ŎR; RŮLE, PŬLL; EXIST; €=K; Ġ=J; Ş=Z; ÇH=SH.

nu′mer ous	rav′en ous	vig′or ous
o dor ous	om i nous	val or ous
hu mor ous	res in ous	am or ous
ri ot ous	glut ton ous	clam or ous
trai tor ous	bar ba rous	tim or ous
per vi ous	ul cer ous	sul phur ous
treach er ous	slan der ous	vent ur ous
haz ard ous	pon der ous	rapt ur ous
pit e ous	mur der ous	ar du ous
plen te ous	gen er ous	mis chiev ous
im pi ous	pros per ous	stren u ous
vil lain ous	ran cor ous	sin u ous
mem bra nous	rig or ous	tyr an nous

No. 95.—X C V.

WORDS OF TWO SYLLABLES, ACCENTED ON THE SECOND.

ap pēaşe′	re pōşe′	es chēat′	re hēar′
dis pleaşe	pro poşe	re peat	be smear
diş ease	im poşe	en treat	ap pear
e rāse	€om poşe	re treat	tat tŏo
pre mīşe	trans poşe	un lōose	en trăp
sur mişe	a būşe, v.	de bạuch	in wrap
de spişe	ae €uşe	re €all	un shĭp
a rişe	ex €uşe, v.	be fall	e quip
€om prişe	re fuşe	with al	en €ămp
chas tişe	ef fuşe	fore stall	de €amp
ad vişe	dîf fuşe	fore warn	un stŏp
de vişe	suf fuşe	de fault	ū şûrp
re vişe	in fuşe	as sault	un €làsp
dis ġuişe	€on fuşe	pa paw	de bär
fōre €lōşe	a muşe	with draw	un bar
in €loşe	re €ruit	a sleep	a far
dis €loşe	de fēat	en dēar	ap plạuşe

BÄR, LÁST, CÂRE, FALL, WHAT; HÊR, PREY, THÈRE; ĞET; BÏRD, MARÏNE; LIŊK;

No. 96.—XCVI.
MONOSYLLABLES IN TH.

IN THE FOLLOWING WORDS, **th** HAS THE ASPIRATED SOUND,
AS IN THINK, THIN.

thēme	thōle	trŏth	tĭlth
three	throe	nôrth	smith
thāne	throve	slŏth	truths
thrīçe	teeth	thought	thạw
thrōne	threw (throo)	thôrn	thrall
thrōw	thrīve	thrŏb	thwart
trụth	mēath	throng	warmth
yọuth	thrĕad	thong	swath
hēath	thresh	thĭng	päth
rụth	thrift	think	bäth
shēath	thrŭst	thin	läth
bōth	thrum	thănk	wräth
oath	dĕpth	thĭck	heärth
quoth	wĭdth	thrill	tōoth
growth	filth	thŭmb	bĭrth
blowth	frith	thump	mĭrth
forth	plinth	lĕngth	third
fourth	spilth	strength	thirst
thiẽf	thwăck	hăth	thirl
thieve	brŏth	wĭthe	worth
fäith	eloth	thătch	mŏnth
thīgh	froth	thĭll	south
thrōat	lōth	thĕft	mouth
dŏth	mŏth	thrŭsh	drouth

IN THE FOLLOWING, THE NOUNS HAVE THE ASPIRATED, AND
THE VERBS THE VOCAL SOUND OF **th.**

NOUNS.	VERBS.	NOUNS.	VERBS.
elŏth	elōthe	shēath	shēathe
bäth	bāthe	wreath	wreathe
mouth	mouth	swạth	swāthe
brĕath	brĕathe	teeth	teeth

MOVE, SÓN, WOLF, FŎOT. MŎŌN. ÔR ; RṲLE, PṲLL ; EXIST ; Ҫ=K ; Ġ=J ; Ş=Z ; ҪH—SH.

Cambric is a kind of thin muslin.
A fire was burning on the hearth.
Many kings have been thrown down from their thrones.
A tiger has great strength, and is very ferocious.
A manly youth will speak the truth.
Keep your mouth clean, and save your teeth.
The water in the canal is four feet in depth.
A toothbrush is good to brush your teeth.
The length of a square figure is equal to its breadth.
The breadth of an oblong square is less than its length.
Plants will not thrive among thorns and weeds.
The thresher threshes grain, as wheat, rye, oats.
A severe battle thins the ranks of an army.
Youth may be thoughtful, but it is not very common.
One good action is worth many good thoughts.
A piece of cloth, if good, is worth what it will bring.
Drunkards are worthless fellows, and despised.
Bathing houses have baths to bathe in.
We breathe fresh air at every breath.

No. 97.—XCVII,

WORDS OF TWO SYLLABLES, ACCENTED ON THE FIRST.

băl' last	eŏm' plex	Tūeş' day	vĕr' y
fĭl bert	vēr tex	Wĕdneş day	drĭz zly
eŏn ҫert	vôr tex	Thûrş day	griş ly
ĕf fort	eŏn vex	mĭd wāy	g̅uĭlt y
pûr pōrt	lär y̆nx	găng wāy	păn şy
trăn script	ăf flux	päth wāy	frĕn zy
eŏn script	eŏn flux	ĕs say	quĭn şy
bănk rupt	ĕf flux	eŏm fort	g̅ip sy
ĕld est	ĭn flux	eŏv ert	tip sy
neph ew*	eŏn text	bŏm băst	drŏp sy
sĭn ew	bōw lĭne	eōurt ship	serŭb by
lănd tăx	mĭd dāy	flĭm şy	shrub by
sy̆n tax	Sŭn day	elŭm şy	stub by
ĭn dex	Mŏn day	swĕl try	nut meg

* Pronounced nĕf' yu̟.

BÄR, LÀST, €ÂRE, FALL, WHAT; HĒR, PRĘY, THÉRE; ŌĘT; BĬRD, MARĪNE; LĬNK:

ŏff' ing	hēar' sāy	dāi' ly	frāil' ty
stŭff' ing	drēar y	dai şy	dain ty
brī ny	wēar y	ēa şy	eām brie
nōşe gāy	quē ry	trea ty	shōul der

No. 98.—XCVIII.

IN THE FOLLOWING, THE **O** OF THE DIGRAPH **OW** HAS ITS
FIRST OR LONG SOUND.

bŏr' rōw	bĭl' lōw	hăr' rōw	wĭn' dōw
ĕl bow	hŏl low	spăr row	win now
fel low	ăr row	yăr row	wil low
fŏl low	fär row	yĕl low	mĕl low
eăl low	năr row	tăl low	mŏr row
mĕad ow	mal low	fal low	sor row
shăd ow	pĭl low	shal low	bŭr row
hal low	min now	fŭr row	swăl low
bĕl low	măr row	wĭd ow	wąl low

Filberts are small nuts growing in hedges.

A ship or boat must have ballast to prevent it from over-setting.

The sinews are the tendons that move the joints of the body. The tendon of the heel is the main sinew that moves the foot.

From the shoulder to the elbow there is only one bone in the arm, but from the elbow to the hand there are two bones.

The light is on one side of the body, and the shadow on the other.

In old times there was no glass for windows.

The farmer winnows chaff from the grain.

The callow young means the young bird before it has feathers.

Fallow ground is that which has lain without being plowed and sowed.

A shallow river will not float ships. Some places in the Ohio are at times too shallow for large boats.

Cattle in South America are hunted for their hides and tallow.

MŌVE, SÓN, WǪLF, FŎŎT, MŌŌN, ÔR ; RU̱LE, PU̱LL ; E̱XIST ; Є=K ; Ġ=J ; Ş=Z ; ȻH=SH.

Tallow is the fat of oxen, cows, and sheep.

Apples and peaches are ripe when they are mellow, but hard
apples keep better than mellow ones.

The bull bellows and paws the ground.

Friday is just as lucky a day as any other.

No. 99.—XCIX.

WORDS OF TWO SYLLABLES, ACCENTED ON THE FIRST.

rāṣ′ūre	wee′vil	mōurn′ful	spōrts′man
sēiz ure	snōw ball	fēar ful	brāin păn
trēa tīse	brīde well	cheer ful	mŏn ster
līke wīṣe	mōle hill	rīght ful	free stōne
dōor ēase	fē rīne	fru̱it ful	mīle stone
stâir ease	mīnd fu̱l	bōast ful	grāve stone
sēa hôrse	pēaçe ful	ạw ful	hāil stone
brī dal	hāte ful	law ful	hȳ phen
feū dal	wake ful	plāy dāy	ạu tumn
ōat mēal	ḡu̱ile ful	thrạll dŏm	au burn
spī ral	dōle ful	wạtch man	sauçe păn
flō ral	shāme ful	watch fu̱l	wạr fâre
neū tral	bane ful	free dŏm	fāç īle
plū ral	tūne ful	bọ şom	sērv ĭle
pōrt al	hōpe ful	lūke wạrm	dăe tȳl
bru̱ tal	eâre ful	trī form	dŭe tīle
vī tal	īre ful	glōw worm	mis sīle
ē qual	dire ful	dē işm	dŏç īle
sûr feĭt	ūse ful	ōak um	rĕp tīle
ăn ḡel	grāte ful	quo rum	fēr tīle
ăn cient	spīte ful	strā tum	hŏs tīle
wēa şel	wāste ful	sēa man	sĕx tīle
jew el	fāith ful	free man	flex īle
new el	yọuth ful	fōre man	vĕrd ūre
erew el	gāin ful	yeŏ man	ôrd ūre
[kru̱′el]	pain ful	sāleş man	fĭg ūre
trē foil	spōŏn ful	states man	in jūre

BÄR, LÃST, GÂRE, FĄLL, WHĄT; HẼR, PRẸY, THÈRE; ĜET; BĪRD, MARÏNE; LIṉK;

eŏn′ jure	frăet′ ūre	môr′ tĭse	lĕg′ ate
pēr jure	eŭlt ūre	prăe tĭçe	frĭg ate
plĕaş ure	fīxt ūre	trav erse	in grāte
meaş ūre	eăm phor	ad verse	phȳṣ ie
treaş ūre	grand sīre	pack hôrse	jŏn quil
çĕn sure	prŏm ĭse	rĕf ūse	sŭb tĭle
press ūre	ăn ĭse	măn dāte	fĕr ụle
fĭs sūre	tûr key	ăg ate	eŏn dor

A treatise is a written composition on some particular subject.

Oatmeal is the meal of oats, and is very good food.

An egg is nearly oval in shape.

A newel is the post round which winding stairs are formed.

Crewel is a kind of yarn, or twisted worsted.

A jewel is often hung in the ear. The Jews formerly wore,
   and some nations still wear, jewels in the nose.

Trefoil is a grass of three leaves.

Weevils in grain are very destructive vermin.

To be useful is more honorable than to be showy.

A hyphen is a little mark between syllables or words, thus,
   hy-phen, attorney-general.

A spiral line winds and rises at the same time.

It is a mean act to deface the figures on a milestone.

No pleasure is equal to that of a quiet conscience.

Let us lay up for ourselves treasures in heaven, where neither
   moth nor rust can corrupt.

No. 100.—C.

ORDS OF FOUR SYLLABLES, ACCENTED ON THE SECOND.

ad vĕnt′ ūr oŭs	pre çĭp′ i toŭs
a nŏn y mous	ne çĕs si tous
sȳ non y mous	am phĭb i ous
un ğĕn er ous	mĭ răe ū lous
mag năn i mous	a nal o gous
ū nan i mous	per fĭd i ous
as păr a gus	fas tid i ous

MOVE, SÒN, WOLF, FÒOT, MOÒN, ÒR ; RŲLE, PŲLL ; EXIST ; €=K ; Ġ=J ; Ș=Z ; ÇH=SH

in sĭd´i oŭs	in tĕl´li ġent
in vid i ous	ma lev o lent
€on spie ū ous	be nev o lent
per spie ū ous	pre dĭe a ment
pro mis eu ous	dis păr aġe ment
as sid ū ous	en €oŭr aġe ment
am big ū ous	en frăn chĭşe ment
€on tig ū ous	dis fran chĭşe ment
mel lif lu ous	en tan gle ment
su pēr flu ous	ae knŏwl edġ ment
in ġĕn ū ous	es tăb lish ment
€on tĭn ū ous	em bĕl lish ment
in €ŏn gru ous	ae €ŏm plish ment
im pĕt ū ous	as ton ish ment
tu mŭlt ū ous	re lĭn quish ment
vo lupt ū ous	im pĕd i ment
tem pĕst ū ous	ha bĭl i ment
sig nĭf i €ant	im priş on ment
ex trăv a gant	em băr rass ment
pre dŏm i nant	in tĕg ū ment
in tol er ant	e mŏl ū ment
ī tĭn er ant	pre ĕm i nent
in hăb it ant	in €ŏn ti nent
€on €ŏm i tant	im pēr ti nent
ir rĕl e vant	in dĭf fer ent
be nef i çent	ir rĕv er ent
mag nĭf i çent	om nĭp o tent
mu nif i çent	mel lif lu ent
€o in çi dent	çīr €ŭm flu ent
non rĕş i dent	ae €ou ter ment
im prŏv i dent	€om mū ni €ant

An anonymous author writes without signing his name to his composition.

Synonymous words have the same signification. Very few words in English are exactly synonymous.

BÄR, LÁST, CÂRE, FALL, WHAT; HĔR, PREY, THÉRE; ĜET, BÎRD. MARĬNE; LĬNK;

Precipitous signifies steep; the East and West rocks in New Haven are precipitous.

An amphibious animal can live in different elements. The frog lives in air, and can live in water for a long time.

A miraculous event is one that can not take place according to the ordinary laws of nature. It can take place only by the agency of divine power.

Assiduous study will accomplish almost any thing that is within human power.

An integument is a cover. The skin is the integument of animal bodies. The bones also have integuments.

Young persons are often improvident—far more improvident than the little ants.

No. 101.—C I.
WORDS OF FOUR SYLLABLES, ACCENTED ON THE SECOND, AND LEFT UNMARKED.

as per′i ty	do cil′i ty	e nor′ mi ty
se ver i ty	a gil i ty	ur ban i ty
pros per i ty	fra gil i ty	cu pid i ty
aus ter i ty	ni hil i ty	tur gid i ty
dex ter i ty	hu mil i ty	va lid i ty
in teg ri ty	ste ril i ty	ca lid i ty
ma jor i ty	vi ril i ty	so lid i ty
pri or i ty	scur ril i ty	ti mid i ty
mi nor i ty	duc til i ty	hu mid i ty
plu ral i ty	gen til i ty	ra pid i ty
fa tal i ty	fer til i ty	stu pid i ty
vi tal i ty	hos til i ty	a rid i ty
mo ral i ty	tran quil li ty	flo rid i ty
mor tal i ty	ser vil i ty	fe cun di ty
bru tal i ty	pro pin qui ty	ro tun di ty
fi del i ty	ca lam i ty	com mod i ty
sta bil i ty	ex trem i ty	ab surd i ty
mo bil i ty	sub lim i ty	lo cal i ty
no bil i ty	prox im i ty	vo cal i ty
fa cil i ty	con form i ty	ras cal i ty

MOVE, SÒN, WOLF, FÒOT, MÒON, ÒR ; RULE, PULL ; EXIST ; ∈=K ; ġ=J ; ṣ=z ; ÇH=SH.

re al′ i ty	de spond′ en cy	hy poc′ ri sy
le gal i ty	e mer gen cy	ti moc ra cy
re gal i ty	in clem en cy	im pi e ty
fru gal i ty	con sist en cy	va ri e ty
for mal i ty	in solv en cy	e bri e ty
car nal i ty	de lin quen cy	so bri e ty
neu tral i ty	mo not o ny	pro pri e ty
as cend en cy	a pos ta sy	sa ti e ty

The winters in Lapland are severe. The people of that country dress in furs, to protect themselves from the severity of the cold.

Major signifies more or greater; minor means less.

A majority is more than half; a minority is less than half.

Plurality denotes two or more; as, a plurality of worlds.

In grammar, the plural number expresses more than one; as, two *men*, ten *dogs*.

A majority of votes means more than half of them.

When we say a man has a plurality of votes, we mean he has more than any one else.

Members of Congress and Assembly are often elected by a plurality of votes.

Land is valued for its fertility and nearness to market.

Many parts of the United States are noted for the fertility of the soil.

The rapidity of a stream sometimes hinders its navigation.

Consistency of character, in just men, is a trait that commands esteem.

Humility is the prime ornament of a Christian.

No. 102.—CII.

WORDS OF FIVE SYLLABLES, ACCENTED ON THE SECOND.

eo tĕm′ po ra ry	de ĕlăm′ a to ry
ex tem po ra ry	ex ĕlam a to ry
de rŏg a to ry	in flam ma to ry
ap pĕl la to ry	ex plan a to ry
eon sŏl a to ry	de ĕlar a to ry
de făm a to ry	pre par a to ry

dis pĕn′ sa to ry	ob sẽrv′ a to ry
sub sĭd i a ry	con serv a to ry
in çĕn di a ry	pro hĭb it o ry
stī pen di a ry	pre mŏn i to ry
e pĭs to la ry	re poṣ i to ry
vo căb ū la ry	sup poṣ i to ry
im ăġ i na ry	le ġĭt i ma çy
pre lĭm i na ry	in vĕt er a çy
con fĕe tion er y	sub sẽrv i en çy
un neç es sa ry	de ġĕn er a çy
he red i ta ry	con fĕd er a çy
in vŏl un ta ry	ef fem i na çy
re sĭd ū a ry	in del i ea çȳ
tu mult ū a ry	in hăb it an çy
vo lupt ū a ry	ae còm pa ni ment

Addison and Pope were cotemporary authors, that is, they lived at the same time.

A love of trifling amusements is derogatory to the Christian character.

Epistolary correspondence is carried on by letters.

Imaginary evils make no small part of the troubles of life.

Hereditary property is that which descends from ancestors.

The Muskingum is a subsidiary stream of the Ohio.

A man who willfully sets fire to a house is an incendiary.

An observatory is a place for observing the heavenly bodies with telescopes.

An extemporary discourse is one spoken without notes or premeditation.

Christian humility is never derogatory to character.

Inflame, signifies to heat, or to excite.

Strong liquors inflame the blood and produce diseases.

The prudent good man will govern his passions, and not suffer them to be inflamed with anger.

Intemperate people are exposed to inflammatory diseases.

A conservatory is a large greenhouse for the preservation and culture of exotic plants.

MOVE, SÒN, WOLF, FOOT, MOON, ÔR ; RULE, PULL ; EXIST ; €=K ; Ġ—J ; S̲=Z ; ÇH=SH.

No. 103.—CIII.

WORDS OF SIX SYLLABLES, ACCENTED ON THE FOURTH, OR
ANTEPENULT.

ma te ri ăl′i ty	€om press i bĭl′i ty
il lib er al i ty	€om pat i bil i ty
ū ni ver sal i ty	de stru€t i bil i ty
in hos pi tal i ty	per çep ti bil i ty
in stru ment al i ty	re s̲ist i bil i ty
spir it ū al i ty	€om bus ti bil i ty
im prob a bĭl i ty	in flex i bil i ty
im pla €a bil i ty	dis sim i lăr i ty
mal le a bil i ty	par tie ū lar i ty
in flam ma bil i ty	ir reg ū lar i ty
in €a pa bil i ty	in fe ri ŏr i ty
pen e tra bil i ty	su pe ri or i ty
im mu ta bil i ty	im pet ū os i ty
in €red i bil i ty	ġen er al ĭs si mo
il leġ i bil i ty	dis çi plin ā ri an
re fran ġi bil i ty	pre des ti na ri an
in fal li bil i ty	an te di lū vi an
dĭ vis̲ i bil i ty	het e ro ġē ne oŭs
in sen si bil i ty	me di a tō ri al
im pos si bil i ty	in quis̲ i to ri al

No. 104.— CIV.

WORDS OF THREE SYLLABLES, ACCENTED ON THE FIRST.

bĕn′ e fit	ĭn′ tel le€t	sŭp′ pli €ant
ăl pha bet	çir €um spe€t	pēr ma nent
păr a pet	pĭck pŏ€k et	mĭs €re ant
sŭm mer set	flow er et	tēr ma gant
mĭn ū €t	lĕv er et	ĕl e gant
pŏl ў pus	pen ny weight	lĭt i gant
ĭm pe tus	€at a pult	ăr ro gant
€at a ra€t	mĕn di €ant	ĕl e phant

BÄR, LÅST, €ÂRE, F₄LL, WH₄T; HĒR, PRE̱Y, THȆRE; ĠET; BĪRD, MARĬNE; LIꞐK;

sȳe′ o phant	ĭn′ do lent	sĭm′ i lar
pĕt ū lant	tûr bu lent	pŏp ū lar
ăd a mant	sŭe eu lent	tăb ū lar
€óv e nant	fĕe ū lent	glŏb ū lar
€ŏn so nant	es €u lent	sĕe ū lar
pēr ti nent	ŏp ū lent	ŏe ū lar
tŏl er ant	vĭr u̯ lent	joe ū lar
€ôr mo rant	flăt ū lent	çĭr eu lar
ĭg no rant	lĭg a ment	mŭs eu lar
€ŏn ver sant	pär lia ment	rĕg ū lar
mĭl i tant	fĭl a ment	çel lu lar
ăd ju tant	ärm a ment	ăn nu lar
rĕl e vant	săe ra ment	seap ū lar
ĭn no çent	tĕst a ment	spĕc ū lar
ăe çi dent	măn aġe ment	€ŏn su lar
ĭn çi dent	ĭm ple ment	€ăp su lar
dif fi dent	€ŏm ple ment	tĭt ū lar
€ŏn fi dent	€om pli ment	sŭb lu nar
rĕs̱ i dent	băt tle ment	çĭm e ter
pres̱ i dent	sĕt tle ment	băs̱ i lisk
prŏv i dent	ten e ment	€an ni bal
ĭn di ġent	ĭn €re ment	€ŏch i nĕal
nĕg li ġent	ĕm brȳ o	mär tin gal
ăm bi ent	pärt ner ship	hŏs pi tal
prĕv a lent	fĕl lōw ship	pĕd es tal
pes ti lent	€ăl en dar	tū bu lar
ex çel lent	vĭn e gar	jū gu lar
red o lent	in su lar	fū ner al

No. 105.—C V.

WORDS OF FIVE SYLLABLES, ACCENTED ON THE THIRD.

am bi gū′ i ty	im por tū′ ni ty
€on ti gū i ty	op por tū ni ty
€on tra rī e ty	per pe tū i ty

MŎVE, SÒN, WOLF, FŎŎT, MŎŎN, ÔR; RỤLE, PỤLL; EXIST; ℭ=K; Ġ=J; S̤=Z; ℭH=SH.

su per flū′ i ty	puṉet ū āl′ i ty
in ere du li ty	mūt ū al i ty
in se eu ri ty	in fi dĕl i ty
im ma tu ri ty	prob a bil i ty
per spi eu i ty	in a bil i ty
as si du i ty	du ra bil i ty
eon ti nu i ty	dis a bil i ty
in ġe nu i ty	in sta bil i ty
in eon grụ i ty	mu ta bil i ty
fran ġi bĭl i ty	ered i bil i ty
fal li bil i ty	tan ġi bil i ty
fēa s̤i bil i ty	so cia bil i ty *(so-sha-)*
vis̤ i bil i ty	traet a bil i ty
sen si bil i ty	pla ea bil i ty
pos si bil i ty	in ū til i ty
plạu s̤i bil i ty	in çi vil i ty
im be çil i ty	ū ni fôrm i ty
in do çil i ty	non eon form i ty
vol a til i ty	eon san guĭn i ty
ver sa til i ty	siṉ gu lăr i ty
ea pa bil i ty	joe ū lar i ty
in si pid i ty	reg ū lar i ty
il le găl i ty	pop ū lar i ty
prod i gal i ty	me di ŏe ri ty
eor di al i ty	in sin çĕr i ty
per son al i ty	sin ū ŏs i ty
prin çi pal i ty	eu ri os i ty
lib er al i ty	an i mos i ty
ġen er al i ty	ġen er os i ty
im mo ral i ty	flex i bĭl i ty
hos pi tal i ty	im mo bil i ty
im mor tal i ty	sol ū bil i ty
in e quạl i ty	vol ū bil i ty
sen sū ăl i ty *(sen-shụ-)*	mag na nim i ty

BÄR, LÁST, CÂRE, FALL, WHĄT; HĒR, PRĘY, THÊRE; ŌRT; BÏRD, MARÏNE; LIŊK;

ū na nĭm′ i ty
in hu măn i ty
ar is tŏe ra çy
in ad vĕr ten çy

phra şe ŏl′ o ġy
os te ol o ġy
a er ol o ġy
nɔ to rī e ty

No. 106.—CVI.

WORDS OF THREE SYLLABLES, ACCENTED ON THE SECOND.

çes sā′ tion	plan tā′ tion	de trăe′ tion
lī ba tion	no ta tion	eon trae tion
pro ba tion	ro ta tion	pro trae tion
va ea tion	quo ta tion	dis trae tion
lo ea tion	temp ta tion	ex trae tion
vo ea tion	prī va tion	eon nĕe tion
gra da tion	sal va tion	af fee tion
foun da tion	e qua tion	eon fee tion
ere a tion	vex a tion	per fee tion
ne ga tion	tax a tion	in fee tion
pur ga tion	sa na tion	sub jee tion
mī gra tion	eom plē tion	de jee tion
ob la tion	se ere tion	re jee tion
re la tion	eon ere tion	in jee tion
trans la tion	ex ere tion	ob jee tion
for ma tion	e mō tion	pro jee tion
stag na tion	pro mo tion	e lee tion
dam na tion	de vo tion	se lee tion
eär na tion	pro pŏr tion	re flee tion
vī bra tion	ap pŏr tion	eol lee tion
nar ra tion	ab lū tion	in spee tion
pros tra tion	so lū tion	dĭ ree tion
du ra tion	pol lū tion	eor ree tion
pul sa tion	dĭ lū tion	dis see tion
sen sa tion	at trăe tion	de tee tion
die ta tion	re frae tion	af flĭe tion
çī ta tion	sub trae tion	re strie tion

MȮVE, SȮN, WȮLF, FŎŎT, MŌŌN, ȮR; RŪLE, PŪLL; EXIST; ᴄ=ᴋ; ᴳ ᴶ; ş=z; ᴄʜ ꜱʜ.

ᴄon vĭe′ tion	de prĕs′ sion	re tĕn′ tion
ᴄom pŭl sion	im pres sion	ᴄon ten tion
ex pul sion	op pres sion	dis ten tion
ᴄon vul sion	sup pres sion	at ten tion
ex păn sion	ex pres sion	in ven tion
as çĕn sion	pos ses sion	ᴄon ven tion
de sçen sion	sub mĭs sion	de çep tion
dĭ men sion	ad mis sion	re çep tion
sus pen sion	e mis sion	ᴄon çep tion
dis sen sion	re mis sion	ex çep tion
pre ten sion	ᴄom mis sion	per çep tion
sub mĕr sion	o mis sion	as çrĭp tion
e mer sion	per mis sion	de sᴄrip tion
im mer sion	dis mis sion	in sᴄrip tion
as per sion	ᴄon ᴄŭs sion	pre sᴄrip tion
dis per sion	dis ᴄus sion	pro sᴄrip tion
a ver sion	re ăᴄ tion	re dĕmp tion
sub ver sion	ᴄon jŭn̄e tion	ᴄon sŭmp tion
re ver sion	in jun̄e tion	a dŏp tion
dĭ ver sion	ᴄom pun̄e tion	ab sȯrp tion
in ver sion	de ᴄŏᴄ tion	e rŭp tion
ᴄon ver sion	ᴄon ᴄoᴄ tion	eor rup tion
per ver sion	in frăᴄ tion	de şĕr tion
ᴄom păs sion	ab dŭᴄ tion	in ser tion
aᴄ çĕs sion	de duᴄ tion	as ser tion
se çes sion	re duᴄ tion	ex er tion
ᴄon çes sion	se duᴄ tion	ᴄon tȯr tion
pro çes sion	in duᴄ tion	dis tor tion
ᴄon fes sion	ob struᴄ tion	ex tĭn̄e tion
pro fes sion	de struᴄ tion	ex tĕn sion
ag gres sion	in struᴄ tion	ex tȯr tion
dĭ gres sion	ᴄon struᴄ tion	ir rŭp tion
pro gres sion	de tĕn tion	ᴄom plĕx ion
re gres sion	in ten tion	de flŭx ion

BÄR, LÀST, CÂRE, FALL, WHAT; HÊR, PRĘY, THÈRE; GĔT; BÌRD, MARÌNE; LĬNK,

No. 107--CVII.

WORDS OF FOUR SYLLABLES, ACCENTED ON THE THIRD.

pub li ca′ tion	lit i ga′ tion	dis til la′ tion
rep li ca tion	mit i ga tion	per co la tion
im pli ca tion	in sti ga tion	vī o la tion
com pli ca tion	nav i ga tion	im mo la tion
ap pli ca tion	pro mul ga tion	des o la tion
sup pli ca tion	pro lon ga tion	con so la tion
ex pli ca tion	ab ro ga tion	con tem pla tion
rep ro ba tion	sub ju ga tion	leg is la tion
ap pro ba tion	fas çi na tion	trib ū la tion
per tur ba tion	me di a tion	pec ū la tion
in cu ba tion	pal li a tion	spec ū la tion
ab di ca tion	ex pi a tion	cal cu la tion
ded i ca tion	va ri a tion	çir cu la tion
med i ta tion	de vi a tion	mod ū la tion
in di ca tion	ex ha la tion	reg ū la tion
vin di ca tion	con ge la tion	gran ū la tion
del e ga tion	mu ti la tion	stip ū la tion
ob li ga tion	in stal la tion	pop ū la tion
al le ga tion	ap pel la tion	grat ū la tion
ir ri ga tion	con stel la tion	re tar da tion

Legislation is the enacting of laws, and a legislator is one who makes laws.

God is the divine legislator. He proclaimed his ten commandments from Mount Sinai.

In free governments the people choose their legislators.

We have legislators for each State, who make laws for the State where they live. The town in which they meet to legislate, is called the seat of government. These legislators, when they are assembled to make laws, are called the legislature.

The people should choose their best and wisest men for their legislators.

It is the duty of every good man to inspect the moral conduct

MŎVE, SŎN, WŎLF, FŎŎT, MŎŎN, ÔR; RŪLE, PŪLL; EXIST; €=K; Ġ=J; Ş=Z, ÇH=SH.

of the man who is offered as a legislator at our yearly elec-
tions. If the people wish for good laws, they may have
them, by electing good men.

The legislative councils of the United States should feel their
dependence on the will of a free and virtuous people.

Our farmers, mechanics, and merchants, compose the strength
of our nation. Let them be wise and virtuous, and watch-
ful of their liberties. Let them trust no man to legislate
for them, if he lives in the habitual violation of the laws
of his country.

No. 108.—CVIII.

WORDS OF THREE SYLLABLES, ACCENTED ON THE FIRST.

dĕf′i nīte	dĕs′ti tūte	mī′€ro seōpe
ăp po şīte	ĭn sti tūte	ăn te lōpe
ŏp po şīte	€ŏn sti tūte	prō to tȳpe
ĭn fi nīte	pros ti tūte	hĕm is phēre
hȳp o €rĭte	pros e lȳte	ăt mos phēre
păr a sīte	bär be €ūe	€ŏm mo dōre
ŏb so lēte	rĕş i dūe	sȳe a mōre
ĕx pe dīte	ves ti būle	vŏl a tĭle
ree on dīte	rĭd i €ūle	vēr sa tĭle
săt el līte	mŭs €a dīne	mer €an tĭle
ĕr e mīte	brĭg an tīne	ĭn fan tĭle
ăp pe tīte	€ăl a mīne	dis çi plĭne
an e€ dōte	çĕl an dīne	măs €u līne
prŏs e €ūte	sēr pen tīne	fĕm i nĭne
pēr se €ūte	tûr pen tīne	ne€ tar ĭne
ĕx e €ūte	pôr €u pīne	ġen ū ĭne
ăb so lūte	ăn o dȳne	ber yl lĭne
dĭs so lūte	tĕl e seōpe	fā vor īte
sŭb sti tūte	hŏr o seōpe	pū €r ĭle

An anecdote is a short story, or the relation of a particular
incident.

Ridicule is not often the test of truth.

BĂP, LĂST, CÂRE, FALL, WHĄT; HĔR, PRĔY, THÊRE; ĞET; BĬRD, MARĬNE; LIŊK;

No. 109.—CIX.

WORDS OF TWO SYLLABLES, ACCENTED ON THE SECOND.

con dĕnse′	re ṣŏlve′	re märk′	con fĕr′
im mense	diṣ ṣolve	un måsk	trans fer
de fense	e volve	ea băl	se çern
pre pense	de volve	re bĕl	con çern
of fense	re volve	fâre well	diṣ çern*
dis pense	con volve	un fûrl	sub ôrn
pre tense	a bōde	de fôrm	a dôrn
col lăpse	un nĕrve	re form	for lorn
im mĕrse	ob ṣerve	in form	ad joûrn
as perse	sub serve	con form	re turn
dis perse	de ṣerve	per form	fōre rŭn
a verse	re ṣerve	trans form	era văt
re verse	pre ṣerve	con dĕmn	co quĕt†
in verse	con serve	in tēr	a băft
con verse	her sĕlf	a ver	be sĕt
per verse	my self	ab hôr	a lŏft
trans verse	at tăch	oc cûr	un ăpt
in dôrse	de tach	in cur	con tĕmpt
re morse	en rĭch	con cur	at tempt
un horse	re trĕnch	re cur	a dŏpt
dis bûrse	in trench	de mur	ab rŭpt
de tĕrge	dis pătch	a lås	cor rupt
dĭ verge	mis match	a mĕnd	a pärt
mis ğĭve	a frĕsh	de fĕr	de part
out live	re fresh	re fer	im part
for ğive	de bärk	pre fer	a mŏng
ab ṣōlve	em bark	in fer	be lŏng

The fixed stars are at immense distances from us. They are so
   distant that we can not measure the number of miles.

When fogs and vapors rise from the earth, and ascend one or
   two miles high, they come to a cold part of the air. The

* Pronounced *diz-zĕrn′*.   † Pronounced *co-kĕt′*.

MOVE, SÓN, WOLF, FOOT, MOON, ÔR; RULE, PULL; EXIST; G=K; G=J; S=Z; CH=SH.

cold there condenses these vapors into thick clouds, which fall in showers of rain.

Noah and his family outlived all the people who lived before the flood.

The brave sailors embark on board of ships, and sail over the great and deep sea.

The time will soon come when we must bid a last farewell to this world.

The bright stars without number adorn the skies.

When our friends die, they will never return to us; but we must soon follow them.

God will forgive those who repent of their sins, and live a holy life.

Thy testimonies, O Lord, are very sure; holiness becometh thine house for ever.

Do not attempt to deceive God; nor to mock him with solemn words, whilst your heart is set to do evil.

A holy life will disarm death of its sting.

God will impart grace to the humble penitent.

No. 110.—C X.

WORDS OF THREE SYLLABLES, ACCENTED ON THE SECOND.

de mean' or	re tire' ment
re main der	ac quire ment
en tiçe ment	im peach ment
en fôrçe ment	en croach ment
di vôrçe ment	con çeal ment
in dūçe ment	con geal ment
a gree ment	at tain ment
en gāge ment	de pō nent
de file ment	op po nent
in çite ment	com po nent
ex çite ment	ad jā çent
re fine ment	in dē çent
con fine ment	viçe ġe rent
e lōpe ment	en rōll ment

im pru' dent   de pärt' ment
in hēr ent   ad jŭst ment
ad hēr ent   in vēst ment
co hēr ent   a bŭt ment
at tēnd ant   as sĭst ant
as çend ant   in çēs sant
de fend ant   re lŭe tant
in tes tĭneş   im pôr tant
pro bŏs çis   re şĭst ant
el lĭp sis   in con stant
syn ŏp sis   in cŭm bent
com mànd ment   pu trĕs çent
a mĕnd ment   trans çend ent
bóm bärd ment   de pend ent
en hànçe ment   in dŭl ġent
ad vançe ment   re ful ġent
a mērçe ment   ef ful ġent
in frĭnge ment   e mul ġent
de tăch ment   as trĭn ġent
at tach ment   re strĭn ġent
in trĕnch ment   e mēr ġent
re trench ment   de ter ġent
re fresh ment   ab hŏr rent
diş cērn ment (-zẽrn'-)   con cŭr rent
pre fer ment   con sĭst ent
a màss ment   re şŏlv ent
al lŏt ment   de lĭn quent
a pärt ment   re cŭm bent

Demeanor signifies behavior or deportment.
Remainder is that which remains or is left.
An enticement is that which allures.
Divorcement signifies an entire separation.
Elopement is a running away or private departure.
Impeachment signifies accusation.
Retirement is a withdrawing from company.

MOVE, SÒN, WOLF, FÒOT, MOON, ÔR ; RULE, PULL ; EXIST ; Є=K ; Ġ=J ; S̬=Z ; ĊH=SH.

A deponent is one who makes oath to any thing.

A vicegerent is one who governs in place of another.

A proboscis is a long tube or snout from the mouth or jaw.

An ellipsis is an omission of a word.

Amercement is a penalty imposed for a wrong done, not a fixed fine, but at the mercy of the court.

A synopsis is a collective view of things.

Refulgent is applied to things that shine.

A contingent event is that which happens, or which is not expected in the common course of things.

No. 111.—C X I.

WORDS OF THREE SYLLABLES, ACCENTED ON THE FIRST. **a,** UNMARKED, IN THE TERMINATION **ate,** HAS AN OBSCURE OR SHORTENED SOUND OF LONG **a,** LIKE SHORT **e.**

dĕs′ o lāte, v.	ĭn′ ti māte, v.	vĕn′ er āte
ăd vo cāte, v.	ĕs ti māte, v.	tem per ate
vĕn ti lāte	făs çi nāte	ŏp er āte
tĭt il lāte	ôr di nate	ăs per ate
sçin til lāte	fŭl mi nāte	dĕs per ate
pēr co late	nŏm i nāte	ĭt er āte
ĭm mo lāte	ġēr mi nāte	ĕm i grāte
spĕc ū lāte	per son āte	trăns mi grāte
căl cu lāte	păs sion ate	as pi rāte, v.
çir cu lāte	fôrt ū nate	dĕc o rāte
mŏd ū lāte	dĭs si pāte	pēr fo rāte
rĕg ū lāte	sĕp a rāte, v.	eòr po rate
ŭn du lāte	çel e brāte	pĕn e trāte
ĕm ū lāte	des e crāte	pēr pe trāte
stĭm ū lāte	con se crāte	är bi trāte
grăn ū lāte	ĕx e crāte	ăc cu rate
stĭp ū lāte	vēr ber ate	lam i nate
cŏp ū lāte	ŭl çer āte	ĭn du rāte, v.
pop ū lāte	mŏd er āte, v.	săt ū rāte
con su late	ăg gre gate	sŭs çi tāte
sŭb li māte, v.	vēr te brāte	mĕd i tāte
ăn i māte, v.	ġĕn er āte	ĭm i tāte

BÃR, LÁST, €ÂRE, FĄLL, WHĄT; HẼR, PRẸY, THÈRE; ĞET; BĪRD, MARÏNE; LIŊK;

ĭr′ ri tāte	săl′ i vāte	sĭt′ ū ate
hĕṣ i tāte	eŭl ti vāte	ĕst ū āte
grăv i tāte	eăp ti vāte	ĕx pi āte
ăm pu tāte	rĕn o vāte	dē vi āte
ĕx ea vāte	ĭn no vāte	vī o lāte
ăg gra vāte	ăd e quate	rụ mi nāte
grad ū āte	flŭet ū āte	lū eu brāte

An advocate is one who defends the cause or opinions of another, or who maintains a party in opposition to another.

Ardent spirits stimulate the system for a time, but leave it more languid.

Men often toil all their lives to get property, which their children dissipate and waste.

We should emulate the virtuous actions of great and good men.

Moderate passions are most conducive to happiness, and moderate gains are most likely to be durable.

Abusive words irritate the passions, but "a soft answer turneth away wrath."

Discontent aggravates the evils of calamity.

Violent anger makes one unhappy, but a temperate state of the mind is pleasant.

No. 112.—CXII.

WORDS OF TWO SYLLABLES, ACCENTED ON THE FIRST. **ain**, UNMARKED, IS SOUNDED AS **in**; **ot**, UNMARKED, AS **ut**.

chĭl′ blain	ăn′ nals	măn′ ners	ĕnd′ less
vil lain	ĕn trails	nĭp pers	zĕal oŭs
môrt māin	mĭt tens	sçĭṣ ṣors	jĕal ous
plănt ain	sŭm mons	eär eass	pŏmp ous
vẽr vāin	fŏr çeps	eŭt lass	wŏn drous
eûr tain	pĭnch ers	eóm pass	lĕp rous
dŏl phin	glăn ders	măt rass	mŏn strous
sóme tīmeṣ	jäun dĭçe	mat tress	nẽrv ous
trĕss eṣ	snŭf fers	ab sçess	tŏr ment
trăp pings	stăg ḡers	lär ḡess	vĕst ment

MOVE, SÓN, WOLF, FÓŎT, MOÒN, ÒR; RŪLE, PŬLL; EXIST; Ç=K; Ġ=J; Ṣ=Z; ÇH=SH.

sẽr′ pent	sŏlv′ ent	făg′ ot	rĕd′ hŏt
tŏr rent	ⱦon vent	mag got	zĕal ot
ⱦŭr rent	fĕr ment	bĭg ot	tăp rōot
ăb sent	sŭn bûrnt	spig ot	gràss plŏt
prĕṣ ent	ăb bot	in got	bŭck et
ăd vent	tûr bot	blŏod shŏt	bū glŏss

Chilblains are sores caused by cold.

A curtain is used to hide something from the view.

The colors of the dolphin in the water are very beautiful.

The ladies adorn their heads and necks with tresses.

A matrass is a chemical vessel used for distilling, etc.; but a mattress is a quilted bed.

Annals are history in the order of years.

A cutlass is a broad curving sword.

A largess is a donation or gift.

A bigot is one who is too strongly attached to some religion, or opinion.

An abscess is a collection of matter under the skin.

Good manners are always becoming; ill manners are evidence of low breeding.

A solvent is that which dissolves something. Warm tea and coffee are solvents of sugar.

Solvent, an adjective, signifies able to pay all debts.

A summons is a notice or citation to appear.

No. 113.—CXIII.

WORDS OF THREE SYLLABLES, ACCENTED ON THE FIRST.

ⱦăl′ o mel	ăl′ ⱦo hol	gär′ ni tūre
çĭt a del	vĭt ri ol	fûr ni tūre
in fi del	păr a sol	sĕp ul tūre
sĕn ti nel	sī ne ⱦūre	păr a dīṣe
măck er el	ĕp i ⱦūre	mĕr chan dīṣe
ⱦŏck er el	lĭg a tūre	ĕn ter prīṣe
ⱦod i çil	sig na tūre	hănd ker chĭef
dom i çile	ⱦûr va tūre	[haṉk′er chĭf]
dăf fo dil	fòr feit ūre	sĕm i brēve

ăn' ti pōde	Stȳg' i an	wāy' fär ing
rĕe om pense	hôrt ū lan	fū ġi tĭve
hŏl ly hock	hŭs̯ band man	pu ni tĭve
ăl ka lī	ġĕn tle man	nu tri tĭve
hĕm i stie͟h	mŭs̯ sul man	ē go tis̯m
a̯u to graph	a̯l der man	prō to €ol
păr a graph	joûr ney man	dū pli €ate
ĕp i taph	bĭsh op ric	rō s̯e ate
ăv e nūe	elĕr ġy man	fū mi gāte
rĕv e nūe	€oŭn try man	mē di āte, *v.*
ret i nūe	vĕt er an	me di um
dĕs pot is̯m	ăl €o ran	ō di um
păr ox ys̯m	wón der f̯ul	o pi um
mī €ro €os̯m	sŏr rōw ful	prē mi um
mĭn i mum	ăn a gram	spō li āte
pĕnd ū lum	ĕp i gram	o pi ate
măx i mum	mŏn o gram	o vert ūre
tȳm pa num	dī a gram	jū ry man
pĕl i €an	ū ni vẽrse	Pu̯ ri tan
guär di an	sēa fär ing	phĭl o mel

Calomel is a preparation of mercury made by sublimation, that is, by being raised into vapor by heat and then condensed.

A citadel is a fortress to defend a city or town.

A codicil is a supplement or addition to a will.

An infidel is one who disbelieves revelation.

An epicure is one who indulges his appetite to excess, and is fond of delicacies.

Alcohol is spirit highly refined by distillation.

Despotism is tyranny or oppressive government.

The despotism of government can often be overthrown; but for the despotism of fashion there is no remedy.

A domicile is the place of a man's residence.

Mackerel signifies spotted. A mackerel is a spotted fish.

The glanders is a disease of horses.

The jaundice is a disease characterized by a yellow skin.

A loquacious companion is sometimes a great torment.

MŌVE, SŎN, WǪLF, FŎŌT, MŌŌN. ŌR; RŪLE, PŬLL; EXIST; ᴄ=ᴋ; ġ=ᴊ; s̩=ᴢ; ᴄʜ=ꜱʜ.

No. 114.—C X I V.

THE SOUND OF **a** IN **all** (= **aw**) AND IN **what** (= **ŏ**).

au' thor	squan' der	slaugh' ter	wan' der
sau çy	plaud it	al ter	draw ers
gaud y	brawn y	fal ter	wal nut
taw ny	quar ry	quar ter	eau sey
taw dry	flaw y	law yer	pal try
fault y	saw pĭt	saw yer	draw băck
pau per	law sūit	haw thôrn	al mōst
squad ron	wa ter	seal lop	want ing
sau çer	daugh ter	wal lop	war ren

The saucy stubborn child displeases his parents.

The peacock is a gaudy, vain, and noisy fowl.

The skin of the Indian is of a tawny color.

Paupers are poor people who are supported by a public tax.

Twenty-five cents are equal to one quarter of a dollar.

It is the business of a lawyer to give counsel on questions of law, and to manage lawsuits.

Walnuts are the seeds of walnut trees.

The Tartars wander from place to place without any settled habitation.

No. 115.—C X V.

WORDS OF TWO SYLLABLES, ACCENTED ON THE FIRST.

mĭs' sĭve	sprĭnk' ling	gŏs' ling
eăp tĭve	twink ling	nûrs ling
fĕs tĭve	shil ling	făt ling
eŏs tĭve	săp ling	bant ling
măg pīe	strĭp ling	seant ling
sòme thing	dŭmp ling	nĕst ling
stŏck ing	där ling	hĕr ring
mĭd dling	star ling	ŏb long
world ling	stēr ling	hĕad long

BĀR, LȦST, CÂRE, FALL, WHAT; HÊR, PREY, THÉRE; ĜET; BĪRD, MARĪNE; LIŊK;

fûr′ long	pärch′ ment	plāin′ tǐve
hĕad āehe	pleas ant	mō tǐve
tōōth āçhe	peas ant	spōrt ǐve
heärt āehe	dīs tant	hīre ling
ŏs trich	in stant	yēar ling
gȧl lant	eŏn stant	dāy spring
dôr mant	ĕx tant	trī umph
tĕn ant	sex tant	tri glў̆ph
preg nant	lăm bent	tru ant
rem nant	ae çent	är dent
pen nant	ad vent	màs sǐve
flīp pant	erĕs çent	păs sǐve
quȧd rant	sêr aph	stat ūe
är rant	stā tǐve	stat ūte
wȧr rant	na tǐve	vîrt ūe

No. 116.—CXVI.

WORDS OF TWO SYLLABLES, ACCENTED ON THE FIRST.

mō′ tion (-shun)	frăe′ tion	ŭne′ tion
no tion	trae tion	fune tion
lo tion	mĕn tion	june tion
po tion	pen sion	sue tion
pōr tion	çes sion	spŏn sion
nā tion	ten sion	tôr sion
ra tion	mĕr sion	mǐs sion
sta tion	ver sion	eăp tion
măn sion	sĕs sion	ŏp tion
pas sion	lee tion	flĕe tion
fae tion	dǐe tion	aue tion
ae tion	fie tion	eau tion

Lection is a reading, and lecture is a discourse.
Lectures on chemistry are delivered in our colleges.
A lotion is a washing or a liquid preparation.
A ration is an allowance daily for a soldier.

MOVE, SON, WOLF. FOOT, MOON, OR; RULE, PULL; EXIST; ᴄ=ᴋ; ġ=ᴊ; ş=ᴢ; ᴄʜ=sʜ.

A mansion is a place of residence, or dwelling.
A fraction is a part of a whole number.
Fiction is a creature of the imagination.
Caution is prudence in the avoidance of evil.
Auction is a sale of goods by outcry to the highest bidder.
Option is choice. It is at our option to make ourselves respectable or contemptible.

No. 117.—CXVII.

WORDS OF FOUR SYLLABLES, ACCENTED ON THE SECOND.

su prĕm′a çy	eom pŭl′so ry	pro lĭx′i ty
the ŏe ra çy	ol fāe to ry	un çēr tain ty
de moe ra çy	re frae to ry	im mŏd est y
eon spĭr a çy	re fĕe to ry	dis hon est y
ġe ŏg ra phy	dĭ ree to ry	so lĭl o quy
bi og ra phy	eon sĭs to ry	hu măn i ty
eoş mog ra phy	ī dŏl a try	a mĕn i ty
ste nog ra phy	ġe om e try	se ren i ty
zo og ra phy	im mĕn si ty	vĭ çĭn i ty
to pog ra phy	pro pen si ty	af fin i ty
tȳ pog ra phy	ver bŏs i ty	dĭ vin i ty
hȳ drog ra phy	ad vēr si ty	in dĕm ni ty
phĭ los o phy	dĭ ver si ty	so lem ni ty
a eăd e my	ne çĕs si ty	fra tēr ni ty
e eŏn o my	ī den ti ty	e ter ni ty
a năt o my	eon eăv i ty	bär băr i ty
zo ŏt o my	de prav i ty	vul gar i ty
e pĭph a ny	lon ġĕv i ty	dis par i ty
phĭ lăn thro py	ae elĭv i ty	çe lĕb ri ty
mis an thro py	na tiv i ty	a lăe ri ty
pe rĭph e ry	ae tiv i ty	sin çēr i ty
är til le ry	eap tiv i ty	çe ler i ty
hȳ drŏp a thy	fes tiv i ty	te mer i ty
de lĭv er y	per plĕx i ty	in teg ri ty
dis eŏv er y	eon vex i ty	dis tĭl ler y

BĀR, LȦST, ÇȂRE, FALL, WHĄT; HẼR, PRẸY, THẼRE; ĞET; BȊRD, MARȊNE; LIꞐK;

Theocracy is government by God himself. The government of the Jews was a theocracy.

Democracy is a government by the people.

Hydropathy, or water cure, is a mode of treating diseases by the copious use of pure water.

Geography is a description of the earth.

Biography is a history of a person's life.

Cosmography is a description of the world.

Stenography is the art of writing in shorthand,

Zoögraphy is a description of animals; but zoölogy means the same thing, and is generally used.

Topography is the exact delineation of a place or region.

Typography is the art of printing with types.

Hydrography is the description of seas and other waters, or the art of forming charts.

Philanthropy is the love of mankind; but misanthropy signifies a hatred of mankind.

The olfactory nerves are the organs of smell.

Idolatry is the worship of idols. Pagans worship gods of wood and stone. These are their idols. But among Christians many persons worship other sorts of idols. Some worship a gay and splendid dress, consisting of silks and muslins, gauze and ribbons; some worship pearls and diamonds; but all excessive fondness for temporal things is idolatry.

No. 118.—CXVIII.

WORDS OF FOUR SYLLABLES, ACCENTED ON THE SECOND.

ju rĭd' i eal	fa nät' i çiṣm	ob lĭv' i on
eon viv i al	ex ôr di um	in eŏg ni to
dī ăg o nal	mil lĕn ni um	eo pärt ner ship
pen tag o nal	re pŭb lie an	dis sĭm i lar
tra dĭ tion al	me rĭd i an	ver näe ū lar
in tĕn tion al	un năt ū ral	o rae ū lar
per pet ū al	eon jĕet ūr al	or bĭe ū lar
ha bĭt ū al	çen trĭp e tal	par tie ū lar
e vĕnt ū al	eon tin ū al	ir rĕg ū lar
un mēr çi ful	ef fĕet ū al	bī vălv ū lar

MOVE, SON, WOLF, FOOT, MOON, ÔR; ȨLE, PULL; EXIST; ç=K; ġ=J; ṣ=z; ǫH=sн.

un pŏp′ ū lar   a năl′ y̆ sis   ex tĕm′ po re
trī ăn gu lar   de lĭr i oŭs   en tăb la tūre
pa rĭsh ion er   in dŭs tri ous   dis çŏm fit ūre
dī ăm e ter   il lus tri ous   pro çŏn sul ship
ad mĭn is ter   las çĭv i ous   dis çon so late
em băs sa dor   ob liv i ous   a pos to late
pro ġĕn i tor   a nŏm a lous   ob sē qui oŭs
çom pŏṣ i tor   e pĭt o mīze   oe eā ṣion al
me trop o lis   a pŏṣ ta tīze   pro pōr tion al
e phĕm e ris   im môr tal īze   heb dŏm a dal

No. 119.—CXIX.

WORDS OF FOUR SYLLABLES, ACCENTED ON THE SECOND. **a,** UNMARKED, IN **ate**, DOES NOT HAVE ITS FULL LONG SOUND.

as sĭm′ i lāte   çon tăm′ i nāte
prog nŏs tie āte   dis sĕm i nāte
per ăm bu lāte   re erĭm i nāte
e jaç ū lāte   a bŏm i nāte
im maç ū lāte   pre dom i nāte
ma trĭç ū lāte   in tĕm per ate
ġes tiç ū lāte   re ġen er āte, v.
in ŏç ū lāte   çŏ ŏp er āte
çο ăg ū lāte   ex ăs per āte
de pŏp ū lāte   çom mĭṣ er āte
çon grăt ū lāte   in vĕt er ate
ea pĭt ū lāte   re ĭt er āte
ex pŏst ū lāte   ob lit er āte
a măl ga māte   e văç ū āte
ex hĭl a rāte   at tĕn u āte, v.
le ġit i māte, v.   ex ten ū āte
ap prŏx i māte   in ăd e quate
çon çăt e nāte   ef fĕet ū āte
sub ôr di nāte, v.   per pet ū āte
o rĭġ i nāte   as săs sin āte

BÄR, LÅST, CÂRE, FALL, WHĂT; HẼR, PREY, THÊRE; GĔT; BĪRD, MARĪNE; LĬNK;

pro erăs′ ti nāte	in dĭe′ a tĭve
pre dĕs ti nāte, *v.*	pre rŏg a tĭve
eom păs sion āte, *v.*	ir rĕl a tĭve
dis pas sion ate	ap pel la tĭve
af fĕe tion ate	eon tem pla tĭve
un fôrt ū nate	su pēr la tĭve
e măn çi pāte	ăl ter na tĭve
de līb er āte, *v.*	de elăr a tĭve
in eär çer āte	eom par a tĭve
eon fĕd er āte, *v.*	im pĕr a tĭve
eon sĭd er ate	in dem ni fỹ
pre pŏn der āte	per sŏn i fỹ
im mod er ate	re stōr a tĭve
ae çĕl er āte	dis qual i fỹ

No. 120.— C X X.

WORDS OF FOUR SYLLABLES, ACCENTED ON THE SECOND.

al lū′ vi on	sa lū′ bri oŭs	luẋ ū′ ri oŭs
pe trō le um	im pē ri ous	vo lu mi nous
çe rụ le an	mys te ri ous	o bē di ent
le vī a than	la bō ri ous	ex pe di ent
lī brā ri an	in glo ri ous	in gre di ent
a gra ri an	çen so ri ous	im mū ni ty
pre ea ri oŭs	vie to ri ous	eom mu ni ty
vī ea ri ous	no to ri ous	im pu ni ty
ne fa ri ous	uẋ o ri ous	eom plā çen çy
gre ga ri ous	in jū ri ous	in dē çen çy
o va ri ous	pe nū ri ous	di plō ma çy
op prō bri ous	ū ṣū ri ous*	trans pâr en çy

A library is a collection of books.

A librarian is a person who has charge of a library.

The laborious bee is a pattern of industry.

That is precarious which is uncertain. Life and health are precarious.

* Pronounced *yoo-zhoo′ ri-oŭs.*

MOVE, SÒN, WOLF, FÒÒT, MOON, ÔR ; RŪLE, PŲLL ; EXIST ; €=K ; ġ=J ; ₰=Z ; ÇH=SH.

Vicarious punishment is that which one person suffers in the place of another.

Gregarious animals are such as herd together, as sheep and goats.

Salubrious air is favorable to health.

A covetous man is called penurious.

Escape or exemption from punishment is impunity.

Do nothing that is injurious to religion, to morals, or to the interest of others.

We speak of the transparency of glass, water, etc.

No. 121.—CXXI.

WORDS OF SEVEN SYLLABLES, HAVING THE ACCENT ON THE FIFTH.

im ma te ri ăl′ i ty
in di viṣ i bĭl i ty
in di vid ū ăl i ty
in €om pat i bĭl i ty
in de struet i bil i ty
im per çep ti bil i ty
ir re ṣist i bil i ty
in €om bus ti bil i ty

im pen e tra bĭl′ i ty
in el i ġi bil i ty
im mal le a bil i ty
per pen die ū lăr i ty
in €om press i bĭl i ty
in de fen si bil i ty
val e tu di nā ri an
an ti trin i ta ri an

WORDS OF EIGHT SYLLABLES, ACCENTED ON THE SIXTH.

un in tel li ġi bĭl′ i ty   in €om pre hen si bĭl′ i ty

The immateriality of the soul has rarely been disputed.

The indivisibility of matter is supposed to be demonstrably false.

It was once a practice in France to divorce husband and wife for incompatibility of tempers; a practice soon found to be incompatible with social order.

The incompressibility of water has been disproved.

We can not doubt the incomprehensibility of the divine attributes.

Stones are remarkable for their immalleability.

The indestructibility of matter is generally admitted.

Asbestus is noted for its incombustibility.

A valetudinarian is a sickly person.

BÄR, LÀST, CÂRE, FALL, WHAT; HÊR, PREY, THÉRE; ĠET; BÍRD, MARÍNE; LINK:

No. 122.—CXXII.

WORDS IN WHICH th HAS ITS ASPIRATED SOUND.

ē' ther

jā' çinth

thē' sis

ze' nith

thĭck' et

thŭn' der

this' tle

thrŏs' tle

throt' tle

thĭrst' y

thrĭft' y

lĕngth' wīse

thrēat' en ing

au' thor

au' thor īze

au thŏr' i ty

au thŏr' i ta tĭve

mĕth' od

ăn' them

dĭph' thong

[dĭf' thong]

ĕth' ics

păn' ther

Sab' bath

thĭm' ble

Thûrṣ' day

trĭph' thong

in thrall'

a thwart'

be trŏth'

thĭr' ty

thŏr' ough

thīr' teen

thou' ṣand

ā' the iṣm

thē' o ry

the' o rem

hȳ' a çinth

eăth' o lic

ap' o theġm

thŭn' der bōlt

ĕp' i thet

lăb' ў rinth

lĕth' ar ġy

pleth' o ry

pleth' o ric

sўm' pa thy

ăm' a ranth

am' e thȳst

ap' a thy

æs thĕt' ics

thīr' ti eth

sўn' the sis

pan thē' on

e the' re al

eăn' tha ris

ea thē' dral

ū re' thra

au thĕn' tic

pa thet' ic

syn thet' ic

a eăn' thus

ath lĕt' ic

me theg' lin

ea thär' tic

a the ĭst' ic

the o rĕt' ic al

me thŏd' ic al

math e măt' ics

le vī' a than

en thū' ṣi aṣm

an tĭp' a thy

a rĭth' me tic

an tith' e sis

mis ăn' thro py

phĭ lan' thro py

ean thär' i dēṣ

the ŏc' ra çy

the ol' o ġy

the od' o līte

ther mom' e ter

ea thol' i con

mў thol' o ġy

or thog' ra phy

hȳ poth' e sis

lĭ thog' ra phy

lĭ thot' o my

a poth' e ca ry

ap o thē' o sis

pōl' ў the iṣm

bib li o thē' cal

ich thy ŏl' o ġy

or ni thol' o ġy

MOVE, SON, WOLF, FOOT, MOON, OR ; RULE, PULL ; EXIST ; Є=K ; Ġ=J ; Ş=Z ; ÇH=SH.

No. 123.—CXXIII.

WORDS IN WHICH **th** HAS ITS VOCAL SOUND.

ei′ ther	neth′ er	broth′ er
nei ther	weth er	wor thy (wûr thў)
hea then	prith ee	moth er
cloth ier (-yer)	bur then	smooth er
rath er	south ern	oth er
fath om	teth er	with ers
gath er	thith er	be neath′
hith er	with er	be queath
fur ther	lath er	with draw
breth ren	fä ther	an oth′ er
whith er	far thing	to ḡeth er
wheth er	fur thest	there with al′
leath er	poth er	nev er the less
feath er	broth el	

The heathen are those people who worship idols, or who know
not the true God.

Those who enjoy the light of the gospel, and neglect to observe
its precepts, are more criminal than the heathen.

All mankind are brethren, descendants of common parents.
How unnatural and wicked it is to make war on our brethren, to conquer them, or to plunder and destroy them.

It is every man's duty to bequeath to his children a rich
inheritance of pious precepts.

No. 124.—CXXIV.

WORDS OF THREE SYLLABLES, ACCENTED ON THE SECOND.

ac com′ plish	di min′ ish	ex tin′ ḡuish
es tab lish	ad mon ish	re lin quish
em bel lish	pre mon ish	ex cul pate
a bol ish	as ton ish	con trib ute
re plen ish	dis tin ḡuish	re mon strançe

BÄR, LÀST, ĠÂRE, FALL, WHĄT; HÊR, PRĘY, THÈRE; ĠET; BÎRD, MARÏNE; LIŅK;

em broid′ er	mo mĕnt′ oŭs	trī ŭmph′ ant
re join der	por tĕnt ous	as sāil ant
ADJECTIVES.	a bŭn dant	so nō roŭs
e nor moŭs	re dun dant	a çē tous
diṣ ăs trous	dis eôr dant	eon eā vous

A man who saves the fragments of time, will accomplish a
  great deal in the course of his life.

The most refined education does not embellish the human
  character like piety.

Laws are abolished by the same power that made them.

Wars generally prove disastrous to all parties.

We are usually favored with abundant harvests.

Most persons are ready to exculpate themselves from blame.

Discordant sounds are harsh, and offend the ear.

No. 125.—C X X V.

WORDS OF FIVE SYLLABLES, ACCENTED ON THE THIRD.

in ter mē′ di ate	e qui pŏn′ der ate
dis pro pōr tion ate	pär ti çip i al
çer e mō ni al	in di vid ū al
mat ri mo ni al	in ef fĕet ū al
pat ri mo ni al	in tel leet ū al
an ti mo ni al	pu sil lăn i moŭs
tes ti mo ni al	dis in ġĕn ū oŭs
im ma tē ri al	in sig nĭf i eant
maġ is te ri al	e qui pŏn der ant
min is te ri al	çīr eum ăm bi ent
im me mō ri al	an ni vēr sa ry
sen a to ri al	pär lia mĕnt a ry
die ta to ri al	tes ta ment a ry
e qua to ri al	al i ment a ry
in ar tĭe ū late	sup ple ment a ry
il le ġit i mate	el e ment a ry
in de tĕrm in ate	sat is fãe to ry

MOVE, SŎN, WOLF, FŎŌT, MŌŌN, ÖR; RŲLE, PŲLL; EXIST; €=K; Ġ=J; Ṣ=Z; ǪH=SH.

€on tra dĭe′ to ry	hom o ġē′ ne oŭs
val e die to ry	€on tu me li ous
in tro dŭe to ry	ae ri mō ni ous
trig o nŏm e try	par si mo ni ous
a re om e try	del e tē ri ous
mis çel lā ne oŭs	mer i tō ri ous
sub ter ra ne ous	dis o bē di ent
sue çe da ne ous	in ex pe di ent
sī mul ta ne ous	€on ti nū i ty
in stan ta ne ous	im pro prī e ty

Senate originally signified a council of elders; for the Romans committed the public concerns to men of age and experience. The maxim of wise men was—old men for counsel, young men for war. But in modern times the senatorial dignity is not always connected with age.

The bat is the intermediate link between quadrupeds and fowls. The orang-outang is intermediate between man and quadrupeds.

Bodies of the same kind or nature are called homogeneous.

Reproachful language is contumelious or contemptuous.

Bitter and sarcastic language is acrimonious.

Simultaneous acts are those which happen at the same time.

Many things are lawful which are not expedient.

No. 126.—CXXVI.

dĕlve	eăsh	smăsh	pĭsh	tĕxt
twelve	dash	rash	wish	twĭxt
nērve	gash	€rash	gŭsh	mi<u>n</u>x
eûrve	hash	trash	hush	sphi<u>n</u>x
ĕlf	lash	flĕsh	blush	chānġe
shelf	flash	mesh	€rush	mānġe
self	plash	fresh	frush	rānġe
pelf	slash	dĭsh	tush	grānġe
ăsh	mash	fish	nĕxt	fōrġe

BÄR, LȦST, ĈȦRE, FALL, WHAT; HĒR, PRĘY, THÈRE; ĜET; BĬRD, MARĪNE; LIŊK;

bāste	flūte	līght	nīght	frounçe
chaste	mute	blīght	wīght	rounçe
haste	brute	plīght	rīght	trounçe
waste	fīght	sīght	tīght	ehȧṣm
lūte	brīght	slīght	blowze	prīṣm

MONOSYLLABLES WITH **th** VOCAL.

the	thȳ	thĕm	tīthe	smooth
thōṣe	thĕn	thençe	līthe	soothe
thĭs	thŭs	theṣe	wrīthe	they
thȧt	thou	thȧn	seȳthe	thêre
thīne	thee	blīthe	thoúgh	thêir

THE FOLLOWING, WHEN NOUNS, HAVE THE ASPIRATED SOUND OF **th** IN THE SINGULAR NUMBER, AND THE VOCAL IN THE PLURAL.

bäth	bäthṣ	swath	swathṣ	mouth	mouthṣ
läth	läthṣ	elōth	elōthṣ	wrēath	wrēathṣ
päth	päthṣ	mōth	mōthṣ	shēath	shēathṣ

Twelve things make a dozen.

To delve is to dig in the ground.

When the nerves are affected the hands shake.

Turf is a clod of earth held together by the roots of grass.

Surf is the swell of the sea breaking on the shore.

Cash formerly meant a chest, but it now signifies money.

An elf is an imaginary being or a being of the fancy.

A flash of lightning sometimes hurts the eyes.

Flesh is the soft part of animal bodies.

Blushes often manifest modesty, sometimes shame.

Great and sudden changes sometimes do hurt.

A grange is a farm and farmhouse.

A forge is a place where iron is hammered.

A rounce is the handle of a printing press.

To frounce is to curl or frizzle, as the hair.

Great haste often makes waste.

It is no more right to steal apples or watermelons from another's garden or orchard, than it is to steal money from his desk. Besides, it is the meanest of all low tricks to

MOVE, SON, WOLF, FOOT, MOON, OR; RULE, PULL; EXIST; ∈═K; Ġ═J; S═Z; CH═SH.

creep into a man's inclosure to take his property. How much more manly is it to ask a friend for cherries, peaches, pears, or melons, than it is to sneak privately into his orchard and steal them. How must a boy, and much more a man, blush to be detected in so mean a trick!

No. 127.—CXXVII.

IN THE FOLLOWING WORDS, **h** IS PRONOUNCED BEFORE **w**; THUS *whale* IS PRONOUNCED hwāle; *when*, hwen.

whāle	whĕt	whĭz	whĭp stŏck
whēat	whĭch	whêre	whis per
wharf	whilk	whey	whis ky
what	whiff	whĕr' ry	whis ker
wheel	whig	wheth er	whis tle
wheeze	whim	whet stōne	whith er
whee' dle	whin	whĭf fle	whit lōw
whīne	whip	whig ḡish	whit tle
while	whĕlm	whig ḡiṣm	whīrl
white	whelp	whim per	whirl pōol
whi' ten	when	whĭm ṣey	whirl wind
white wash	whençe	whin ny	whirl băt
whi tish	whĭsk	whip côrd	whirl i ḡig
whi ting	whist	whip gráft	wharf age
whȳ	whit	whip ṣaw	wharf in ḡer

IN THE FOLLOWING WORDS **w** IS SILENT.

who	*who* ĕv' er
whom	*who* so ĕv' er
whose	*whom* so ĕv' er
whōle	*whōle'* sāle
whōop	*whōle* sŏme

Whales are the largest of marine animals. They afford us oil for lamps and other purposes.

Wheat is a species of grain that grows in most climates, and the flour makes our finest bread.

BÄR, LÀST, ÇÂRE, FALL, WHAT; HÊR, PREY, THÉRE; ĞET; BÎRD, MARÌNE; LIŊK;

Wharves are structures built for the convenience of lading and unlading ships.

Wheels are most admirable instruments of conveyance; carts, wagons, gigs, and coaches run on wheels.

Whey is the thin watery part of milk.

Bad boys sometimes know what a whip is by their feelings. This is a kind of knowledge which good boys dispense with.

White is not so properly a color as a want of all color.

One of the first things a little boy tries to get is a knife, that he may whittle with it. If he asks for a knife and it is refused, he is pretty apt to whimper.

The love of whisky has brought many a strong fellow to a disgraceful death.

Whiskers are thought by some to afford protection to the throat in cold weather.

No. 128.—CXXVIII.

IN THE FOLLOWING WORDS, X PASSES INTO THE SOUND OF GZ.

ex ăet′	ex ăg′ ger āte	ex ôr′ di um
ex alt′	ex am′ ĭne	ex ŏt′ ie
ex ĕmpt′	ex am′ ple	ex ĕm′ plar
ex ērt′	ex an′ i māte	ex′ em pla ry
ex haust′	ex as′ per āte	ex em′ pli fȳ
ex hôrt′	ex ĕe′ ū tĭve	ex emp′ tion
ex īle′, v.	ex ee′ ū tor	ex ŏn′ er āte
ex ĭst′	ex ee′ ū trix	ex ôr′ bi tançe
ex ŭlt′	ex hĭb′ it	ex or′ bi tant
ex hāle′	ex ist′ ençe	ex ū′ ber ant

The word exact is an adjective signifying nice, accurate, or precise; it is also a verb signifying to demand, require, or compel to yield.

Astronomers can, by calculating, foretell the exact time of an eclipse, or of the rising and setting of the sun.

It is useful to keep very exact accounts.

A king or a legislature must have power to exact taxes or duties to support the government.

An exordium is a preface or preamble.

MOVE, SÒN, WOLF, FÔOT, MOÒN, ÔR ; RŪLE, PŪLL ; EXIST ; Ç=K ; Ġ=J ; Ș=Z ; ÇH=SH.

"Take away your exactions from my people." *Ezek.* xlv. 9.

To exist signifies to be, or to have life. The soul is immortal; it will never cease to exist.

We must not exalt ourselves, nor exult over a fallen rival.

It is our duty to exert our talents in doing good.

We are not to expect to be exempt from evils.

Exhort one another to the practice of virtue.

Water is exhaled from the earth in vapor, and in time the ground is exhausted of water.

An exile is one who is banished from his country.

In telling a story be careful not to exaggerate.

Examine the Scriptures daily and carefully, and set an example of good works.

An executor is one appointed by a will to settle an estate after the death of the testator who makes the will.

The President of the United States is the chief executive officer of the government.

Officers should not exact exorbitant fees for their services.

Charitable societies exhibit proofs of much benevolence.

The earth often produces exuberant crops.

Every man wishes to be exonerated from burdensome services.

No. 129.—CXXIX.

IN THE FOLLOWING WORDS, **tian** AND **tion** ARE PRONOUNCED NEARLY **chun.**

băs′ tion	fŭs′ tian	com bŭs′ tion
Chrĭs tian	con ġĕs′ tion	in dĭ ġĕs′ tion
mĭx tion	dĭ ġĕs tion	ex haus′ tion
quĕs tion	ad mĭx tion	sug ġĕs tion

IN THE FOLLOWING WORDS, **i** IN AN UNACCENTED SYLLABLE AND FOLLOWED BY A VOWEL, HAS A LIQUID SOUND, LIKE **y** CONSONANT; THUS *alien* IS PRONOUNCED āl′yen, AND *clothier,* clōth′ yer.

āl′ ien (-yen)	sāv′ ior (-yur)	sēn′ ior (-yur)
cōurt ier	pāv ior	bĭl ioŭs
clōth ier	jūn ior	bill ion

BÄR, LÅST, CÂRE, FALL, WHẠT; HĒR, PRĘY, THÈRE; ĞET; BĨRD, MARĪNE; LIŊK;

bĭll′iard̰s	văl′ iant	ɛom păn′ion
ĕull ion	ȯn ion	ras ɛal ion
mĭll ion	bu̱ll ion	do mĭn ion
mȧn ion	āl ien āte	mo dĭll ion
mĭll ionth	bĭl ia ry	o pĭn ion
pĭll ion	brĭll ian ẹy	re bĕll ion
pȧn ion	brĭll iant ly	re bell iŏŭs
rȯn ion	mĭl ia ry	ẹĭ vĭl ian
seull ion	văl iant ly	dis ūn ion
trĭll ion	val iant ness	be hāv ior
trŭnn ion	ɛom mūn′ion	pe ɛūl iar
brĭll iant	ver mĭl ion	in tăɡl io
fĭl ial	pa vĭl ion	se raɡl io
ɛŏll ier	pȱs tĭll ion	fa mĭl iar īze
pănn ier	fa mil iar	o pĭn ion ist
pŏn iard	bat tăl ion	o pĭn ion ā ted

No. 130.—C X X X

IN THE FOLLOWING WORDS, THE SYLLABLES **sier** AND **zier** ARE PRONOUNCED **zher** OR **zhur. sion** ARE PRONOUNCED **zhun,** AND **sia** ARE PRONOUNCED **zha.**

brā′ ṣier	pro fū′ ṣion	il lū′ ṣion
gla zier	a brā ṣion	in fu ṣion
gra zier	ɛol lū ṣion	in vā ṣion
hō ṣier	ɛon ɛlu ṣion	suf fū ṣion
o ṣier	ɛon fu ṣion	dis suā ṣion
ɛro ṣier	ɛor rō ṣion	per ṣua ṣion
fū ṣion	oe ɛā ṣion	am brȯ ṣiȧ
af fu′ ṣion	per va ṣion	am bro ṣial
ɛo hē ṣion	e lū ṣion	ob tru ṣion
ad he ṣion	dif fu ṣion	de tru ṣion
de lū ṣion	dis plō ṣion	in tru ṣion
e rō ṣion	ex plo ṣion	pro tru ṣion
e vā ṣion	ef fū ṣion	ex tru ṣion

MǪVE, SȮN, WǪLF, FŎŎT, MŌŌN, ȮR ; RỤLE, PỤLL ; EX̱IST ; Є=K ; Ġ=J ; S̱=Z ; ǪH=SH̱

IN SOME OF THE FOLLOWING WORDS, THE TERMINATING SYL-
LABLE IS PRONOUNCED **zhun,** AND IN OTHERS THE VOWEL
ĭ MAY BE CONSIDERED TO HAVE THE SOUND OF **y.**

ab sçĭş′şion	pro vĭş′ion	in çĭş′ion
eol lĭş ion	re vĭş ion	mis prĭş ion
de çĭş ion	re sçĭş ion	pre vĭş ion
de rĭş ion	eon çĭş ion	e lў̆ş ian
e lĭş ion	ex çĭş ion	çîr eum çĭş′ion
pre çĭş ion	dĭ vĭş ion	sub dĭ vĭş ion

No. 131.—CXXXI.

WORDS IN WHICH **є** BEFORE **h** HAS THE SOUND OF **k.**

Єhrīst	єhĕm′ist	ăṉ′eho rīte
єhў̄le	Єhrĭst mas	äreh i teet
sehēme	Єhrĭs tian	areh i trăve
āehe	dis tieh	areh e tȳpe
єhăş̇m	ĕeh o	hĕp tar ehy
єhrĭş̇m	єhrŏn ie	măeh i nāte
єhôrd	sehĕd ūle	Єhrĭs ten dŏm
єhȳme	păs ehal	brăeh i al
lŏeh	єhŏl er	laeh rў̆ mal
sehōōl	єhō rist	sae eha rĭne
ehoir (*kwïr*)	sehŏl ar	sў̄ṉ ehro niş̇m
єhō′rus	mon areh	Mĭeh ael mas
eho ral	stŏm aeh	єhŏr is ter
är єhīveş̱	ăṉ′ar ehy	єhron i ele
єhā os	єhrў̆s o līte	ôr ehes trả
ĕp oeh	єhăr ae ter	pă tri areh
ī ehor	eat e ehiş̇m	eū eha rist
ō eher	pĕn ta teūeh	єhi mē′rả
tro ehee	sep ul eher	pa rō єhĭ al
ăṉ ehor	teeh nie al	eha mē le on

BÄR, LÁST, CÂRE, FALL, WHAT; HÊR, PRĘY, THÊRE; ĞET; BĪRD, MARĪNE; LIŊK;

ehro măt′ ie	syn ĕe′ do ehe	the ŏm′ a ehy
me ehan ie	mo näreh ie al	mĕl′ an ehol y
eha ŏt ie	bron ehŏt o my	pā tri äreh y
seho lăs tie	ehro nol o ġy	hī er areh y
ea ehĕx y	ehī rog ra phy	ŏl i gar ehy
eha lўb e ate	eho rog ra phy	eat e ehĕt′ ie al
a năeh ro nism	ehro nom e ter	ieh thў ŏl o ġy

Experience keeps a dear school, but fools will learn in no other.

Chyle is the milky fluid separated from food by digestion, and from this are formed blood and nutriment for the support of animal life.

An epoch is a fixed point of time from which years are reckoned. The departure of the Israelites from Egypt is a remarkable epoch in their history.

A patriarch is the father of a family. Abraham was the great patriarch of the Israelites.

Sound striking against an object and returned, is an echo.

The stomach is the great laboratory of animal bodies, in which food is digested and prepared for entering the proper vessels, and nourishing the body. If the stomach is impaired and does not perform its proper functions, the whole body suffers.

No. 132.—CXXXII.

WORDS IN WHICH g, BEFORE e, i AND y, HAS ITS HARD OR CLOSE SOUND.

ḡear	ēa′ ḡer	erăg′ ḡed	ḡĭb′ boŭs
ḡeese	mēa ḡer	dĭg ḡer	ḡid dy
ḡĕld	ḡew gąw	dig ḡing	ḡig gle
ḡĭft	tī ḡer	rig ḡing	ḡig gling
ḡive	tō ḡed	rigḡed (rĭgd)	ḡig gler
ḡig	bĭg ḡin	rig ḡer	ḡiz zard
ḡild	brăg ḡer	flăg ḡing	ḡim let
ḡimp	dag ḡer	flag ḡy	ḡirl ish
ḡĭrd	erag ḡy	sŏg ḡy	jăg ḡed
ḡĭrth	bŭg ḡy	ḡĭb ber ish	jăg ḡy

MǬVE, SǑN, WǪLF, FǑǑT, MŎŎN. ǑR ; RŬLE, PŬLL ; EXIST ; ᴄ=ᴋ ; ġ=ᴊ ; ṣ=ᴢ ; ᴄʜ=ꜱʜ.

lĕgged *	twĭgged *	nŏg′ ġin	găg′ ġing
leg′ ġin	twĭg′ ġy	tär ġet	bragged *
pĭg ġer y	wăg ġing	flŏgged *	brag′ ġing
quăg ġy	wag ġish	flog′ ġing	bag ġing
rag ġed	au ġer	ġĭft ed	ġĕld ing
trĭg ġer	bŏg ġy	hŭgged *	ġĭld ing
serăg ġed	fog ġy	hug ġing	ġild ed
serag ġy	ᴄlogged *	shrugged *	ġild er
shag ġy	ᴄlog ġing	shrug′ ġing	swăg ġer
shag ġed	ᴄlog ġy	rug ġed	swag ġy
slŭg ġish	ᴄogged *	tugged *	ġīrd le
lug ġer	băg′ ġy	tug′ ġing	ġird er
snăg ġed	dŏg ġed	lugged *	be ġĭn′
snag ġy	dog ġish	lug′ ġing	wăgged *
sprĭg ġy	jogged *	mug ġy	wag′ ġer y
stăg ġer	jog′ ġing	făgged *	lŏg ġer hĕad
stag ġerṣ	jog ġer	fag′ ġing	to ġĕth′ er

No. 133.—CXXXIII.

IN THE FOLLOWING, ᴄ OR ɡ ENDING A SYLLABLE HAVING A PRIMARY OR A SECONDARY ACCENT, IS SOUNDED AS ꜱ AND ᴊ RESPECTIVELY.

măġ′ ie	tăç′ it	păç′ i fȳ
traġ ie	aġ i tāte	paġ i nal
aġ ĭle	lĕġ i ble	rĕġ i çīde
aç id	vĭġ i lant	reġ i men
dĭġ it	rĕġ i ment	reġ is ter
făç ĭle	preç e dent	speç i fȳ
fraġ ĭle	preç i pĭçe	măç er āte
frĭġ id	reç i pe	maġ is trāte
riġ id	deç i mal	maġ is tra çy
plăç id	deç i māte	traġ e dy
vĭġ il	lăç er āte	vĭç i naġe

* The starred words are pronounced as one syllable.

BÄR, LȦST, CÂRE, FȦLL, WHẠT; HẼR, PRẸY, THÈRE; ŌET; BÏRD, MARÏNE; LIŊK;

vĕġ′ e tāte	pär tĭç′ i pāte	ạu then tĭç′ i ty
veġ e ta ble	sim plĭç i ty	e las tiç i ty
lŏġ ie	me dĭç i naȷ	du o dĕç i mo
proç ess	so liç i tūde	in ea pă̆ç i tāte
eoġ i tāte	trī plĭç i ty	ab o rĭġ i naȷ
proġ e ny	ver tiç i ty	ee çen triç i ty
iȷ lĭç′ it	rus tiç i ty	mu çi lăġ i noŭs
im plĭç it	ex ăġ ġer āte	mul ti plĭç i ty
e liç it	mor daç i ty	per spi eăç i ty
ex pliç it	pub lĭç i ty	per ti naç i ty
so liç it	o pă̆ç i ty	taç i tûr ni ty
im ăġ ĭne	ra paç i ty	maġ is tē ri aȷ
ạu daç i ty	sạ gaç i ty	a trŏç′ i ty
ea paç i ty	bel lĭġ er ent	fe roç i ty
fu gaç i ty	o rĭġ i naȷ	ve loç i ty
lo quaç i ty	ar miġ er oŭs	rℏī noç e rŏs
men daç i ty	ver tiġ i nous	reç i proç′ i ty
iȷ lĕġ i ble	re frĭġ er ate	im aġ in ā′ tion
o rĭġ i nāte	reç i tā′ tion	ex aġ ġer a tion
so liç i tor	veġ e ta tion	re frĭġ er a tion
fe liç i ty	aġ i ta tion	so lĭç i ta tion
mu nĭç i paȷ	eoġ i ta tion	fe lĭç i ta tion
an tiç i pāte	o le ăġ i noŭs	leġ er de māin′

No. 134.—CXXXIV.

WORDS IN WHICH **ce, ci, ti** AND **si**, ARE SOUNDED AS **sh.**

Grē′ cian	eŏn′ sciençe	nŭp′ tial
grā cioŭs	eăp tioŭs	pär tial
spa cious	fae tious	es sĕn′ tial
spē cious	fĭe tious	po ten tial
spe ciēṣ	lŭs cious	pro vĭn cial
sō cial	frăe tious	pru dĕn tial
ġĕn tian	eạu tious	eom mēr cial
tẽr tian	eŏn scious	im pär tial

MOVE, SÓN, WOLF, FÓOT, MÓON, ÓR ; RULE, PULL ; EXIST ; €=K ; Ġ=J ; Ş=Z ; ÇH=SH.

sub stăn' tial   fe rō' cioŭs   lī çĕn' tioŭs
€on fi dĕn' tial   lo quā cious   in ĕau tious
pen i ten tial   ra pa cious   ef fi eā' cions
prov i den tial   sa ga cious   os ten ta tious
rev e ren tial   te na cious   per spi €a cious
e qui nŏ€ tial   vex a tious   per ti na cious
in flu ĕn tial   vī va cious   €on sci ĕn tious
pes ti len tial   vo ra cious   pā' tient
au dā' cioŭs   ve ra cious   quō tient
€a pa cious   erus ta ceous   ān cient
fa çē tious   €on tĕn tious   trăn sient
fal lā cious   in fee tious   pär ti ăl' i ty
a trō cious   sen ten tious   ĭm par ti al' i ty

No. 135.—C X X X V.

WORDS IN WHICH **ci** AND **ti** ARE SOUNDED AS **sh**, AND IN
PRONUNCIATION ARE UNITED TO THE PRECEDING SYLLABLE.

prē' cioŭs (*presh'-*)   mo nĭ' tion   ma ġĭ' cian
spĕ cial (*spĕsh' al*)   mu nĭ tion   ma lĭ cioŭs
vĭ cioŭs   €on trĭ tion   mi lĭ tiă
ad dĭ' tion   at trĭ tion   mu şĭ cian
am bĭ tion   nu trĭ tion   of fĭ cial
aus pĭ cious   €og nĭ tion   pa trĭ cian
of fĭ cious   ig nĭ tion   pär tĭ tion
€a prĭ cious   €on dĭ tion   per dĭ tion
nu trĭ tious   de fĭ cient   per nĭ cious
de lĭ cious   de lĭ cioŭs   pe tĭ tion
am bĭ tious   dis €rē tion   pro fĭ cient
fa€ tĭ tious   e dĭ tion   phў şĭ cian
fi€ tĭ tious   ef fĭ cient   po şĭ tion
den tĭ tion   fla ġĭ tioŭs   pro pĭ tioŭs
fru ĭ tion   fru ĭ tion   se dĭ tion
es pĕ cial   ju dĭ cial   se dĭ tioŭs
op tĭ cian   lo ġĭ cian   sol stĭ tial

suf fĭ′ cient	ap po şĭ′ tion	av a rĭ′ cioŭs
sus pĭ cioŭs	eb ul lĭ tion	in au spĭ cioŭs
vo lĭ tion	er u dĭ tion	ben e fĭ cial
ab o lĭ′ tion	ex hi bĭ tion	eo a lĭ tion
ae qui şĭ tion	im po şĭ tion	eom pe tĭ tion
ad mo nĭ tion	op po şĭ tion	eom po şĭ tion
ad ven tĭ tioŭs	prej ū dĭ cial	def i nĭ tion
am mu nĭ tion	pol i tĭ cian	dem o lĭ tion
pre mo nĭ tion	prep o şĭ tion	dep o şĭ tion
dis qui şĭ tion	prop o şĭ tion	dis po şĭ tion
in qui şĭ tion	pro hi bĭ tion	prae tĭ′ tion er
rep e tĭ tion	su per fĭ cial	a rith me tĭ′cian
in hi bĭ tion	su per stĭ tion	ae a de mĭ cian
ex po şĭ tion	sup po şĭ tion	ġe om e trĭ cian
ap pa rĭ tion	sur rep tĭ tioŭs	in ju dĭ′ cioŭs
är ti fĭ cial	mĕr e trĭ cioŭs	de fĭ′ cien çy

No. 136.—CXXXVI.

IN THE FOLLOWING WORDS, **ci** AND **ti** ARE PRONOUNCED LIKE **shi**, AS *associate* (as so shĭ′āte).

as sō′ ci āte	ne gō′ ti āte	ex eru′ ci āte
eon sō ci āte	in sā ti āte	pro pĭ ti āte
ap prē ci āte	an nŭn ci āte	e nŭn ci āte
de pre ci āte	lĭ çen ti ate	de nŭn ci āte
e mā ci āte	sub stan ti āte	dis sō ci āte
ex pa ti āte	no vĭ ti ate	sā′ ti āte
in gra ti āte	of fĭ ci āte	vĭ ti āte

No. 137.—CXXXVII.

THE FOLLOWING WORDS, ENDING IN **ic**, MAY HAVE, AND SOME OF THEM OFTEN DO HAVE, THE SYLLABLE **al** ADDED AFTER **ic**, AS *comic, comical*; AND THE ADVERBS IN **ly** DERIVED FROM THESE WORDS ALWAYS HAVE **al**, AS IN *classically*.

eau′ stie	elĭn′ ie	erĭt′ ie	ŏth′ ie
çĕn tric	cŏm ie	eū bie	eth nie
elăs sie	eon ie	çўn ie	lŏg ie

MOVE, SÒN, WOLF, FŎOT, MOÒN, ÒR; RŪLE, PŬLL; EXIST; Ç=K; Ġ=J; Ş=Z; ÇH=SH.

lўr′ ie	ŏp′ tie	stăt′ ie	trăġ′ ie
măġ ie	*phthĭş* ie	stō ie	tўp ie
mū şie	skĕp tĭe	stўp tie	rŭs tie
mўs tie	sphĕr ie	tŏp ie	grăph ie

WORDS OF THREE SYLLABLES, ACCENTED ON THE SECOND. THESE MAY RECEIVE THE TERMINATION **al** FOR THE AD-JECTIVE, AND TO THAT MAY BE ADDED **ly** TO FORM THE ADVERB; AS, *agrestic, agrestical, agrestically.*

a ĕrŏn′ ye	ġe nĕr′ ie	Pla tŏn′ ie
a grĕs tie	ġўm năs tie	*pneū* măt ie
al ehem ie	har mŏn ie	po lĕm ie
as çet ie	He brā ie	prag măt ie
ath let ie	hĕr mĕt ie	pro lĭf ie
ạu then tie	hўs ter ie	pro phĕt ie
bär băr ie	ī rŏn ie	*rh*ap sŏd ie
bo tan ie	in trĭn sie	ro măn tie
ea thär tie	la eŏn ie	ru bĭf ie
elas sĭf ie	lu çĭf ie	sa tĭr ie
eoş mĕt ie	mag nĕt ie	*sch*iş măt ie
dī dăe tie	mag nĭf ie	seho las tie
do mĕs tie	ma jĕs tie	seor bū tie
dog măt ie	me ehăn ie	so phĭs tie
dra mat ie	mo nas tie	sper măt ie
Drụ ĭd ie	mor bĭf ie	sta lăe tie
dys pĕp tie	nu mĕr ie	stig mat ie
ee çen trie	ob stet rie	sўm mĕt rie
ee lee tie	or găn ie	syn ŏd ie
ee stăt ie	os sĭf ie	ter rĭf ie
e lĕe trie	pa çĭf ie	the ist ie
em pĭr ie	pa thĕt ie	tў răn nie
ĕr răt ie	pe dănt ie	e lăs tie
fa nat ie	phleg mat ie	bòm bast ie
fo rĕn sie	phre nĕt ie	sta tĭst ie

BÄR, LÁST, CÂRE, FALL, WHAT; HĒR, PREY, THÉRE; ĜET; BÎRD, MARÎNE; LIŊK;

WORDS OF FOUR SYLLABLES, ACCENTED ON THE THIRD.

ae a dĕm′ ie	dol o rĭf′ ie	par a lў̆t′ ie
al chem ĭst ie	em blem ăt ie	par a phrăst ie
al pha bĕt ie	en er ḡĕt ie	par a sĭt ie
ap o plee tie	e nig măt ie	par en thĕt ie
an a lŏg̈ ie	ep i lĕp tie	par a bŏl ie
an a lў̆t ie	ep i dem ie	path o log ie
an a tŏm ie	ep i sŏd ie	pe ri od ie
ap os tol ie	eū cha rĭst ie	phil o log ie
a rith mĕt ie	ex e ḡĕt ie	phil o soph ie
as tro lŏg̈ ie	frig̈ or ĭf ie	phil an throp ie
as tro nom ie	ḡe o lŏg̈ ie	Phar i sā ie
a the ĭst ie	ḡe o mĕt rie	prob lem ăt ie
at mos phĕr ie	hem is phĕr ie	pu ri tan ie
bar o met rie	his tri ŏn ie	pyr a mĭd ie
be a tĭf ie	hyp o crĭt ie	pyr o tĕeh nie
bī o grăph ie	hў̄ per bŏl ie	sçī en tĭf ie
eab a lĭst ie	hў̄ po stăt ie	sye o phănt ie
Cal vin ist ie	hў̄ po thĕt ie	syl lo g̈ĭs tie
eaş ū ist ie	id i ŏt ie	sym pa thĕt ie
eat e chĕt ie	in e lăst ie	sys tem ăt ie
eat e g̈ŏr ie	Jae o bīn ie	tal iş man ie
ehro no log ie	math e măt ie	the o lŏg̈ ie
dem o erăt ie	met a phŏr ie	the o erăt ie
dī a bŏl ie	met a phў̄s ie	the o rĕt ie
dī a lĕe tic	myth o lŏg̈ ie	to po grăph ie
dip lo măt ie	ne o tĕr ie	tў̄ po graph ie
dī a mĕt rie	or tho grăph ie	zo o lŏg̈ ie
dī ū ret ie	pan the ĭst ie	ḡe o çĕn trie

Thermometrical observations show the temperature of the air
   in winter and summer.
The mineralogist arranges his specimens in a scientific manner.

MOVE, SON, WOLF, FOOT, MOON, ÔR; RULE, PULL; EXIST; ₵=K; Ġ=J; Ş=Z; ÇH=SH.

WORDS OF FIVE SYLLABLES, ACCENTED ON THE FOURTH.

an ti scor bū′ tie	gen e a lŏg′ ie
ar is to crăt ie	lex i co grăph ie
char ac ter ĭs tie	mon o syl lăb ie
ce ele ṣi ăs tie	or ni tho lŏġ ie
en thu ṣi as tie	os te o lŏġ ie
en to mo lŏġ ie	phyṣ i o lŏġ ie
ep i gram măt ie	ieh thy̆ o lŏġ ie

THE FOLLOWING WORDS RARELY OR NEVER TAKE THE TERMINATION al.

quad răt′ ie	găl′ lie	plăs′ tie
eăth′ o lie	Gŏth ie	pŭb lie
çe phăl′ ie	hy̆m nie	Pū nie
cha ŏt ie	ī tăl′ ie	re pŭb′ lie
con çĕn trie	me dal lie	tăe′ tie
e lē′ ġĭ ae	me te ŏr′ ie	äre tie
ce stăt′ ie	me tăl′ lie	pĕp tie
ĕp′ ie	O ly̆m pie	e lăs′ tie
ex ŏt′ ie	par e gŏr′ ie	çy̆s′ tie

THE FOLLOWING WORDS USUALLY OR ALWAYS END IN al.

bĭb′ li eal	il lŏġ′ ie al	eŏm′ ie al
ea nŏn′ ie al	in ĭm i eal	mĕt ri eal
ehĭ mĕr ie al	me thŏd ie al	phy̆ṣ ie al
elĕr′ ie al	fär′ çi eal	prăe ti eal
eŏṣ mi eal	mĕd i eal	răd i eal
eŏr ti eal	trŏp ie al	vĕr ti eal
do mĭn′ i eal	top ie al	vôr ti eal
fĭn′ i eal	drop si eal	whĭm ṣi eal

THE FOLLOWING WORDS NEVER TAKE THE TERMINATION al.

ap o strŏph′ ie	plĕth′ o rie	ear bŏn′ ie
ehŏl′ er ie	ear bŏl′ ie	tûr′ mer ie
lū na tie	sul phū rie	oph thăl′ mie

WORDS ENDING IN an, en, OR on, IN WHICH THE VOWEL IS MUTE OR SLIGHTLY PRONOUNCED.

ärt′i şan   eoûr′te şan   ŏr′i şon
bĕn i şon   gär ri son   pär′ti şan
ea păr′i son   çĭt i zen   ū′ni son
eom par i son   dĕn i zen   vĕn′i şon*

WORDS ENDING IN ism, RETAINING THE ACCENT OF THEIR PRIMITIVES.

mo năs′ti çişm   prŏp a gand′işm
re ŏl′o ĝişm   per i pa tĕt′i çişm
ăt′ti çişm   pro vīn′cial işm
gŏth i çişm   ăn′gli çişm
pa rāl′o ĝişm   van dal işm
A mĕr i ean işm   gal li çişm
ĕp′i eū rişm   pĕd a gog işm
Jĕş ū it işm   pū ri tan işm
lĭb er tin işm   Preş by tē′ri an işm
ma tē′ri al işm   păr′a sit işm
mŏn′o the işm   par al lel işm
năt ū ral işm   fā vor it işm
pā tri ot işm   so çīn′i an işm
pŏl y the işm   pa răeh ro nişm
prŏs e lyt işm   re pŭb lie an işm
phăr i sa işm   see tā ri an işm
Prŏt est ant işm   seho lăs ti çişm

No. 138.—CXXXVIII.

WORDS ENDING IN ize, ACCENTED ON THE FIRST SYLLABLE.

au′thor īze   mŏr′al īze   măg′net īze
băs tard ize   drăm a tize   mŏd ern ize
çĭv il ize   ĕm pha size   ăg o nize
eăn on ize   găl van ize   pŭl ver ize
lē gal ize   hĕr bo rize   stĕr il ize

* Pronounced ven i-zn or ven′zn.

MOVE, SÒN, WOLF, FŎOT, MOON, ÒR; RŲLE, PŲLL; EXIST; €=K; Ġ=J; Ş=Z; ÇH=SH.

sŭb′si dīze   ôr′ gan īze   drăm′ a tīze
tyr an nize   păt ron ize   ıẽr til ize
sys tem ize   săt ir ize   ī dol ize
mĕth od ize   tăn tal ize   mĕl o dize
joûr nal ize   vō cal ize   mes mer ize
bru tal ize   eau ter ize   pō lar ize
eōl o nize   bär bar ize   rē al ize
ĕn er ġize   bŏt a nize   thē o rize
ē qual ize   dăs tard ize   trăn quil ize
hū man ize   dĕt o nize   tĕm po rize
Ju da ize   dŏg ma tize   Rō man ize

No. 139.—CXXXIX.

WORDS OF FOUR AND FIVE SYLLABLES, RETAINING THE ACCENT OF THEIR PRIMITIVES.

ăl′ eo hol īze   ġĕn′ er al īze   păn′ e ġyr īze
ăl le go rize   lĭb er al ize   pŏp ū lar ize
a năth′ e ma tize ma tē′ ri al ize prŏs e ly tize
ăn′ i mal ize   me mō ri al ize pū ri tan ize
e pĭs′ to lize   mĭn′ er al ize   re pŭb lie an ize
bĕs′ tial ize   mo nŏp′ o lize   sĕe ū lar ize
e nĭg′ ma tize   năt′ ū ral ize   sen sū al ize *
ehăr′ ae ter ize ŏx y ġen ize   spĭr it ū al ize
e thē′ re al ize par tĭe′ū lar ize vŏl a til ize

It is almost impossible to civilize the American Indians.
We should never tyrannize over those weaker than ourselves.
Sometimes, when a person is bitten by a rattlesnake, the doctor will cauterize or sear the wound.

No. 140.—CXL.

THE COMBINATION **ng** REPRESENTS, IN SOME WORDS, A SIMPLE ELEMENTARY SOUND, AS HEARD IN *sing, singer, long;* IN OTHER WORDS, IT REPRESENTS THE SAME ELEMENTARY

* Pronounced *sĕn′ shu-al-īze.*

BÄR, LÀST, ÇÂRE, FALL, WHAT; HËR, PREY, THÉRE; ĜET; BÏRD, MARĪNE; LIŊK;

SOUND FOLLOWED BY THAT OF **g** HARD (HEARD IN *go, get*)
AS IN *finger, linger, longer.*

THE FOLLOWING HAVE THE SIMPLE SOUND.

a' móng	hăng' er	sĭng' ing	strŭng
băng	hang man	sŏng	strĭng' ing
brĭng	hang nail	sŭng	strŏng
bring' ing	hŭng	slăng	strong' ly
bŭng	kĭng	slĭng	swĭng
clăng	ling	sling' er	swing' er
clĭng	lŏng	slŭng	swing ing
cling' ing	lŭngs	sprĭng	swŭng
clŭng	păng	sprăng	tăng
dung	prŏng	spring' er	thĭng
făng	răng	spring ing	thŏng
flĭng	rĭng	stĭng	tòngue
fling' er	ring' ing	sting' er	twăng
fling ing	ring let	sting ing	wrĭng
flŭng	rŭng	stŭng	wring' er
găng	săng	strĭng	wring ing
hăng	sĭng	stringed	wrŏng
hanged	sing' er	string er	wrŏnged

IN THE FOLLOWING WORDS, **n**, ALONE, REPRESENTS THE
SOUND OF **ng**, AND IS MARKED THUS, **n̠**.

an̠' ḡer	elan̠' gor	jan̠' gler
an̠ gry	eŏn̠ go	jan̠ gling
an̠ gle	dăn̠ gle	jĭn̠ gle
an̠ gler	dĭn̠ gle	lăn̠ guid
an̠ gli ean	făn̠ gle	lăn̠ guish
an̠ gli çişm	fĭn̠ ḡer	lŏn̠ ḡer
ăn̠ gli çīze	fŭn̠ gus	lŏn̠ ḡest
ăn̠ guish	hŭn̠ ḡer	măn̠ gle
ăn̠ gu lar	hŭn̠ gry	măn̠ gler
brăn̠ gle	ĭn̠ gle	măn̠ go
bŭn̠ gle	jăn̠ gle	mĭn̠ gle

MŎVE, SŎN, WOLF, FŎOT, MŌON, ŎR; RŪLE, PŪLL; EXIST; ꞓ=K; Ġ= J; Ṣ=Z; ĊH=SH.

mŏn̄' ḡer	lĭn̄' ḡer	e lŏn̄' gāte
mŏn grel	tăn gle	lĭn̄' ḡ·r ing
strŏn̄ ḡer	tĭn gle	sȳ rĭn̄' ḡä
strŏn̄ ḡest	wrăn gle	străn' gu ry

No. 141.—CXLI.

IN THE FOLLOWING WORDS THE **d, t** AND **u,** PREFERABLY TAKE THEIR REGULAR SOUNDS; AS IN *capture, verdure,* PRONOUNCED *capt'yoor, vĕrd'yoor.* MANY SPEAKERS, HOWEVER, SAY *kap'choor, vĕr'jur.*

eăpt' ūre	moist' ūre	seŭlpt' ūre
çĭn̄et ūre	nāt ūre	stăt ūre
erēat ūre	nûrt ūre	ġĕst ūre
eŭlt ūre	ôrd ūre	strĭet ūre
fĕat ūre	păst ūre	strŭet ūre
frăet ūre	pĭet ūre	sūt ūre
fūt ūre	pŏst ūre	tĕxt ūre
joint ūre	pŭn̄et ūre	tĭn̄et ūre
jŭn̄et ūre	răpt ūre	tôrt ūre
lĕet ūre	rŭpt ūre	vĕnt ūre
mĭxt ūre	serĭpt ūre	vĕrd ūre

The lungs are the organs of respiration. If any substance, excess air, is inhaled and comes in contact with the lungs, we instantly cough. This cough is an effort of nature to free the lungs.

A finger signifies a taker, as does fang. We take or catch things with the fingers, and fowls and rapacious quadrupeds seize other animals with their fangs.

A pang is a severe pain. Anguish is violent distress.

A lecture is a discourse read or pronounced on any subject: it is also a formal reproof.

The Bible, that is, the Old and the New Testament, contains the Holy Scriptures.

Discourage cunning in a child: cunning is the ape of wisdom.

Whatever is wrong is a deviation from right, or from the just laws of God or man.

Anger is a tormenting passion, and so are envy and jealousy. To be doomed to suffer these passions long, would be as severe a punishment as confinement in the state prison.

An anglicism is a peculiar mode of speech among the English.

Love is an agreeable passion, and love is sometimes stronger than death.

How happy men would be if they would always love what is right and hate what is wrong.

No. 142.—CXLII.

g AND **k** BEFORE **n** ARE ALWAYS SILENT.

gnär	knāv′ ish	knŏck′ er
gnärl	knāv ish ly	knōll
gnăsh	knāv ish ness	knŏt
gnat	knēad	knot′ grȧss
gnaw	knee	knot′ ted
gnō′ mon	kneel	knot′ ty
gnŏs ties	knīfe	knot′ ti ly
gnos ti çişm	knight	knot′ ti ness
knäb	knight ĕr′ rant	knout
knack	knight′ hŏŏd	knōw
knag	knight ly	know′ a ble
knag ḡy	knĭt	known
knap	knit′ ter	know′ ing
knap săck	knit′ ting	know′ ing ly
knap weed	knŏb	knŏwl′ edge
knell	knobbed	knŭck′ le
knāve	knob′ by	knûrl
knāv′ er y	knock	knurl y

Knead the dough thoroughly, if you would have good bread.

The original signification of *knave* was 'a boy'; but the word now signifies 'a dishonest person.'

In Russia, the knout is used to inflict stripes on the bare back.

MOVE, SÒN, WOLF, FÓÓT, MŌŌN, ÔR; RULE, PULL; EXIST; €=K; Ġ=J; ₷=Z; ÇH=SH.

No. 143.—CXLIII.

IN THE FOLLOWING WORDS, **ch** HAS THE SOUND OF **sh**, AND IN MANY OF THEM **i** HAS THE SOUND OF **e** LONG.

çhāiṣe	€ap ū çhïn′	€av a liēr′
çha grĭn′	mag a zïne	quạr′an tïne
çham pāiṛn	sub ma rïne	man da rïn′
çhĭ €āne	trans ma rïne	€ash iēr′
çhĭ €ān′er y	bòm ba zïne	ma rïne
çhev a liēr′	brig a diēr	€a prïçe
çhĭv′al ry	€an non niēr	po lïçe
çhăn de liēr′	€ap a pīe	fas çïne
çhe mïṣe′	€är bin iēr	fron tiēr

No. 144.—CXLIV.

IN THE FOLLOWING WORDS, THE VOWEL **a** IN THE DIGRAPH **ea**, HAS NO SOUND, AND **e** IS EITHER SHORT, OR PRONOUNCED LIKE **e** IN *term*; THUS, *bread, tread, earth, dearth*, ARE PRONOUNCED *brĕd, trĕd, ērth, dērth*.

brĕad	hĕalth	hĕav′en	pĕaṣ′ant
dead	wealth	leav en	pleaṣ ure
head	stealth	heav y	meaṣ ūre
tread	€leanṣe	read y	treaṣ ūre
dread	ĕarl	health y	treach er y
stead	pearl	wealth y	en dĕav′or
thread	earn	feaᵗh er	re hēarse′
spread	learn	leaᵗh er	thrĕat′en
breast	yearn	leaᵗh ern	break fast
breadth	mĕant	tread le	stead fast
breath	dreamt	jeal oŭs	mead ōw
ēarth	realm	jeal oŭs y	pēarl ash
dearth	ēar′ly	zeal oŭs	stĕalth y
thrĕat	earn est	zeal oŭs ly	stead y
sweat	re sēarch′	zeal ot	stealth ful
sēarch	€lean′ly	pleaṣ ant	health ful

BÄR, LȦST, ÇÂRE, FĄLL, WHAT; HËR, PRĘY, THÊRE; ĢET; BÏRD, MARĪNE; LIŊK;

No. 145.—C X L V.

IN THE FOLLOWING, **g** IS SILENT.

P. stands for past tense; PPR. for participle of the present tense.

VERBS.	P.	PPR. AGENT.	VERBS.	P.	PPR. AGENT.
sīgn	ed	ing er	re sīgn	ed	ing er
as sign'	ed	ing er	im pūgn	ed	ing er
¢on sign	ed	ing er	op pūgn	ed	ing er
de sign	ed	ing er	ar rāign	ed	ing er
ma lign	ed	ing er	coun ter sīgn	ed	ing

Adjectives and Nouns.

¢on dīgn'	poign'ant	fōr'eign	ĕn'sīgn
be nīgn	ma līgn'	sŏv er eign	¢am pāign'

IN THE FOLLOWING, THE SOUND OF **g** IS RESUMED.

as sig nā'tion	in dĭg'ni ty	im prĕg'na ble
des ig nā tion	in dig nant	op pūg nan çy
reṣ ig nā tion	dĭg'ni ty	re pug nant
be nĭg'nant	dig ni fȳ	re pug nan çy
be nig ni ty	prĕg nant	sīg'ni fȳ
ma lig ni ty	preg nan çy	sig ni fi eā'tion
ma lig nant	im prĕg'nāte	sig nĭf'i eant

No. 146.—C X L V I.

WORDS IN WHICH **e, i,** AND **o,** BEFORE **n,** ARE MUTE. THOSE WITH **v** ANNEXED, ARE OR MAY BE USED AS VERBS, ADMITTING **ed** FOR THE PAST TIME, AND **ing** FOR THE PARTICIPLE.

bā'¢on	brā'zen	bĭd'den
bēa ¢on	brō ken	slăck'en, *v.*
beech en	blăck en, *v.*	bound en
bā sin	băt ten, *v.*	bŭt ton, *v.*
bēat en	bĕck on, *v.*	broạd en, *v.*
bĭt ten	bûr den, *v.*	chō ṣen
blā zon	bûr then, *v.*	¢lō ven

No. 147.—CXLVII.

THE DOG.

This dog is the mastiff. He is active, strong, and used as a watchdog. He has a large head and pendent ears. He is not very apt to bite; but he will sometimes take down a man and hold him down. Three mastiffs once had a combat with a lion, and the lion was compelled to save himself by flight.

THE STAG.

The stag is the male of the red deer. He is a mild and harmless animal, bearing a noble attire of horns, which are shed and renewed every year. His form is light and elegant, and he runs with great rapidity. The female is called a hind; and the fawn or young deer, when his horns appear, is called a pricket or brocket.

THE SQUIRREL.

The squirrel is a beautiful little animal. The gray and black squirrels live in the forest and make a nest of leaves and sticks on the high branches. It is amusing to see the nimble squirrel spring from branch to branch, or run up and down the stem of a tree, and dart behind it to escape from sight. Little ground squirrels burrow in the earth. They subsist on nuts, which they hold in their paws, using them as little boys use their hands.

FABLE I.

OF THE BOY THAT STOLE APPLES.

An old man found a rude boy upon one of his trees stealing apples, and desired him to come down; but the young saucebox told him plainly he would not. "Won't you?" said the old man, "then I will fetch you down;" so he pulled up some turf or grass and threw at him; but this only made the youngster laugh, to think the old man should pretend to beat him down from the tree with grass only.

"Well, well," said the old man, "if neither words nor grass will do, I must try what virtue there is in stones;" so the old man pelted him heartily with stones, which soon made the young chap hasten down from the tree and beg the old man's pardon.

MORAL.

If good words and gentle means will not reclaim the wicked, they must be dealt with in a more severe manner.

FABLE II.

THE COUNTRY MAID AND HER MILK PAIL.

When men suffer their imagination to amuse them with the prospect of distant and uncertain improvements of their condition, they frequently sustain real losses, by their inattention to those affairs in which they are immediately concerned.

A country maid was walking very deliberately with a pail of milk upon her head, when she fell into the following train of reflections: "The money for which I shall sell this milk, will enable me to increase my stock of eggs to three hundred. These eggs, allowing for what may prove addle, and what may be destroyed by vermin, will produce at least two hundred and fifty chickens. The chickens will be fit to carry to market about Christmas, when poultry always bears a good price; so that by May Day I can not fail of having money enough to purchase a new gown. Green!—let me consider—yes, green becomes my complexion best, and green it shall be. In this dress I will go to the fair, where all the young fellows will strive to have me for a partner; but I shall perhaps refuse every one of them, and, with an air of disdain, toss from them." Transported with this triumphant thought, she could not forbear acting with her head what thus passed in her imagination, when down came the pail of milk, and with it all her imaginary happiness.

FABLE III.

THE TWO DOGS.

Hasty and inconsiderate connections are generally attended with great disadvantages; and much of every man's good or ill fortune, depends upon the choice he makes of his friends.

A good-natured Spaniel overtook a surly Mastiff, as he was traveling upon the highroad. Tray, although an entire stranger to Tiger, very civilly accosted him; and if it would be no interruption, he said, he should be glad to bear him company on his way. Tiger, who happened not to be altogether in so growling a mood as usual, accepted the proposal; and they very amicably pursued their journey together. In the midst of their conversation, they arrived at the next village, where Tiger began to display his malignant disposition, by an unprovoked attack upon every dog he met. The villagers immediately sallied forth with great indignation to rescue their respective favorites; and falling upon our two friends, without distinction or mercy, poor Tray was most cruelly treated, for no other reason than his being found in bad company.

FABLE IV.

THE PARTIAL JUDGE.

A farmer came to a neighboring lawyer, expressing great concern for an accident which he said had just happened. "One of your oxen," continued he, "has been gored by an unlucky bull of mine, and I should be glad to know how I am to make you reparation." "Thou art a very honest fellow," replied the lawyer, "and wilt not think it unreasonable that I expect one of thy oxen in return." "It is no more than justice," quoth the farmer, "to be sure; but what did I say?—I mistake —it is *your* bull that has killed one of *my* oxen." "Indeed!" says the lawyer, "that alters the case: I must inquire into the affair; and if—" "And *if!*" said the farmer; "the business I find would have been concluded without an *if*, had you been as ready to do justice to others as to exact it from them."

FABLE V.

THE CAT AND THE RAT.

A certain cat had made such unmerciful havoc among the vermin of her neighborhood, that not a single rat or mouse dared venture to appear abroad. Puss was soon convinced that if affairs remained in their present state, she must ere long starve. After mature deliberation, therefore, she resolved to have recourse to stratagem. For this purpose, she suspended herself from a hook with her head downward, pretending to be dead. The rats and mice, as they peeped from their holes, observing her in this dangling attitude, concluded she was hanging for some misdemeanor, and with great joy immediately sallied forth in quest of their prey. Puss, as soon as a sufficient number were collected together, quitting her hold, dropped into the midst of them; and very few had the fortune to make

good their retreat. This artifice having succeeded so well, she was encouraged to try the event of a second. Accordingly, she whitened her coat all over by rolling herself in a heap of flour, and in this disguise she lay concealed in the bottom of a meal tub. This stratagem was executed in general with the same effect as the former. But an old experienced rat, altogether as cunning as his adversary, was not so easily insnared. "I don't quite like," said he, "that white heap yonder. Something whispers me there is mischief concealed under it. 'Tis true, it may be meal, but it may likewise be something that I should not relish quite as well. There can be no harm at least in keeping at a proper distance; for caution, I am sure, is the parent of safety."

FABLE VI.

THE FOX AND THE BRAMBLE.

A fox, closely pursued by a pack of dogs, took shelter under the covert of a bramble. He rejoiced in this asylum, and for

a while, was very happy; but soon found that if he attempted
to stir, he was wounded by the thorns and prickles on every
side. However, making a virtue of necessity, he forebore to
complain, and comforted himself with reflecting that no bliss
is perfect; that good and evil are mixed, and flow from the
same fountain. These briers, indeed, said he, will tear my
skin a little, yet they keep off the dogs. For the sake of the
good, then, let me bear the evil with patience; each bitter has
its sweet; and these brambles, though they wound my flesh,
preserve my life from danger.

FABLE VII.

THE BEAR AND THE TWO FRIENDS.

Two friends, setting out together upon a journey which led
through a dangerous forest, mutually promised to assist each
other, if they should happen to be assaulted. They had not
proceeded far, before they perceived a bear making toward
them with great rage.

There were no hopes in flight; but one of them, being very
active, sprang up into a tree; upon which the other, throwing
himself flat on the ground, held his breath and pretended to
be dead; remembering to have heard it asserted that this
creature will not prey upon a dead carcass. The bear came
up and after smelling of him some time, left him and went on.
When he was fairly out of sight and hearing, the hero from
the tree called out,—" Well, my friend, what said the bear?
He seemed to whisper you very closely." "He did so," replied
the other, "and gave me this good advice, never to associate with
a wretch, who, in the hour of danger, will desert his friend."

"Henry, tell me the number of days in a year." "Three hundred and sixty-five." "How many weeks in a year?" "Fifty-two." "How many days in a week?" "Seven." "What are they called?" "Sabbath or Sunday, Monday, Tuesday, Wednesday, Thursday, Friday, Saturday." The Sabbath is a day of rest, and called the Lord's day, because God has commanded us to keep it holy. On that day we are to omit labor and worldly employments, and devote the time to religious duties, and the gaining of religious knowledge.

"How many hours are there in a day or day and night?" "Twenty-four." "How many minutes in an hour?" "Sixty." "How many seconds in a minute?" "Sixty." Time is measured by clocks and watches; or by dials and glasses.

The light of the sun makes the day, and the shade of the earth makes the night. The earth revolves from west to east once in twenty-four hours. The sun is fixed or stationary; but the earth turns every part of its surface to the sun once in twenty-four hours. The day is for labor, and the night is for sleep and repose. Children should go to bed early in the evening, and all persons, who expect to thrive in the world, should rise early in the morning.

♦ ♦ ♦

No. 148.—CXLVIII.

WORDS NEARLY, BUT NOT EXACTLY, ALIKE IN PRONUNCIATION.

Ac cept', to take.
ex cept, to take out.

af fect, to impress.
ef fect, what is produced.

ac cede, to agree.
ex ceed, to surpass.

pre scribe, to direct.
pro scribe, to banish.

ac cess, approach.
ex cess, superfluity.

al lu'sion, hint, reference.
il lu sion, deception.
e lu sion, evasion.

acts, deeds.
ax, a tool for cutting.

as say', trial of metals.
es say', to try.

af fu'sion, a pouring on.
ef fu sion, a pouring out.

al lowed', admitted, granted.
a loud, with a great voice.

er'rand, a message.
er rant, wandering.

ad di'tion, something added.
e di tion, publication.

bal'lad, a song.
bal let, a dance.   [vote.
bal lot, a ball for voting, or a

chron'i cal, of long continu-
chron i cle, a history.   [ance.

clothes, garments.
close, conclusion.

con'sort, husband or wife.
con cert, harmony.

de scent', a falling, a slope.
dis sent, a differing.

de cease', death.
dis ease, sickness.

MŎVE, SŎN, WŎLF, FŎŎT, MŌŌN, ÒR; RŪLE, PŬLL; EXIST; C as K; G as J; S as Z; CH as SH.

e lic' it, to call forth.
il lic' it, unlawful.
  im merge', to plunge.
  e merge, to come forth.
fat, fleshy.
vat, a tub or cistern.
  gest' ure, motion.
  jest er, one who jests.
i' dle, not employed.
i dol, an image.
  im pos' tor, a deceiver.
  im post ure, deception.
naugh' ty, bad.
knot ty, full of knots.
  in gen' u ous, frank.
  in ge ni ous, skillful.
line, extension in length.

loin, part of an animal.
loom, a frame for weaving.
loam, a soft loose earth.
med' al, an ancient coin.
med dle, to interpose.
  pint, half a quart.
  point, a sharp end.
rad' ish, a garden vegetable.
red dish, somewhat red.
  since, at a later time.
  sense, faculty of perceiving.
ten' or, course continued.
ten ure, a holding.
  tal' ents, ability.
  tal ons, claws.
val' ley, low land.
val ue, worth.

WORDS SPELLED ALIKE, BUT PRONOUNCED DIFFERENTLY.

Au' gust, the eighth month.
au gust', grand.
  bow (ow as in cow), to bend.
  bōw, for shooting arrows.
bass, a tree; a fish.
băss, lowest part in music.
  con jure', to entreat.
  con' jure, to use magic art.
des' ert, a wilderness.
des sert', fruit, etc., at dinner.
  gal' lant, brave, gay.
  gal lant', a gay fellow.
gill, the fourth of a pint.
gill, part of a fish.
  hin' der, to stop.
  hind er, further behind.
in' va lid, one not in health.
in val' id, not firm or binding.
  low'er (ow as in cow), to be dark.
  lōw er, not so high.
live, to be or dwell.

live, having life.
  mow (ow as in cow), a pile of hay.
  mōw, to cut with a scythe.
read, to utter printed words.
read [red], past tense of read.
  rec' ol lect, to call to mind.
  re col lect', to collect again.
re form', to amend.
re' form, to make anew.
  rec' re ate, to refresh.
  re cre ate', to create anew.
rout, defeat and disorder.
route, a way or course.
  slough, a place of mud.
  slough [sluff], a cast skin.
tär' ry, like tar.
tăr ry, to delay.
  tēars, water from the eyes.
  teârs, [he] rends.
wind, air in motion.
wīnd, to turn or twist.

WORDS PRONOUNCED ALIKE, BUT SPELLED DIFFERENTLY.

ail, to be in trouble.
ale, malt liquor.
  air, the atmosphere.
  heir, one who inherits.
all, the whole.
awl, an instrument.

al' tar, a place for offerings.
al ter, to change.
  ănt, a little insect.
  äunt, a sister to a parent.
ark, a vessel.
arc, part of a circle.

BÄR, LÅST, €ÂRE, F ALL, WH AT; HÊR, PRÊY, THÊRE; ĞET; BÎRD, MARÎNE; LIŅK;

as cent', steepness.
as sent, agreement.
  au' ger, a tool.
  au gur, one who foretells.
bail, surety.
bale, a pack of goods.
  ball, a sphere.
  bawl, to cry aloud.
base, low, vile
bass or base, in music.
  beer, a liquor.
  bier, a carriage for the dead.
bin, a box.
been, participle of be.
  ber' ry, a little fruit.
  bu ry, to inter.
beat, to strike.
beet, a root.
  blew, did blow.
  blue, a dark color.
boar, a male swine.
bore, to make a hole.
  bow, to bend the body.
  bough, a branch.
bell, to ring.
belle, a fine lady.
  beau, a gay gentleman.
  bow, to shoot with.
bread, a kind of food.
bred, educated.
  bur' row, for rabbits.   [town.
  bor ough, an incorporated
by, near at hand.
buy, to purchase.
bye, a dwelling.
  bay, an inlet of water.
  bey, a Turkish governor.
be, to exist.
bee, an insect.
  beach, sea-shore.
  beech, a tree.
boll, a pod of plants.
bowl, an earthen vessel.
bole, a kind of clay.
  but, a conjunction.
  butt, two hogsheads.
brake, a weed.
break, to part asunder.
  Cain, a man's name.
  cane, a shrub or staff.
call, to cry out, or name.
caul, a net inclosing the bowels.

can' non, a large gun.
can on, a law of the church.
ces' sion, a grant.
ses sion, the sitting of a court.
  can' vas, coarse cloth.
  can vass, to examine.
ceil, to make a ceiling.
seal, to fasten a letter.
  seal' ing, setting a seal.
  ceil ing, of a room.
cens' er, an incense pan.
cen sor, a critic.
  course, way, direction.
  coarse, not fine.
cote, a sheep-fold.
coat, a garment.
  core, the heart.
  corps, a body of soldiers.
cell, a hut.
sell, to dispose of.
  cen' tu ry, a hundred years.
  cen tau ry, a plant.
chol' er, wrath.
col lar, for the neck.
  cord, a small rope.
  chord, a line.
cite, to summon.
site, situation.
sight, the sense of seeing.
  com' ple ment, a full number.
  com pli ment, act of polite-
    ness.
cous' in, a relation.
coz en, to cheat.
  cur' rant, a berry.
  cur rent, a stream.
deer, a wild animal.
dear, costly.
  cask, a vessel for liquids.
  casque, a helmet.
ce' dar, a kind of wood.
ce der, one who cedes.
  cede, to give up.
  seed, fruit, offspring.
cent, the hundredth part of a
    dollar.
sent, ordered away.
scent, a smell.
  cel' lar, the lowest room.
  sell er, one who sells.
clime, a region.
climb, to ascend.

MOVE, SÒN, WOLF, FOÒT, MOON, ÔR ; RULE, PULL ; EXIST ; €=K ; Ġ=J ; S=Z ; ÇH=SH.

coun' cil, an assembly.
coun sel, advice.

 sym' bol, a type.
 cym bal, a musical instrument.

col' or, hue.
cul ler, one who selects.

 dam, to stop water.
 damn, to condemn.

dew, falling vapors.
due, owing.

 die, to expire.
 dye, to color.

doe, a female deer.
dough, bread not baked.

 fane, a temple.
 feign, to dissemble.

dire, horrid.
dy er, one who colors.

 dun, to urge for money.
 dun, a brown color.
 done, performed.

dram, a drink of spirit.
drachm, a small weight.

 e lis' ion, the act of cutting off.
 e lys ian, blissful, joyful.

you, second person.
yew, a tree.
ewe, a female sheep.

 fair, handsome.
 fare, customary duty.

feat, an exploit.
feet, plural of foot.

 freeze, to congeal.
 frieze, in a building.

hie, to hasten.
high, elevated, lofty.

 flea, an insect.
 flee, to run away.

flour, of rye or wheat.
flow er, a blossom.

 forth, abroad.
 fourth, in number.

foul, filthy.
fowl, a bird.

 gilt, with gold.
 guilt, crime.

grate, iron bars.
great, large.

 grown, increased.
 groan, an expression of pain.

hail, to call; also frozen rain.

hale, healthy.

 hart, a beast.
 heart, the seat of life.

hare, an animal.
hair, the fur of animals.

 here, in this place.
 hear, to hearken.

hew, to cut.
hue, color.

 him, objective of he.
 hymn, a sacred song.

hire, wages.
high er, more high.

 heel, the hinder part of the foot.
 heal, to cure.

haul, to drag.
hall, a large room.

 I, myself.
 eye, organ of sight.

isle (ile), an island.
aisle, of a church.

 in, within.
 inn, a tavern.

in dite', to compose.
in dict, to prosecute.

 kill, to slay.
 kiln, for burning bricks.

knap, a protuberance.
nap, a short sleep.

 knave, a rogue.
 nave, of a wheel.

knead, to work dough.
need, necessity.

 kneel, to bend the knee.
 neal, to heat.

knew, did know.
new, fresh, not old.

 know, to understand.
 no, not.

knight, a title.
night, darkness.

 knot, a tie.
 not, no, denying.

lade, to fill, to dip.
laid, placed.

 lain, did lie.
 lane, a narrow street.

leek, a root.
leak, to run out.

 less' on, a reading.
 les sen, to diminish.

BÄR, LÂST, ĈÂRE, FĄLL, WHĄT; HÊR, PRĘY, THÈRE; ǦET; BĪRD, MARĪNE; LIŊK;

li' ar, one who tells lies.
li er, one who lies in wait.
lyre, a harp.
  led, did lead.
  lead, a heavy metal.
lie, an untruth.
lye, water drained through ashes.
  lo, behold.
  low, humble; not high.
lac, a gum.
lack, want.
  lea, grass-land.
  lee, opposite the wind.
leaf, of a plant.
lief, willingly.
  lone, solitary.
  loan, that is lent.
lore, learning.
low er, more low.
  lock, a catch to a door.
  loch, a lake.
main, ocean; the chief.
mane, of a horse.
  made, finished.
  maid, an unmarried woman.
male, the he kind.
mail, armor; bag for letters.
  man' ner, mode of action.
  man or, lands of a lord.
meet, to come together.
meat, flesh, food.
mete, measure.
  mean, low, humble.
  mien, countenance.
mewl, to cry.
mule, a beast.
  mi' ner, one who works in a mine.
  mi nor, less, or one under age.
moan, to grieve.
mown, cut down.
  moat, a ditch.
  mote, a speck.
more, a greater portion.
mow er, one who mows.
  mite, an insect.
  might, strength.
met' al, gold, silver, etc.
met tle, briskness.
  nit, egg of an insect.
  knit, to join with needles.
nay, no.

neigh, as a horse.
  aught, any thing.
  ought, morally owed, should.
oar, a paddle.
ore, of metal.
  one, a single thing.
  won, did win.
oh, alas.
owe, to be indebted.
  our, belonging to us.
  hour, sixty minutes.
plum, a fruit.
plumb, a lead and line.
  pale, without color.
  pail, a vessel.
pain, distress.
pane, a square of glass.
  pal' ate, part of the mouth.
  pal let, painter's board; a bed.
pleas, pleadings.
please, to give pleasure.
  pole, a long stick.
  poll, the head.
peel, to pare off the rind.
peal, sounds.
  pair, a couple.
  pare, to cut off the rind.
  pear, a fruit.
plain, even or level.
plane, to make smooth.
  pray, to implore.
  prey, booty, plunder.
prin' ci pal, chief.
prin ci ple, rule of action.
  prof' it, advantage.
  proph et, a foreteller.
peace, quietude.
piece, a part.
  pan' el, a square in a door.
  pan nel, a kind of saddle.
raise, to lift.
raze, to demolish.
  rain, water falling from clouds.
  reign, to rule.
rap, to strike.
wrap, to fold together.
  read, to peruse.
  reed, a plant.
red, a color.
read, did read.
  reek, to emit steam.
  wreak, to revenge.

rest, to take ease.
wrest, to take by force.
rice, a sort of grain.
rise, source, beginning.
rye, a sort of grain.
wry, crooked.
ring, to sound; a circle.
wring, to twist.
rite, ceremony.
right, just.
write, to make letters with a pen.
wright, a workman.
rode, did ride.
road, the highway.
rear, to raise.
rear, the hind part.
rig′ ger, one who rigs vessels.
rig or, severity.
ruff, a neck-cloth.
rough, not smooth.
rote, repetition of words.
wrote, did write.
roe, a female deer.
row, a rank.
roar, to sound loudly.
row er, one who rows.
rab′ bet, to cut, as the edge of a board, in a sloping manner.
rab bit, an animal.
sail, the canvas of a ship.
sale, the act of selling.
sea, a large body of water.
see, to behold.
sa′ ver, one who saves.
sa vor, taste or odor.
seen, beheld.
scene, part of a play.
seine, a fish net.
sen′ ior (*sēn′ yur*), older.
seign ior, a Turkish king.
seam, where the edges join.
seem, to appear.
shear, to cut with shears.
sheer, clear, unmixed.
sent, ordered away.
cent, a small coin.
scent, smell.
shore, sea-coast.
shore, a prop.
so, in such a manner.
sow, to scatter seed.

sum, the whole.
some, a part.
sun, the fountain of light.
son, a male child.
stare, to gaze.
stair, a step.
steel, hard metal.
steal, to take by theft.
suck er, a young twig.
suc′ cor, help.
slight, to despise.
sleight, dexterity.
sole, of the foot.
soul, the spirit.
slay, to kill.
sley, a weaver's reed.
sleigh, a carriage on runners.
sloe, a fruit.
slow, not swift.
stake, a post.
steak, a slice of meat.
stile, steps over a fence.
style, fashion, diction.
tacks, small nails.
tax, a rate, tribute.
throw, to cast away.
throe, pain of travail.
tare, an allowance in weight.
tear, to rend.
tēar, water from the eyes.
tier, a row.
team, of horses or oxen.
teem, to produce.
tide, flux of the sea.
tied, fastened.
their, belonging to them.
there, in this place.
the, definite adjective.
thee, objective case of *thou*.
too, likewise.
two, twice one.
toe, extremity of the foot.
tow, to drag.
vail, a covering.
vale, a valley.
vial, a little bottle.
viol, a fiddle.
vane, to show which way the wind blows.
vein, for the blood.
vice, sin.
vise, a griping instrument.

BÄR, LÀST, CÂRE, FALL, WHAT; HẼR, PREY, THÉRE; GĔT; BĪRD, MARÏNE; LIŊK;

wait, to tarry.
weight, heaviness.

wear, to carry, as clothes.
ware, merchandise.

waste, to spread.
waist, a part of the body.

way, road, course.

weigh, to find the weight.

week, seven days.
weak, not strong.

wood, timber.
would, past time of *will*.

weather, state of the air.
wether, a sheep.

What *ails* the child?
Ale is a fermented liquor, made from malt.
The *awl* is a tool used by shoemakers and harness-makers.
All quadrupeds that walk and do not leap, walk upon four legs.
The Prince of Wales is *heir* to the crown of England.
We breathe *air*.
The moon *alters* its appearance every night.
The Jews burned sacrifices upon an *altar* of stone.
Cruel horsemen *beat* their horses.
Molasses may be made from *beets*.
A fine *beau* wears fine clothes.
The *rainbow* is caused by the sun's shining upon the falling rain.
Beer may be made from malt and hops.
They bore the body to the grave on a *bier*.
The great *bell* in Moscow, weighs two hundred and twenty tons.
The *belles* and the *beaux* are fond of fine shows.
Black*berries* and raspberries grow on briers.
The farmer, when he plants seeds, *buries* them in the ground.
Wheat is a *better* grain than rye.
One who lays a wager is a *bettor*.
The wind *blew*.
The color of the sky is *blue*.
Your father's or your mother's sister is your *aunt*.
The little *ants* make hillocks.
Carpenters bore holes with an *auger*.
An *augur* foretells.
Boys love to play *ball*.
Children *bawl* for trifles.
Bears live in the woods.
An oak *bears* acorns.

We *bear* evils.
Trees *bare* of leaves.
Beech wood makes a good fire.
The waves beat on the *beach*.
A wild *boar* is a savage beast.
Miners *bore* holes in rocks, and burst them with powder.
The *boll* of plants is a seed vessel.
Eat a *bowl* of bread and milk.
The planks of vessels are fastened with copper *bolts*.
Millers separate the bran from the flour by large sieves called *bolts*.
The breech of a gun is its *butt* or club end.
A ram *butts* with his head.
We import *butts* of spirits.
Brakes are useless weeds.
We *break* flax and hemp in dressing.
Well-*bred* people do not always eat wheat *bread*.
A *butt* contains two hogsheads; but a barrel, 31½ gallons.
We judge of people's motives *by* their actions.
We can not *buy* a seat in heaven with our money.
Clothiers smooth their clothes with *calenders*.
Almanac makers publish new *calendars* every year.
Sails are made of *canvas*.
Inspectors *canvass* votes.
The courts of New York hold their *sessions* in the City Hall.
Since the *cession* of Florida, the United States have been bounded on the south by the Gulf of Mexico.
We *call* the membrane that covers the bowels a *caul*.
Live fish are kept in the water, near our fish markets, in *caufs*.
Consumptive people are afflicted with bad *coughs*.

MOVE, SÒN, WOLF. FOOT, MOON, ÔR; RULE, PULL; EXIST; ç=K; ġ=J; ş=Z; çH=SH.

Brass *cannon* are more costly than iron.

Church laws are *canons*.

Farmers are *sellers* of apples and cider, which are put into *cellars*.

A *liar* is not believed.

The *lyre* is a musical instrument.

Galileo *made* the telescope.

A charming *maid* or maiden.

The Missouri is the *main* branch of the Mississippi.

A horse's *mane* grows on his neck.

The *male* bird has a more beautiful plumage than the female.

The *mail* is opened at the post-office.

Children should imitate the *manners* of polite people.

The farms of the English nobility are called *manors*.

A *mite* is an insect of little *might*.

Mead is a pleasant drink.

Lying is a *mean* practice.

We *mean* to study grammar.

The Hudson and East rivers *meet* at the Battery.

Salt will preserve *meat*.

Miners work in mines.

Minors are not allowed to vote.

David *moaned* the loss of Absalom.

When grass is *mown* and dried we call it hay.

Forts are surrounded by a *moat*.

Mote is an atom.

A brigade of soldiers is *more* than a regiment.

Mowers mow grass.

Brass is a compound *metal*.

A lively horse is a horse of *mettle*.

Fishes are caught in a *net*.

Clear profits are called *net* gain.

Boats are rowed with *oars*.

Ores are melted to separate the metal from the dross.

A bird *flew* over the house.

The smoke ascends in the *flue*.

Gums *ooze* through the pores of wood.

The tanner puts his hides into *ooze*.

We carry water in *pails*.

Gardens are sometimes surrounded by a fence made of *pales*.

Sick people look *pale*.

Panes of glass are put into window frames.

Pains are distressing.

Shoes are sold by *pairs*.

People *pare* apples to make pies.

Pears are not so common as apples.

A person who has lost his *palate* can not speak plain.

The painter holds his *pallet* in his hand.

The child sleeps on a *pallet*.

The comma is the shortest *pause* in reading.

Bears seize their prey with their *paws*.

Good people love to live in *peace*.

Our largest *piece* of silver coin is a dollar.

The *peak* of Teneriffe is fifteen thousand feet high.

The Jews had a *pique* or ill-will against the Samaritans.

On the Fourth of July, the bells ring a loud *peal*.

The farmer *peels* the bark from trees for the tanner.

The British Parliament is a legislative assembly, consisting of the House of *Peers* and the House of Commons.

Our vessels lie near the *piers* in our harbor.

The carpenter *planes* boards with his plane.

The essential principles of religion are written in *plain* language.

Babylon stood upon an extended *plain*.

Polite people *please* their companions.

The courts of common *pleas* are held in the courthouses.

The builder uses the *plumb* and line to set his walls perpendicular.

Plums grow on trees.

One dollar is *one* hundred cents.

The most depraved gambler *won* the money.

The cat *preys* upon mice.

We should *pray* for our enemies.

The student *pores* over his books day after day.

The Niagara river *pours* down a precipice of a hundred and fifty feet.

BÄR, LÅST, €ÂRE, F̣ALL, WHAT; HẼR, PRĘY, THÊRE; ĞET; BÎRD, MARÎNE; LĮNK;

We sweat through the *pores* of the skin.

The Hudson is the *principal* river of New York.

A man of good *principles* merits our esteem.

There is no *profit* in profane swearing.

The *prophet* Daniel was a prisoner in Babylon.

Panel doors are more expensive than batten doors.

The court *impanel* jurors to judge causes in court.

God sends his *rain* on the just and the unjust.

Horses are guided by the *reins* of the bridle.

Queen Victoria *reigns* over Great Britain and Ireland.

The barber shaves his patrons with a *razor*.

Farmers are *raisers* of grain.

The Laplander *wraps* himself in furs in the winter.

When we wish to enter a house, we *rap* at the door.

Reeds grow in swamps, and have hollow, jointed stems.

We should *read* the Bible with seriousness.

We should often think upon what we have *read*.

The hyacinth bears a beautiful large *red* flower.

Nero *wreaked* his malice upon the Christians.

Brutus held up the dagger *reeking* with the blood of Lucretia.

We *rest* on beds.

The English *wrested* Gibraltar from the Spaniards.

Rice grows in warm climates.

The *rise* of the Missouri is in the Rocky Mountains.

Some ladies are fond of gold *rings*.

The bell *rings* for church.

Washerwomen *wring* clothes.

Riggers rig vessels; that is, fit the shrouds, stays, braces, etc., to the masts and yards.

Hannibal crossed the Alps in the *rigor* of winter.

Baptism is a *rite* of the Christian church.

It is not *right* to pilfer.

Wheelwrights make carts and wagons.

Cumberland *road* leads from Baltimore to Wheeling.

King David *rode* upon a mule.

Children often learn the alphabet by *rote* before they know the letters.

Oliver Goldsmith *wrote* several good histories.

Paste is made of *rye* flour.

Children make *wry* faces when they eat sour grapes.

A *roe* deer has no horns.

Corn is planted in *rows*.

Oarsmen *row* boats with oars.

The joiner *rabbets* boards.

Rabbits are lively animals.

The river Danube runs into the Black *Sea*.

This house is for *sale*.

We *sail* for Liverpool to-morrow.

Owls can not *see* well when the sun shines.

Seals are caught both in the northern and the southern seas.

We *seal* letters with wafers and *sealing wax*.

Masons *ceil* the inner roof with lime mortar.

A plastered *ceiling* looks better than a ceiling made of boards.

We have never *seen* a more dazzling object than the sun in summer.

A thunderstorm is a sublime *scene*.

Fishermen catch shad in *seines*.

The city of Paris stands on the river *Seine*.

John Smith, *Senior*, is father to John Smith, *Junior*.

The Sultan of Turkey is also called the Grand *Seignior*.

The sun *seems* to rise and set.

Neat sewers (sō′erz) make handsome *seams* with their needles.

Sheep-shearers *shear* the wool from the sheep.

When the wolf sees the sheep well guarded he *sheers* off.

Waves dash against the *shore*.

When ship-builders build vessels they *shore* them up with props.

The writer *signs* his name.

Heavy clouds are *signs* of rain.

Mankind *slay* each other in cruel wars.

A *sleigh* or sled runs on snow and ice.

MOVE, SÒN, WOLF, FOOT, MOÒN, ÒR; RULE, PULL; EXIST; C=K; G=J; S=Z; CH=SH.

Children should never *slight* their parents.

Indians live in very *slight* buildings, called wigwams.

Some have a good *sleight* at work.

A *sloe* is a black wild plum.

The sloth is *slow* in moving.

The lark *soars* into the sky.

A boil is a *sore* swelling.

A *sower* sows his seeds.

We all have *some* knowledge.

The *sum* of four and five is nine.

The *sole* of a shoe is the bottom of it.

The sun is the *sole* cause of day.

Our *souls* are immortal.

Tents are fastened with *stakes*.

Beefsteaks are good food.

"A wise *son* makes a glad father."

Without the *sun* all animals and vegetables would die.

The Jews were not permitted to have *stairs* to their altars.

Do not let children *stare* at strangers.

Stiles are steps over fences.

Goldsmith wrote in a clear plain *style*.

Saul *threw* his javelin at David.

The Israelites went *through* the Red Sea.

Tares grow among wheat.

Grocers subtract the *tare* from the gross weight.

Never *tear* your clothes.

The plumb-line hangs *straight* toward the center of the earth.

The *Straits* of Gibraltar separate Spain from Morocco.

Succor a man in distress.

Suckers sprout from the root of an old stock.

Shoemakers drive *tacks* into the heels of shoes.

People pay a heavy *tax*.

Lions have long bushy *tails*.

The *tale* of Robinson Crusoe is a celebrated romance.

Ladies wear sashes round the *waist*.

Foolish children *waste* their time in idleness.

Time *waits* for no one.

Butter is sold by *weight*.

Earthen *ware* is baked in furnaces.

A Turk *wears* a turban instead of a hat.

Sickness makes the body *weak*.

Seven days constitute one *week*.

We *weigh* gold and silver by Troy Weight.

The *way* of a good man is plain.

The *weather* is colder in America than in the same latitudes in Europe.

Among the flock of sheep were twenty fat *wethers*.

Men have a great *toe* on each foot.

Horses *tow* the canal boats.

Tow is hatcheled from flax.

Good scholars love *their* books.

There are no tides in the Baltic Sea.

Women wear *vails*.

The valley of the Mississippi is the largest *vale* in the United States.

The *vane* shows which way the wind blows.

Arteries convey the blood from the heart and *veins*.

A *vial* of laudanum.

A base-*viol* is a large fiddle, and a *violin* is a small one.

We shed *tears* of sorrow when we lose our friends.

Ships often carry two *tiers* of guns.

A *team* of horses will travel faster than a team of oxen.

Farmers rejoice when their farms *teem* with fruits.

The *tide* is caused by the attraction of the moon and sun.

A black ribbon is *tied* on the left arm and worn as a badge of mourning.

Many things are possible which are not practicable. That is possible which can be performed by any means; that is practicable which can be performed by the means which are in our power.

Bank notes are redeemable in cash.

BÄR, LÀST, CÂRE, FALL, WHAT; HÊR, PREY, THÈRE; ÔET; BÎRD, MARÏNE; LIŊK;

No. 149.--CXLIX.

WORDS OF IRREGULAR ORTHOGRAPHY.

WRITTEN.	PRONOUNCED.	WRITTEN.	PRONOUNCED.	WRITTEN.	PRONOUNCED.
any	ĕn′ ny	ghost	gōst	should	shoŏd
many	mĕn′ ny	corps	kōre	debt	dĕt
demesne	de meen′	ache	āke	phlegm	flĕm
bat eau	bat ō′	half	häf	croup	kroŏp
beau	bō	calf	käf	tomb	toŏm
beaux	bōze	calve	käv	womb	woŏm
bu reau	bū′ ro	one	wŭn	wolf	woŏlf
been	bĭn	once	wŭnçe	yacht	yŏt
bu ry	bĕr′ ry	done	dŭn	dough	dō
bu ri al	bĕr′ i al	gone	gŏn	neigh	nā
bus y	bĭz′ zy	folks	fōks	sleigh	slā
isle	īle	ra tio	rā′ sho	weigh	wā
isl and	ī′ land	va lise	va lēçe′	gauge	gāge
does	dŭz	o cean	ō′ shun	bough	bou
says	sĕz	though	thō	slough	slou
said	sĕd	broad	brawd	doubt	dout
lieu	lū	could	koŏd	is sue	ĭsh′ shu
adieu	a dū′	would	woŏd	tis sue	tĭsh′ shu

WRITTEN.	PRONOUNCED.	WRITTEN.	PRONOUNCED.
busi ness	bĭz′ ness	flam beau	flăm′ bo
bus i ly	bĭz′ i ly	right eous	rī′ chus
colonel	kûr′ nel	car touch	kär toŏch
haut boy	hō′ boy	in veigh	in vā′
masque	mâsk	sur tout	sur toŏt′
sou, sous	soŏ	wom an	woŏm′ an
gui tar	gĭ tär′	wom en	wĭm′ en
pur lieu	pûr′ lu	bis cuit	bĭs′ kit
su gar	shoŏg′ ar	cir cuit	sĭr′ kit
vis count	vī′ kount	sal mon	săm′ un
ap ro pos	ap ro pō′	isth mus	ĭs′ mus

MOVE, SÒN, WOLF, FÒÒT, MÒÒN, ÒR; RULE, PULL; EXIST; €=K; Ġ=J; Ş=Z; ÇH=SH.

WRITTEN.	PRONOUNCED.	WRITTEN.	PRONOUNCED.
neigh bor	nā' bur	mort gage	môr' ġĕj
piqu ant	pĭk' ant	seign ior	seen yur
piqu an çy	pĭk' an çy	se ragl io	se răl' yo
ptis an	tĭz' an	asth ma	ăst' má
phthis ic	tĭz' ik	beau ty	bū' ty
sol dier	sōl' jer	beau te ous	bū' te us
vict uals	vĭt' tlş	bdell ium	dĕl' yum
ca tarrh	ka tär'	ca noe	ka nōō'
bou quet	boo kā'	plaid	plăd
bru nette	bru nĕt'	schism	sĭzm
ga zette	ga zĕt'	feoff ment	fĕf' ment
in debt ed	in dĕt' ed	hal cy on	hăl' sí on
lieu ten ant	lu tĕn' ant	mis tle toe	mĭz' zl to
qua drille	kwa drĭl'	psal mo dy	săl' mo dy̆
pneu mat ics	nu măt' iks	bal sam ic	băl săm' ik

IN THE FOLLOWING, **l** IS SILENT.

balk	chalk	talk
ealk	stalk	walk

THE FOLLOWING END WITH THE SOUND OF **f.**

choŭgh	roŭgh	eough	(€awf)
eloŭgh *	sloŭgh †	trough	(trawf)
toŭgh	e noŭgh'	läugh	(läf)

h AFTER **r** IS SILENT.

rheum	rhu' barb
rheu măt' ie	rhĕt' o rie
rheu' ma tişm	rhăp' so dy
rhȳme	rhī nŏç' e ros

g IS SILENT BEFORE **n.**

deign	ed	ing	reign	ed	ing
feign	ed	ing	poign' ant		

* A cleft.   † The cast-off skin of a serpent, etc.

BÄR, LÅST, CÂRE, FALL, WHAT; HẼR, PRẼY, THÉRE; ǴET; BÎRD, MARÏNE; LINK;

l BEFORE m IS SILENT IN THE FOLLOWING.

cälm	bälm′y	psälm
cälm′ly	em bälm′	quälm
cälm ness	älms	quälm ish
be cälm′	älms′ house	psälm ist
bälm	älms ǵīv ing	hōlm

IN THE FOLLOWING, geon AND gion ARE PRONOUNCED AS jun; con, AS un; cheon, AS chun; geous AND gious, AS jus.

blŭd′ǵeon	sûr′ǵeon	pro dĭ′ǵioŭs
dŭd ǵeon	dŭn ǵeon	pŭn′cheon
gŭd ǵeon	pĭǵ eon	trŭn cheon
stûr ǵeon	wĭd ǵeon	seŭtch con
lē ǵion	lŭn cheon	es eŭtch′ eon
rē ǵion	con tā′ǵioŭs	eur mŭd ǵeon
con tā′ǵion	e grē ǵioŭs	gôr′ǵeoŭs
re lĭ ǵion	re lĭ ǵioŭs	sac ri lē′ǵioŭs

IN THE FOLLOWING, ou AND au ARE PRONOUNCED AS aw, AND gh IS MUTE.

bought	ought	wrought
brought	sought	naught
fought	thought	fraught

IN THE FOLLOWING, THE LETTERS ue AT THE END OF THE PRIMITIVE WORD ARE SILENT.

plāgue	vōgue	pïque
vāgue	tóngue	har ăngue′
lēague	mŏsque	ăp′o lōgue
brōgue	in trïgue′	eăt a lōgue
rōgue	o pāque	dï a lŏgue
fa tïgue′	ū nïque	ĕc lŏgue

No. 150.—C L.

1. *Regular verbs form the past tense, and participle of the past, by taking ed, and the participle of the present tense by taking ing; as, called, calling, from call. The letter p. stands for past tense; ppr. for participle of the present tense; and a. for agent.*

	p.	ppr.		p.	ppr.		p.	ppr.
call	ed	ing	pray	ed	ing	al low	ed	ing
turn	ed	ing	cloy	ed	ing	a void	ed	ing
burn	ed	ing	jest	ed	ing	em ploy	ed	ing
plow	ed	ing	a bound	ed	ing	pur loin	ed	ing
sow	ed	ing	ab scond	ed	ing	rep re sent	ed	ing
plant	ed	ing	al lay	ed	ing	an noy	ed	ing

2. *Monosyllabic verbs ending in a single consonant after a single vowel, and other verbs ending in a single consonant after a single vowel and accented on the last syllable, double the final consonant in the derivatives. Thus, abet, abetted, abetting, abettor.*

	p.	ppr.	a.		p.	ppr.	a.		p.	ppr.	a.
a bet	ted	ting	tor	wed	ded	ding		tre pan	ned	ning	ner
fret	ted	ting	ter	bar	red	ring		de fer	red	ring	
man	ned	ning		ex pel	led	ling	ler	ab hor	red	ring	rer
plan	ned	ning	ner	re bel	led	ling	ler	in cur	red	ring	

3. *Verbs having a digraph, diphthong, or long vowel sound before the last consonant, do not double that consonant.*

	p.	ppr.	a.		p.	ppr.	a.		p.	ppr.	a.
seal	ed	ing	er	claim	ed	ing	er	re coil	ed	ing	
heal	ed	ing	er	cool	ed	ing	er	ve neer	ed	ing	
oil	ed	ing	er	ap pear	ed	ing	er	a vail	ed	ing	
hail	ed	ing	er	re peat	ed	ing	er	re strain	ed	ing	er

4. *Verbs ending in two consonants, do not double the last.*

	p.	ppr.	a.		p.	ppr.	a.		p.	ppr.	a.
gild	ed	ing	er	dress	ed	ing	er	re sist	ed	ing	er
long	ed	ing	er	paint	ed	ing	er	con vert	ed	ing	er
watch	ed	ing	er	charm	ed	ing	er	dis turb	ed	ing	er

5. *Verbs ending in a single consonant, preceded by a single vowel, the last consonant or syllable not being accented, ought not to double the last consonant in the derivatives.*

	p.	ppr.		p.	ppr.		p.	ppr.
bi as	ed	ing	lev el	ed	ing	grav el	ed	ing
bev el	ed	ing	coun sel	ed	ing	grov el	ed	ing
can cel	ed	ing	cud gel	ed	ing	par al lel	ed	ing
car ol	ed	ing	driv el	ed	ing	jew el	ed	ing
cav il	ed	ing	du el	ed	ing	kern el	ed	ing
chan nel	ed	ing	e qual	ed	ing	la bel	ed	ing
chis el	ed	ing	gam bol	ed	ing	lau rel	ed	ing

lev el	ed	ing	ri val	ed	ing	mod el	ed	ing
li bel	ed	ing	row el	ed	ing	wag on	ed	ing
mar shal	ed	ing	shov el	ed	ing	clos et	ed	ing
par cel	ed	ing	shriv el	ed	ing	riv et	ed	ing
pen cil	ed	ing	tram mel	ed	ing	lim it	ed	ing
pom mel	ed	ing	trav el	ed	ing	ben e fit	ed	ing
quar rel	ed	ing	tun nel	ed	ing	prof it	ed	ing
rev el	ed	ing	wor ship	ed	ing	buf fet	ed	ing

6 *The name of the agent, when the verb admits of it, is formed in like manner, without doubling the last consonant, as,* caviler, worshiper, duelist, libeler, traveler. *So also adjectives are formed from these verbs without doubling the last consonant, as,* libelous, marvelous.

7. *When verbs end in* e *after* d *and* t, *the final* e *in the past tense and participle of the perfect tense, unites with* d *and forms an additional syllable, but it is dropped before* ing. *Thus,* abate, abated, abating.

ab di cate	d	ing	de grade	d	ing	cor rode	d	ing
ded i cate	d	ing	suf fo cate	d	ing	de lude	d	ing
med i tate	d	ing	ed u cate	d	ing	in trude	d	ing
im pre cate	d	ing	in vade	d	ing	ex plode	d	ing
vin di cate	d	ing	con cede	d	ing	de ride	d	ing

8. *In verbs ending in* e *after any other consonant than* d *and* t, *the past tense is formed by the addition of* d, *and this letter with the final* e *may form a distinct syllable; but usually the* e *is not sounded. Thus* abridged, *is pronounced* abridjd; abased, abäste. *Before* ing, e *is dropped.*

a base	d	ing	pro nounce	d	ing	crit i cise	d	ing
a bridge	d	ing	man age	d	ing	em bez zle	d	ing
con fine	d	ing	re joice	d	ing	dis o blige	d	ing
com pose	d	ing	cat e chise	d	ing	dis fig ure	d	ing
re fuse	d	ing	com pro mise	d	ing	un der val ue	d	ing

Note. *Although* ed *in the past tense and participle is thus blended with the last syllable of the verb, yet when a noun is formed by adding* ness *to such participles, the* ed *becomes a distinct syllable. Thus* blessed *may be pronounced in one syllable; but* bless-ed-ness *must be in three.*

9. *Verbs ending in* ay, oy, ow, ew, *and* ey, *have regular derivatives in* ed *and* ing.

ar ray	ed	ing	al loy	ed	ing	re new	ed	ing
al lay	ed	ing	em ploy	ed	ing	con vey	ed	ing
pray	ed	ing	de stroy	ed	ing	fol low	ed	ing
stray	ed	ing	an noy	ed	ing	be stow	ed	ing
de lay	ed	ing	en dow	ed	ing	con voy	ed	ing

But a few monosyllables, as pay, say, *and* lay, *change* y *into* i, *as* paid, said, laid.

10. *Verbs ending in* y, *change* y *into* i *in the past tense and participle of the perfect, but retain it in the participle of the present tense.*

cry	cried	cry ing	dry	dried	dry ing
de fy	de fied	de fy ing	car ry	car ried	car ry ing
ed i fy	ed i fied	ed i fy ing	mar ry	mar ried	mar ry ing

11. *Verbs ending in* y *change this letter to* i *in the second and third persons, and in the word denoting* the agent. *Thus:*

Solemn Style.			*Familiar Style.*	*Agent.*
I cry	thou criest	he crieth	he cries	crier
I try	thou triest	he trieth	he tries	trier

Past tense.

I cried	thou criedst	he	we	ye	they cried
I tried	thou triedst	he	we	ye	they tried

12. *Verbs ending in* ie *change* ie *into* y *when the termination* ing *of the present participle is added, as* die, dying, lie, lying.

The past tense, and participle of the present, are regular.

died   lied   tied   hied   vied

Formation of the plural number of nouns.

13. *The regular plural of nouns is formed by the addition of* s *to the singular, which letter unites with most consonants in the same syllable, but sounds like* z *after all the consonants except the aspirates* f, p, q, t, k, *or* c *with the sound of* k.

sing.	*plu.*	*sing.*	*plu.*	*sing.*	*plu.*
slab	slabs	roll	rolls	strait	straits
lad	lads	ham	hams	post	posts
chief	chiefs	chain	chains	port	ports
bag	bags	crop	crops	sight	sights
back	backs	tear	tears	sign	signs

a. *When the noun ends in* e, *if* s *will coalesce with the preceding consonant, it does not form an additional syllable.*

bride	brides	knave	knaves	bone	bones
blade	blades	date	dates	cake	cakes
smile	smiles	note	notes	flame	flames

b. *If* s *will not coalesce with the preceding consonant, it unites with* e, *and forms an additional syllable.*

grace	gra ces	maze	ma zes	pledge	pledg es
spice	spi ces	fleece	flee ces	stage	sta ges

14. *When nouns end in* ch, sh, ss, *and* x, *the plural is formed by the addition of* es.

church	churches	bush	bushes	dress	dresses
peach	peaches	glass	glasses	fox	foxes

15. *Nouns ending in* y *after a consonant, form the plural by the changing of* y *into* i, *and the addition of* es; *the termination* ies *being pronounced* ize, *in monosyllables, and* iz *in most other words.*

fly	flies	du ty	du ties	fu ry	fu ries
cry	cries	glo ry	glo ries	ber ry	ber ries
sky	skies	ru by	ru bies	mer cy	mer cies
cit y	cit ies	la dy	la dies	va can cy	va can cies

16. Nouns ending in ay, ey, oy, ow, ew, take s only to form the plural.

day	days	val ley	val leys	boy	boys
way	ways	mon ey	mon eys	bow	bows
bay	bays	at tor ney	at tor neys	vow	vows
de lay	de lays	sur vey	sur veys	clew	clews

17. Nouns ending in a vowel take s or es.

sea	seas	hoe	hoes	woe	woes	pie	pies

18. When the singular ends in f, the plural is usually formed by changing f into v, with es.

life	lives	loaf	loaves	calf	calves
wife	wives	leaf	leaves	half	halves
knife	knives	shelf	shelves	sheaf	sheaves
beef	beeves	wharf	wharves	thief	thieves

Adjectives formed from nouns by the addition of y.

n	a	n	a	n	a	n	a
bulk	y	silk	y	pith	y	rain	y
flesh	y	milk	y	meal	y	hill	y

Some nouns when they take y, lose e final.

flake	flaky	scale	scaly	stone	stony
plume	plumy	smoke	smoky	bone	bony

Adjectives formed from nouns by ly.

n	a	n	a	n	a	n	a
friend	ly	love	ly	man	ly	earth	ly
home	ly	time	ly	cost	ly	lord	ly

Nouns formed from adjectives in y, by changing y into i and taking ness.

a	n	a	n	a	n	a	n
hap py	i ness	la zy	i ness	drow sy	i ness	sha dy	i ness
loft y	i ness	emp ty	i ness	diz zy	i ness	chil ly	i ness

Adverbs formed from adjectives in y, by a change of y into i, and the addition of ly.

a	ad	a	ad	a	ad	a	ad
craft y	i ly	luck y	i ly	loft y	i ly	gloom y	i ly

Adverbs formed from adjectives by the addition of ly.

a	ad	a	ad	a	ad
fer vent	ly	brill iant	ly	em i nent	ly
pa tient	ly	op u lent	ly	per ma nent	ly

Nouns formed from adjectives by adding ness.

a	n	a	n	a	n
au da cious	ness	of fi cious	ness	ra pa cious	ness
ca pa cious	ness	li cen tious	ness	in ge ni ous	ness

Adjectives formed from nouns by less, adverbs by ly, and nouns by ness.

bound	less	ly	ness	blame	less	ly	ness
fear	less	ly	ness	need	less	ly	ness
hope	less	ly	ness	faith	less	ly	ness

Adjectives formed from nouns by ful, *from which adverbs are formed by* ly, *and nouns by* ness.

n	a	ad	n	n	a	ad	n	n	a	ad	n
art	ful	ly	ness	pain	ful	ly	ness	skill	ful	ly	ness
care	ful	ly	ness	grace	ful	ly	ness	peace	ful	ly	ness

The termination ist *added to words denotes* an agent.

art ist   form a list   loy al ist   or gan ist   du el ist   hu mor ist

In some words, y *is changed into* i.

zo ol o gy   zo ol o gist   or ni thol o gy   or ni thol o gist

The prefix ante *denotes* before.

date ante-date	chamber ante-chamber	diluvian ante-diluvian
past ante-past	penult ante-penult	nuptial ante-nuptial

The prefix anti *usually denotes* opposition *or* against.

Christ anti-christ   Christian anti-christian   febrile anti-febrile

Be, *a prefix, generally denotes* intensity; *sometimes* to make, *as* becalm, befoul.

daub be-daub	dew be-dew	friend be-friend	labor be-labor
numb be-numb	moan be-moan	speak be-speak	sprinkle be-sprinkle

The prefix con, *or* co, *denotes* with *or* against; con *is changed into* col *before* l.

co-equal	co-exist	co-habit	con-form
co-eval	co-extend	con-firm	con-join

The prefix counter *denotes* against *or* opposition.

balance counter-balance	act counter-act	evidence counter-evidence
plead counter-plead	work counter-work	part counter-part

The prefix de *denotes* down from; *sometimes it gives* a negative sense.

base de-base	bar de-bar	compose de-compose	cry de-cry
form de-form	fame de-fame	face de-face	garnish de-garnish

Dis *denotes* separation, departure; *hence gives to words* a negative sense.

able dis-able	agree dis-agree	allow dis-allow	belief dis-belief
credit dis-credit	esteem dis-esteem	grace dis-grace	honor dis-honor

Fore *denotes* before *in time, sometimes in place.*

bode fore-bode	father fore-father	know fore-know	noon fore-noon
tell fore-tell	taste fore-taste	warn fore-warn	run fore-run

In, *which is sometimes changed into* il, im, *and* ir, *denotes* in, on, upon, *or against; it gives to adjectives* a negative sense, *as,* infirm; *sometimes it is* intensive; *sometimes it denotes* to make; *as,* bank, imbank; brown, imbrown; bitter, imbitter.

In the following, it gives a negative sense.

material im-material   moderate im-moderate   mutable im-mutable

pure	im-pure	active	in-active	applicable	in-applicable
articulate	in-articulate	attention	in-attention	cautious	in-cautious
defensible	in-defensible	discreet	in-discreet	distinct	in-distinct
religious	ir-religious	reverent	ir-reverent	revocable	ir-revocable

Non *is used as a prefix, giving to words a negative sense.*

appearance	non-appearance	compliance	non-compliance
conformist	non-conformist	resident	non-resident

Out, *as a prefix, denotes* beyond, longer than, *or* more than.

leap	out-leap	live	out-live	venom	out-venom	weigh	out-weigh

Over, *as a prefix, denotes* above, beyond, excess, too much.

balance	over-balance	bold	over-bold	burden	over-burden
charge	over-charge	drive	over-drive	feed	over-feed
flow	over-flow	load	over-load	pay	over-pay

Trans, *a prefix, signifies* beyond, across *or* over.

plant	trans-plant	Atlantic	trans-atlantic

Pre, *as a prefix, denotes* before, in time *or* rank.

caution	pre-caution	determine	pre-determine	eminent	pre-eminent
mature	pre-mature	occupy	pre-occupy	suppose	pre-suppose
conceive	pre-conceive	concert	pre-concert	exist	pre-exist

Re, *a prefix, denotes* again *or* repetition.

assert	re-assert	assure	re-assure	bound	re-bound
dissolve	re-dissolve	embark	re-embark	enter	re-enter
assume	re-assume	capture	re-capture	collect	re-collect
commence	re-commence	conquer	re-conquer	examine	re-examine
export	re-export	pay	re-pay	people	re-people

Un, *a prefix, denotes* not, *and gives to words* a negative sense.

abashed	un-abashed	abated	un-abated	abolished	un-abolished
acceptable	un-acceptable	adjusted	un-adjusted	attainable	un-attainable
biased	un-biased	conscious	un-conscious	equaled	un-equaled
graceful	un-graceful	lawful	un-lawful	supported	un-supported

Super, supra, *and* **sur,** *denote* above, beyond, *or* excess.

abound	super-abound	eminent	super-eminent
mundane	supra-mundane	charge	sur-charge

He seldom lives frugally, who lives by chance, or without method.
Without frugality, none can be rich; and with it, few would be poor.
The most necessary part of learning is to unlearn our errors.
Small parties make up in diligence what they want in numbers.
Some talk of subjects which they do not understand; others praise
  virtue, who do not practice it.
The path of duty is always the path of safety.
Be very cautious in believing ill of your neighbor; but more cautious
  in reporting it.

OF NUMBERS.

FIGURES.	LETTERS.	NAMES.	NUMERAL ADJECTIVES.
1	I	one	first
2	II	two	second
3	III	three	third
4	IV	four	fourth
5	V	five	fifth
6	VI	six	sixth
7	VII	seven	seventh
8	VIII	eight	eighth
9	IX	nine	ninth
10	X	ten	tenth
11	XI	eleven	eleventh
12	XII	twelve	twelfth
13	XIII	thirteen	thirteenth
14	XIV	fourteen	fourteenth
15	XV	fifteen	fifteenth
16	XVI	sixteen	sixteenth
17	XVII	seventeen	seventeenth
18	XVIII	eighteen	eighteenth
19	XIX	nineteen	nineteenth
20	XX	twenty	twentieth
30	XXX	thirty	thirtieth
40	XL	forty	fortieth
50	L	fifty	fiftieth
60	LX	sixty	sixtieth
70	LXX	seventy	seventieth
80	LXXX	eighty	eightieth
90	XC	ninety	ninetieth
100	C	one hundred	one hundredth
200	CC	two hundred	two hundredth
300	CCC	three hundred	three hundredth
400	CCCC	four hundred	four hundredth
500	D	five hundred	five hundredth
600	DC	six hundred	six hundredth
700	DCC	seven hundred	seven hundredth
800	DCCC	eight hundred	eight hundredth
900	DCCCC	nine hundred	nine hundredth
1000	M	one thousand, &c.	one thousandth
1829	MDCCCXXIX	one thousand eight hundred and twenty-nine	

$\frac{1}{2}$ one half.
1-1

$\frac{1}{6}$ one sixth.
1-11111

$\frac{1}{10}$ one tenth.
1-111111111

$\frac{1}{3}$ one third.
1-11

$\frac{1}{7}$ one seventh.
1-111111

$\frac{2}{5}$ two fifths.
11-111

$\frac{1}{4}$ one fourth.
1-111

$\frac{1}{8}$ one eighth.
1-1111111

$\frac{4}{5}$ four fifths.
1111-1

$\frac{1}{5}$ one fifth.
1-1111

$\frac{1}{9}$ one ninth.
1-11111111

$\frac{9}{10}$ nine tenths.
111111111-1

WORDS AND PHRASES FROM FOREIGN LANGUAGES, FREQUENTLY OCCURRING IN ENGLISH BOOKS, RENDERED INTO ENGLISH.

L. stands for Latin, F. for French, S. for Spanish.

Ad captandum vulgus, L. to captivate the populace.

Ad finem, L. to the end.

Ad hominem, L. to the man.

Ad infinitum, L. to endless extent.

Ad libitum, L. at pleasure.

Ad referendum, L. for further consideration.

Ad valorem, L. according to the value.

Alma mater, L. a cherishing mother.

A mensa et thoro, L. from bed and board.

Anglice, L. according to the English manner.

Avalanche, F. a snow-slip: a vast body of snow that slides down a mountain's side.

Auto da fé, S. act of faith; a sentence of the Inquisition for the punishment of heresy.

Beau monde, F. the gay world.

Bona fide, L. in good faith.

Bon mot, F. a witty repartee.

Cap-a-pie, F. from head to foot.

Caput mortuum, L. the dead head; the worthless remains.

Carte blanche, F. blank paper; permission without restraint.

Chef d'œuvre, F. a master-piece.

Comme il faut, F. as it should be.

Compos mentis, L. of sound mind.

Coup de main, F. sudden enterprise or effort.

Dernier ressort, F. the last resort.

Dieu et mon droit, F. God and my right.

Ennui, F. weariness, lassitude.

E pluribus unum, L. one out of, or composed of, many. [*The motto of the United States.*]

Ex, L. out; as, ex-minister, a minister out of office.

Excelsior, L. more elevated. [*The motto of the State of New York.*]

Ex officio, L. by virtue of office.

Ex parte, L. on one side only.

Ex post facto, L. after the deed is done.

Extempore, L. without premeditation.

Fac simile, L. a close imitation.

Fille de chambre, F. a chambermaid.

Fortiter in re, L. with firmness in acting.

Gens d'armes, F. armed police.

Habeas corpus, L. that you have the body. [*A writ for delivering a person from prison.*]

Hic jacet, L. here lies.

Honi soit qui mal y pense, F. shame be to him that evil thinks.

Hotel dieu, F. a hospital.

Impromptu, L. without previous study.

In statu quo, L. in the former state.

In toto, L. in the whole.

Ipse dixit, L. he said.

Ipso facto, L. in fact.

Jet-d'eau, F. a waterspout.

Jeu d'esprit, F. a play of wit.

Lex talionis, L. the law of retaliation; as, an eye for an eye, etc.

Literatim, L. letter for letter.

Locum tenens, L. a substitute.

Magna Charta, L. the great charter.

Maximum, L. the greatest.

Memento mori, L. be mindful of death.

Minimum, L. the smallest.

Mirabile dictu, L. wonderful to tell.

Multum in parvo, L. much in a small compass.

Nem. con., or *nem. dis.*, L. no one dissenting: unanimously.

Ne plus ultra, L. the utmost extent.

Nolens volens, L. whether he will or not.

Nom de plume, F. a literary title.

Non compos mentis, L. not of a sound mind.

Par nobile fratrum, L. a noble pair of brothers.

Pater patriæ, L. the father of his country.

Per annum, L. by the year.

Per diem, L. by the day.

Per cent, L. by the hundred.

Per contra, L. contrariwise.

Per se, L. by itself considered.

Prima facie, L. at the first view.

Primum mobile, L. first cause of motion.

Pro bono publico, L. for the public good.

Pro et con., L. for and against.

Pro patria, L. for my country.

Pro tempore, L. for the time.

Pro re nata, L. as occasion requires; for a special emergency.

Pugnis et calcibus, L. with fists and feet, with all the might.

Quantum, L. how much.

Quantum sufficit, L. a sufficient quantity.

Qui transtulit sustinet, L. he who has borne them sustains them.

Quid nunc, L. a newsmonger.

Re infecta, L. the thing not done.

Sanctum Sanctorum, L. the Holy of Holies

Sang froid, F. in cold blood, indifference.

Sans souci, F. free and easy; without care.

Secundum artem, L. according to art.

Sic transit gloria mundi, L. thus passes away the glory of the world.

Sine die, L. without a day specified.

Sine qua non, L. that without which a thing can not be done.

Soi disant, F. self-styled.

Suaviter in modo, L. agreeable in manner.

Sub judice, L. under consideration.

Sub rosa, L. under the rose, or privately. [good.

Summum bonum, L. the chief

Toties quoties, L. as often as.

Toto cœlo, L. wholly, as far as possible.

Utile dulci, L. the useful with the agreeable.

Vade mecum, L. (lit. *go with me*); a convenient companion; a hand-book.

Veni, vidi, vici, L. I came, I saw, I conquered.

Versus, L. against.

Via, L. by the way of.

Vice versa, L. the terms being exchanged.

Viva voce, L. with the voice.

ABBREVIATIONS EXPLAINED.

Ans. Answer.

A. A. S. Fellow of the American Academy.

A. B. Bachelor of Arts.

Abp. Archbishop.

Acct. Account.

A. D. Anno Domini, the year of our Lord.

Adm. Admiral.

Admr. Administrator.

Admx. Administratrix.

Ala. Alabama.

A. M. Master of Arts; before noon; in the year of the world.

Apr. April.

Ariz. Arizona Ter.

Ark. Arkansas.

Atty. Attorney.

Aug. August.

Bart. Baronet.

B. C. Before Christ.

B. D. Bachelor of Divinity.

Bbl. Barrel; *bbls.* barrels.

Cal. California.

C. Centum, a hundred.

Capt. Captain.

Chap. Chapter.

Col. Colonel.

Co. Company.

Com. Commissioner, Commodore.

Cr. Credit.

Cwt. Hundred weight.

Conn. or *Ct.* Connecticut.

C. S. Keeper of the Seal.

Cl. Clerk, Clergyman.

Colo. Colorado.

Cong. Congress.

Cons. Constable.

Cts. Cents.

Dak. Dakota Ter.

D. C. District of Columbia.

D. D. Doctor of Divinity.

Dea. Deacon.

Dec. December.

Del. Delaware.

Dept. Deputy.

do. Ditto, the same.

Dr. Doctor, *or* Debtor.

D. V. Deo volente, God willing.

E. East.

Ed. Edition, Editor.

E. & O. E. Errors and omissions excepted.

e. g. for example.

Eng. England, English.

Esq. Esquire. [forth.

E'c. et cætera; and so

Ex. Example.

Exec. Executor.

Execx. Executrix.

Feb. February.

Fla. Florida.

Fr. France, French, Frances.

F. R. S. Fellow of the Royal Society [Eng.]

Gen. General.

Gent. Gentleman.

Geo. George.

Ga. or *Geo.* Georgia.

Gov. Governor.

Hon. Honorable.

Hund. Hundred.

H. B. M. His *or* Her Britannic Majesty.

Hhd. Hogshead.
Ibid. In the same place.
Ida. Idaho Ter.
i. e. that is [id est].
id. the same.
Ill. Illinois.
Ind. Indiana.
Ind. Ter. Indian Ter.
Inst. Instant.
Io. Iowa.
Ir. Ireland, Irish.
Jan. January.
Jas. James.
Jac. Jacob.
Josh. Joshua.
Jun. or *Jr.* Junior.
K. King.
Kans. Kansas.
Ky. or *Ken.* Kentucky.
Kt. Knight.
L. or *Ld.* Lord or Lady.
La or *Lou.* Louisiana.
Lieut. Lieutenant.
Lond. London.
Lon. Longitude.
Ldp. Lordship.
Lat. Latitude.
LL.D. Doctor of Laws.
lbs. Pounds.
L. S. Place of the Seal.
M. Marquis, Meridian.
Maj. Major.
Mass. Massachusetts.
Matt. Matthew.
Mch. March.
M. D. Doctor of Medicine.
Md. Maryland.
Me. Maine.
Mich. Michigan.
Mr. Mister, Sir.
Messrs. Gentlemen, Sirs.
Minn. Minnesota.
Miss. Mississippi.

Mo. Missouri.
Mont. Montana Ter.
MS. Manuscript.
MSS. Manuscripts.
Mrs. Mistress.
N. North.
N. B. Take notice.
N. C. North Carolina.
Nebr. Nebraska.
Nev. Nevada.
N. Mex. New Mexico.
N. H. New Hampshire.
N. J. New Jersey.
No. Number.
Nov. November.
N. S. New Style.
N. Y. New York.
O. Ohio.
Obt. Obedient.
Oct. October.
Oreg. Oregon.
O. S. Old Style.
Parl. Parliament.
Pa. or *Penn.* Pennsylvania.
per. by; as, per yard, by the yard.
Per cent. By the hundred.
Pet. Peter.
Phil. Philip.
P. M. Post Master, Afternoon.
P. O. Post Office.
P. S. Postscript.
Ps. Psalm.
Pres. President.
Prof. Professor.
Q. Question, Queen.
q. d. (*quasi dicat*), as if he should say.
q. l. (*quantum libet*), as much as you please.
q. s. (*quantum sufficit*), a sufficient quantity.

Regr. Register.
Rep. Representative.
Rev. Reverend.
Rt. Hon. Right Honorable.
R. I. Rhode Island.
S. South, Shilling.
S. C. South Carolina.
St. Saint.
Sect. Section.
Sen. Senator, Senior.
Sept. September.
Servt. Servant.
S. T. P. Professor of Sacred Theology.
S. T. D. Doctor of Divinity.
ss. to wit, namely.
Surg. Surgeon.
Tenn. Tennessee.
Ter. Territory.
Tex. Texas.
Theo. Theophilus.
Thos. Thomas.
Ult. the last, or the last month.
U. S. United States.
U. S. A. United States of America.
V. (*vide*), See.
Va. Virginia.
viz. to wit, namely.
Vt. Vermont.
Wash. Washington Ter.
Wis. Wisconsin.
Wt. Weight.
Wm. William.
W. Va. West Virginia.
Wyo. Wyoming Territory.
Yd. Yard.
& (*et*). And.
&c. (= *etc.*) And so forth.

PUNCTUATION.

The *comma* (,) indicates a short pause. The *semicolon* (;) indicates a pause somewhat longer than that of a comma; the *colon* (:) a still longer pause; and the *period* (.) indicates the longest pause. The period is placed at the close of a sentence.

The *interrogation* point (?) denotes that a question is asked, as, *What do you see?*

An *exclamation* point (!) denotes wonder, grief, or other emotion.

A *parenthesis* ( ) includes words not closely connected with the other words of the sentence

Brackets or hooks [ ] are sometimes used for nearly the same purpose as the parenthesis, or to include some explanation.

A dash (—) denotes a sudden stop, or a change of subject, and requires a pause, but of no definite length.

A caret ( ) shows the omission of a word or letter, which is placed above the line, the caret being put below, thus, *give me* the *book*.

An apostrophe (') denotes the omission of a letter or letters, thus, lov'd, tho't.

A quotation is indicated by these points " " placed at the beginning and end of the passage.

The index ( ) points to a passage which is to be particularly noticed.

The paragraph (¶) denotes the beginning of a new subject.

The star or asterisk (*), the dagger (†), and other marks (‡, §, ‖), and sometimes letters and figures, are used to refer the reader to notes in the margin.

The diaeresis (¨) denotes that the vowel under it is not connected with the preceding vowel.

CAPITAL LETTERS.

A CAPITAL letter should be used at the *beginning* of a sentence. It should begin all proper *names of persons, cities, towns, villages, seas, rivers, mountains, lakes, ships,* &c. It should begin *every line of poetry,* a *quotation,* and often an important word.

The name or appellation of *God, Jehovah, Christ, Messiah,* &c., should begin with a capital.

The pronoun *I* and interjection *O* are always in capitals.

No. 151.—CLI.

THE LETTER **q** IS EQUIVALENT TO **k.** THE **u** FOLLOWING, AND NOT ITALICIZED, HAS THE SOUND OF **w**, ITALICIZED **u** IS SILENT.

ăq′ue duct	in ĭq′ui tŏus	lĭq′uid āte
ăq uĭ līne	lĭq′uid	liq uid ā′tion
an tĭq′ui ty	lĭq uor	ob lĭq′ui ty
ĕq′ui ty	lĭq ue fy̆	u bĭq ui ty
ĕq ui ta ble	liq ue fãe′tion	pĭq′nant
ĕq ui ta bly	lĭq′ue fī a ble	rĕq ui site
in ĭq′ui ty	lĭq ue fy̆ ing	req ui si′tion

IN THE FOLLOWING WORDS, **t** IS NOT SOUNDED.

chās ten	glĭs′ten	moist′en
hās ten	fȧst′en	ŏft′en
chrĭs ten	lĭst′en	sŏft′en

BÄR, LÀST, CÂRE, FALL, WHAT; HÊR, PREY, THÈRE; GET; BÎRD, MARÏNE; LIŊK;

EI AND IE WITH THE SOUND OF E LONG.

The letters *ei* and *ie* occur in several words with the same sound, that of long *e*, but persons are often at a loss to recollect which of these letters stands first. I have therefore arranged the principal words of these classes in two distinct tables, that pupils may commit them to memory, so that the order may be made as familiar as letters of the alphabet.

WORDS IN WHICH THE LETTER e STANDS BEFORE i.

çēil	disseīze	reçēive
çēiling	ēither	reçēipt
conçēit	invēigle	sēignior
conçēive	lēisure	sēine
deçēit	nēither	sēize
deçēive	obēisançe	sēizin
perçēive	obēisant	sēizūre

WORDS IN WHICH THE LETTER i STANDS BEFORE e.

achiēve	liēf	reliēve
griēve	liēge	retriēve
griēvançe	liēn	shiēld
griēvoŭs	miēn	shiēling
aggriēve	niēçe	shriēk
beliēf	piēçe	siēge
beliēve	piēr	thiēf
briēf	piērçe	thiēve
chiēf	priēst	tiēr
fiēf	reliēf	tiērçe
fiēld	reliēve	wiēld
fiēnd	repriēve	yiēld
brigadiēr	bombardiēr	finançiēr
breviēr	grenadiēr	cavaliēr
fiērçe	cannoniēr	çhevaliēr

SPELLING BOOK. 171

MOVE, SÓN, WOLF, FOOT, MOON, ÔR; RŬLE, PŬLL; EXIST; ç=K; ġ=J; ş=Z; CH=SH.

No 152.—CLII. WORDS DIFFICULT TO SPELL.

(1)

a bey′ançe
a çērb′i ty
āehe (āk)
ae quī ĕsçe′
ā′ er o naut
ăġ′ īle
ălms
ăm a teur′
ăm′ e thȳst
ān′ a lȳze
ān′ o dȳne
ān′ swer
a nŏn′ ȳ moŭs
an tïque′
ăq′ ue duet
āreh ān′ ġel
a skew′
ăv oir du poiş′
āȳe (ăi)

(2)

ban dăn′ à
bàsque (bàsk)
bāss′-vī ol
ba zäar′
bēa′ eon
beaux (bōz)
bïs′ euĭt (-kĭt)
bŏr′ ōugh
bọ′ şom
bruişe (brōoz)
bọu′ doir (-dwòr)

bū′ reau (-rō)
ealk (kawk)
ea prïçe′
ea rouşe′
ea tăs′ tro phe
eau′ eus
ehā′ os (kā′-)

(3)

chärġe′ a ble
ehĭ mē′ ra
çhĭv′ al ry
ehȳle (kīl)
ehȳme (kīm)
çïe′ a trïçe
elïque (kleek)
eō′ eōa (kō′ kō)
eōl′ league
eol lō′ quĭ al
eōmb (kōm)
eŏm′ plai şănçe
eŏn′ duĭt (-dīt)
eon dīgn′
eon va lĕsçe′
eon vey′
eorps (kōr)
eoun′ ter feĭt
eọu′ rĭ er
eoùrt′ e sy
eoùrte′ sy

(4)

eoŭş′ in
eōx′ eōmb

eroup
eruişe
erŭmb
erȳpt
euck′ ōō
eū′ po là
de fï′ cient
dĕm′ a gŏgue
dī′ a lŏgue
dĭl′ i ġençe
dis guişe′
dĭ shĕv′ el
dŏm′ i çīle
dough′ ty
drȧught (drȧft)

(5)

dȳs′ en tĕr y
dȳs pĕp′ sy
ēa′ gle
ef fer vĕsçe′
e lec trī′ cian
ĕl′ e phant
en çȳ elo pē′di à
en frăn′ chĭşe
e quĕs′ tri an
ĕr y sīp′ e las
ĕs′ pi on āġe
ex eru′ ci āte
ex hȧust′
fa tïgue′
fie tĭ′ tioŭs
flȧunt

flo rĕs′ çençe
for bāde′
fŏr′ eign er

(6)
frăn′ chĭse
frīe as see′
fûr′ lōugh
gāy′ e ty
gāuġe
ga zĕlle′
ghàst′ ly
ghōst (gōst)
ghoul (gōōl)
ġĭ rāffe′
glā′ çiēr (-seer)
gnärled
gō′ pher
gôr′ ġeoŭs (-jŭs)
gour′ mänd
gränd′ eūr
gro tĕsque′
guăr an tee′
guăr′ an ty
gŭd ġeon (-jŭn)

(7)
guīl′ lo tïne
guĭn′ ea (gĭn′ e)
guĭse (gīz)
gўp′ sy
heärth
hĕif′ er
hêir′ lōōm (âr′-)
hĕm′ i sphēre

hĕrb′ age
hī e ro glўph′ ie
hōax
hŏugh (hŏk)
how′ itz er
hŏs′ tler
hў′ a çĭnth
hў ē′ nà
hў pĕr′ bo là
īce′ bêrg
ĭch neū′ mon

(8)
ĭch thy ŏl′ o ġy
ī′ çi cle
ī′ dўl
ĭm′ be çīle
in dĭġ′ e noŭs
in ġēn′ ioŭs (-yŭs)
in trïgu′ er
ī′ o dīde
ī räs′ çi ble
jäs′ mïne
jĕop′ ard y
jāve′ lin
joùr′ ney
ju dī′ cioŭs
jūi′ çy
ka leī′ do seōpe
kăn ga rōō′
knĭck′ knack
lăb′ ў rinth

(9)
lär′ ўnx

lĭe′ o rĭçe
lieŭ tĕn′ ant
lĭ tĭġ′ ioŭs
lōath′ sòme
lŭnch′ eon (-ŭn)
lŭs′ cioŭs
lux ū′ ri ançe
lўnx
ma çhĭne′
Ma dēi′ rà
ma ġī′ cian
mal fēa′ sançe
ma lĭ′ cioŭs
ma līgn′
măn′ a cle
man eū′ ver
ma ny (mĕn′ ў)
mär′ riage

(10)
mēa′ ₅les
mē′ di ō cre
mêr′ can tīle
me rĭ′ no
mĕt a môr′phose
mī ăs′ mà
mī lĭ′ tiā
mĭll′ ion âire
mĭs′ chïef
mĭs′ sion a ry
moi′ e ty
mŏn′ eys
mŏn′ eyed (-ĭd)
môrt′ ġage

MŎVE. SŎN. WŎLF. FŎŎT. MŌŌN. ŎR ; RŲLE, PŲLL ; EXIST ; €=K ; Ġ=J ; S̯=Z ; Ç̣H=SH

môr′ tïse

mus täçhe′

mŭs′ çle (-sl)

mu s̯ï′ cian

mus quï′ to (-kē′-)

(11)

nă ph′ thȧ

ne gō′ ti āte

neigh′ bor hŏŏd

neū rȧl′ ġi ȧ

nȳmph

o bēi′ sançe

of fï′ cioŭs

ō′ gre

om nï′ scient

ō′ nȳx

op tï′ cian

ôr′ phan

pæ′ an

păġ′ eant ry

păn e ġȳr′ ie

păr′ a lȳze

păr′ ox ȳs̯m

pā′ tri äreh

pe eūl′ iar

(12)

pe lïsse′ (-lees′)

pēo′ ple

pe rïph′ e ry (-rif′-)

per nï′ cioŭs

per suāde′

phā′ e tŏn

phō′ to graph

phȳs̯′ ie

phȳs̯ i ŏg′ no my

phȳ s̯ïque′

pĭ ăz′ zȧ

pict ūr ĕsque′

pĭġ′ eon

pŏm′ açe

pôr′ phȳ ry

prāi′ rie

pre €ō′ cioŭs

pro dĭġ′ ioŭs

pro fĭ′ cien çy

(13)

prŏph′ e çy

pûr′ lieūs̯

pȳr o tĕeh′ nies

quȧr tĕtte′ (-ĕt′)

quay (kē)

quï′ nīne

quoit

răs̯p′ ber ry

rĕck′ on

ree on noi′ ter

re eruit′

rhăp′ so dy

rheu′ ma tis̯m

rhī nŏç′ e ros

rhu′ bärb

rhȳme

rō′ guish

ru tà-bā′ gȧ

(14)

sā′ ti ate (-shĭ-āt)

seal′ lop

seär la tï′ nȧ

sçĭm′ i ter

sçĭs̯′ s̯ors̯

seoûrġe

seru toire′ (-twôr′)

sçȳthe

sĕn′ sū al (-shu-al)

shrewd

sïl′ hou ĕtte (-ĕt)

slūiçe

sōl′ dier (-jer)

souve′ nïr

sŏv′ er eign

spē′ ciēs̯

sphē′ roid

sphĭnx

stăt ū ĕtte′ (-ĕt′)

(15)

stĕ′ re o tȳpe

stŏm′ aeh

sū per fï′ cial

sûr′ feĭt

tăb leaux′ (-lōz′)

tam bour ïne′

tĕeh′ nie al

tur quois̯′ (-koiz′)

tȳ′ phoid

ū nïque′

văl′ iant

va lïse′

vex ā′ tioŭs

vïl′ lain oŭs

BÄR, LÅST, CÂRE, FALL, WHAT; HÊR, PREY, THÉRE; ĜET; BÎRD, MARÎNE; LIŊK;

	[SPELLED.]	[PRONOUNCED.]
vĭ' ti āte (-shĭ-āt)		
wēird	āid'-de-camp	ād' de kŏng
wrĕs' tle	bay' ou	bī' oo
wrĕtch' ed	belles-let' tres	bel lĕt' tr
yącht (yŏt)	bĭl' let-dọux	bĭl' le doo
(16)	blanc-mange'	blo mŏnj'
băc cha nā' li an	brag ga dō' ci o	brag ga dō' shĭ o
brụ nĕtte' (-nĕt')	buoy' an cy	brooy' an cy
çhăn de liêr'	çham pāgne'	sham pān'
ca tärrh' (-tär')	clăp' bōard	klăb' bōrd
co quĕtte' (-kĕt')	caọut' choục	kōō' chook
cro quet' (-ke')	cärte-blånçhe'	kärt blänsh'
dĭs' tich (-tik)	(18)	
e clăt' (e klä')	cŏn' science	kŏn' shens
ĕl ee mŏs' ỹ na ry	da guĕrre' o tỹpe	da gĕr' o tīp
é lȳte' (ā līt')	däh' liä	d d' yâ
en nụï (ŏng nwē')	dé brïs'	dā brē'
et i quĕtte' (-kĕt')	dĭs çêrn' i ble	dĭz zĕrn' i bl
ĝhĕr' kin	en cōre'	ŏng kōr'
gỹm nā' si um	mād em oi sĕlle'	mād mŏạ zĕl
hĭc cough (-kŭp)	mag nē' si å	mag nē' zhi a
hō'sier y (hō'zher-)	men äg' e rie	men äzh' e rỹ
ĭd i o sỹn' era sy	mĭgn on ĕtte'	mĭn yoạ ĕt'
(17)	nau' se āte	naw' she āt
Ind' ian (-yạn)	pen i tĕn' tia ry	pĕn e tĕn sha rỹ
meer' sçhạum	pōrt măn' teaụ	pōrt măn tō
nạu' seoŭs (-shạs)	ren' dez vọus	rĕn' de voo
nĕph' ew (nĕf' yọo)	rĕs' tau rant	rĕs to rant
phlegm (-flĕm)	rīght' coŭs	rī' chus
psỹ çhŏl' o gy	ser' geant	sär' jent or sĕr'-
queue (kū)	sŭb' tle ty	sŭt' l tỹ
rā' ti o (-shĭ o)	vĭgn ĕtte'	vin yĕt'
săp o nā' ceoŭs	whort' le bĕr ry	hwûrt i bĕr rỹ

The Two Babylons
Alexander Hislop

You may be surprised to learn that many traditions of Roman Catholicism in fact don't come from Christ's teachings but from an ancient Babylonian "Mystery" religion that was centered on Nimrod, his wife Semiramis, and a child Tammuz. This book shows how this ancient religion transformed itself as it incorporated Christ into its teachings....

Religion/History   **Pages:**358

ISBN: *1-59462-010-5*   **MSRP** *$22.95*

QTY

The Go-Getter
Kyne B. Peter

The Go Getter is the story of William Peck.He was a war veteran and amputee who will not be refused what he wants. Peck not only fights to find employment but continually proves himself more than competent at the many difficult test that are throw his way in the course of his early days with the Ricks Lumber Company...

Business/Self Help/Inspirational   **Pages:**68

ISBN: *1-59462-186-1*   **MSRP** *$8.95*

QTY

The Power Of Concentration
Theron Q. Dumont

It is of the utmost value to learn how to concentrate. To make the greatest success of anything you must be able to concentrate your entire thought upon the idea you are working on. The person that is able to concentrate utilizes all constructive thoughts and shuts out all destructive ones...

Self Help/Inspirational   **Pages:**196

ISBN: *1-59462-141-1*   **MSRP** *$14.95*

Self Mastery
Emile Coue

Emile Coue came up with novel way to improve the lives of people. He was a pharmacist by trade and often saw ailing people. This lead him to develop autosuggestion, a form of self-hypnosis. At the time his theories weren't popular but over the years evidence is mounting that he was indeed right all along...

New Age/Self Help   **Pages:**98

ISBN: *1-59462-189-6*   **MSRP** *$7.95*

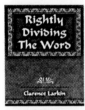

Rightly Dividing The Word
Clarence Larkin

The "Fundamental Doctrines" of the Christian Faith are clearly outlined in numerous books on Theology, but they are not available to the average reader and were mainly written for students. The Author has made it the work of his ministry to preach the "Fundamental Doctrines." To this end he has aimed to express them in the simplest and clearest manner..

Religion   **Pages:**352

ISBN: *1-59462-334-1*   **MSRP** *$23.45*

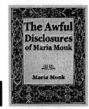

The Awful Disclosures Of
Maria Monk

"I cannot banish the scenes and characters of this book from my memory. To me it can never appear like an amusing fable, or lose its interest and importance. The story is one which is continually before me, and must return fresh to my mind with painful emotions as long as I live..."

Religion   **Pages:**232

ISBN: *1-59462-160-8*   **MSRP** *$17.95*

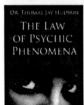

The Law of Psychic Phenomena
Thomson Jay Hudson

"I do not expect this book to stand upon its literary merits; for if it is unsound in principle, felicity of diction cannot save it, and if sound, homeliness of expression cannot destroy it. My primary object in offering it to the public is to assist in bringing Psychology within the domain of the exact sciences. That this has never been accomplished..."

New Age   **Pages:**420

ISBN: *1-59462-124-1*   **MSRP** *$29.95*

As a Man Thinketh
James Allen

"This little volume (the result of meditation and experience) is not intended as an exhaustive treatise on the much-written-upon subject of the power of thought. It is suggestive rather than explanatory, its object being to stimulate men and women to the discovery and perception of the truth that by virtue of the thoughts which they choose and encourage..."

Inspirational/Self Help   **Pages:**80

ISBN: *1-59462-231-0*   **MSRP** *$9.45*

Beautiful Joe
Marshall Saunders

When Marshall visited the Moore family in 1892, she discovered Joe, a dog they had nursed back to health from his previous abusive home to live a happy life. So moved was she, that she wrote this classic masterpiece which won accolades and was recognized as a heartwarming symbol for humane animal treatment...

Fiction   **Pages:**256

ISBN: *1-59462-261-2*   **MSRP** *$18.45*

The Enchanted April
Elizabeth Von Arnim

It began in a woman's club in London on a February afternoon, an uncomfortable club, and a miserable afternoon when Mrs. Wilkins, who had come down from Hampstead to shop and had lunched at her club, took up The Times from the table in the smoking-room...

Fiction   **Pages:**368

ISBN: *1-59462-150-0*   **MSRP** *$23.45*

The Codes Of Hammurabi And
Moses - W. W. Davies

The discovery of the Hammurabi Code is one of the greatest achievements of archaeology, and is of paramount interest, not only to the student of the Bible, but also to all those interested in ancient history...

Religion   **Pages:**132

ISBN: *1-59462-338-4*   **MSRP** *$12.95*

Holland - The History Of Netherlands
Thomas Colley Grattan

Thomas Grattan was a prestigious writer from Dublin who served as British Consul to the US. Among his works is an authoritative look at the history of Holland. A colorful and interesting look at history....

History/Politics   **Pages:**408

ISBN: *1-59462-137-3*   **MSRP** *$26.95*

The Thirty-Six Dramatic Situations
Georges Polti

An incredibly useful guide for aspiring authors and playwrights. This volume categorizes every dramatic situation which could occur in a story and describes them in a list of 36 situations. A great aid to help inspire or formalize the creative writing process...

Self Help/Reference   **Pages:**204

ISBN: *1-59462-134-9*   **MSRP** *$15.95*

A Concise Dictionary of Middle English
A. L. Mayhew
Walter W. Skeat

The present work is intended to meet, in some measure, the requirements of those who wish to make some study of Middle-English, and who find a difficulty in obtaining such assistance as will enable them to find out the meanings and etymologies of the words most essential to their purpose...

Reference/History   **Pages:**332

ISBN: *1-59462-119-5*   **MSRP** *$29.95*

www.bookjungle.com *email: sales@bookjungle.com fax: 630-214-0564 mail: Book Jungle PO Box 2226 Champaign, IL 61825*

QTY

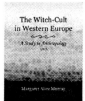

The Witch-Cult in Western Europe
Margaret Murray

The mass of existing material on this subject is so great that I have not attempted to make a survey of the whole of European "Witchcraft" but have confined myself to an intensive study of the cult in Great Britain. In order, however, to obtain a clearer understanding of the ritual and beliefs I have had recourse to French and Flemish sources...

Occult	Pages:308

ISBN: *1-59462-126-8*   MSRP *$22.45*

The Science Of Psychic Healing
Yogi Ramacharaka

This book is not a book of theories it deals with facts. Its author regards the best of theories as but working hypotheses to be used only until better ones present themselves. The "fact" is the principal thing the essential thing to uncover which the tool, theory, is used...

New Age/Health	Pages:180

ISBN: *1-59462-140-3*   MSRP *$13.95*

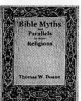

Bible Myths
Thomas Doane

In pursuing the study of the Bible Myths, facts pertaining thereto, in a condensed form, seemed to be greatly needed, and nowhere to be found. Widely scattered through hundreds of ancient and modern volumes, most of the contents of this book may indeed be found; but any previous attempt to trace exclusively the myths and legends...

Religion/History	Pages:644

ISBN: *1-59462-163-2*   MSRP *$38.95*

Tertium Organum
P. D. Ouspensky

A truly mind expanding writing that combines science with mysticism with unprecedented elegance. He presents the world we live in as a multi dimensional world and time as a motion through this world. But this isn't a cold and purely analytical explanation but a masterful presentation filled with similes and analogies...

New Age	Pages:356

ISBN: *1-59462-205-1*   MSRP *$23.95*

Advance Course in Yogi Philosophy
Yogi Ramacharaka

"The twelve lessons forming this volume were originally issued in the shape of monthly lessons, known as "The Advanced Course in Yogi Philosophy and Oriental Occultism" during a period of twelve months beginning with October, 1904, and ending September, 1905."

Philosophy/Inspirational/Self Help	Pages:340

ISBN: *1-59462-229-9*   MSRP *$22.95*

Ambassador Morgenthau's Story
Henry Morgenthau

"By this time the American people have probably become convinced that the Germans deliberately planned the conquest of the world. Yet they hesitate to convict on circumstantial evidence and for this reason all eye witnesses to this, the greatest crime in modern history, should volunteer their testimony..."

History	Pages:472

ISBN: *1-59462-244-2*   MSRP *$29.95*

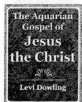

The Aquarian Gospel of Jesus the Christ
Levi Dowling

A retelling of Jesus' story which tells us what happened during the twenty year gap left by the Bible's New Testament. It tells of his travels to the far-east where he studied with the masters and fought against the rigid caste system. This book has enjoyed a resurgence in modern America and provides spiritual insight with charm. Its influences can be seen throughout the Age of Aquarius.

Religion	Pages:264

ISBN: *1-59462-321-X*   MSRP *$18.95*

QTY

Philosophy Of Natural Therapeutics
Henry Lindlahr

We invite the earnest cooperation in this great work of all those who have awakened to the necessity for more rational living and for radical reform in healing methods...

Health/Philosophy/Self Help	Pages:552

ISBN: *1-59462-132-2*   MSRP *$34.95*

A Message to Garcia
Elbert Hubbard

This literary trifle, A Message to Garcia, was written one evening after supper, in a single hour. It was on the Twenty-second of February, Eighteen Hundred Ninety-nine, Washington's Birthday, and we were just going to press with the March Philistine...

New Age/Fiction	Pages:92

ISBN: *1-59462-144-6*   MSRP *$9.95*

The Book of Jasher
Alcuinus Flaccus Albinus

The Book of Jasher is an historical religious volume that many consider as a missing holy book from the Old Testament. Particularly studied by the Church of Later Day Saints and historians, it covers the history of the world from creation until the period of Judges in Israel. It's authenticity is bolstered due to a reference to the Book of Jasher in the Bible in Joshua 10:13

Religion/History	Pages:276

ISBN: *1-59462-197-7*   MSRP *$18.95*

The Titan
Theodore Dreiser

"When Frank Algernon Cowperwood emerged from the Eastern District Penitentiary, in Philadelphia he realized that the old life he had lived in that city since boyhood was ended. His youth was gone, and with it had been lost the great business prospects of his earlier manhood. He must begin again..."

Fiction	Pages:564

ISBN: *1-59462-220-5*   MSRP *$33.95*

Biblical Essays
J. B. Lightfoot

About one-third of the present volume has already seen the light. The opening essay "On the Internal Evidence for the Authenticity and Genuineness of St John's Gospel" was published in the "Expositor" in the early months of 1890, and has been reprinted since...

Religion/History	Pages:480

ISBN: *1-59462-238-8*   MSRP *$30.95*

The Settlement Cook Book
Simon Kander

A legacy from the civil war, this book is a classic "American charity cookbook," which was used for fundraisers starting in Milwaukee. While it has transformed over the years, this printing provides great recipes from American history. Over two million copies have been sold. This volume contains a rich collection of recipes from noted chefs and hostesses of the turn of the century...

How-to	Pages:472

ISBN: *1-59462-256-6*   MSRP *$29.95*

My Life and Work
Henry Ford

Henry Ford revolutionized the world with his implementation of mass production for the Model T automobile. Gain valuable business insight into his life and work with his own auto-biography... "We have only started on our development of our country we have not as yet, with all our talk of wonderful progress, done more than scratch the surface. The progress has been wonderful enough but..."

Biographies/History/Business	Pages:300

ISBN: *1-59462-198-5*   MSRP *$21.95*

www.bookjungle.com email: sales@bookjungle.com fax: 630-214-0564 mail: Book Jungle PO Box 2226 Champaign, IL 61825

QTY

The Rosicrucian Cosmo-Conception Mystic Christianity *by Max Heindel*   ISBN: *1-59462-188-8*   **$38.95**
The Rosicrucian Cosmo-conception is not dogmatic, neither does it appeal to any other authority than the reason of the student. It is: not controversial, but is: sent forth in the, hope that it may help to clear...   New Age Religion Pages 646

Abandonment To Divine Providence *by Jean-Pierre de Caussade*   ISBN: *1-59462-228-0*   **$25.95**
"The Rev. Jean Pierre de Caussade was one of the most remarkable spiritual writers of the Society of Jesus in France in the 18th Century. His death took place at Toulouse in 1751. His works have gone through many editions and have been republished...   Inspirational Religion Pages 400

Mental Chemistry *by Charles Haanel*   ISBN: *1-59462-192-6*   **$23.95**
Mental Chemistry allows the change of material conditions by combining and appropriately utilizing the power of the mind. Much like applied chemistry creates something new and unique out of careful combinations of chemicals the mastery of mental chemistry...   New Age Pages 354

The Letters of Robert Browning and Elizabeth Barret Barrett 1845-1846 vol II   ISBN: *1-59462-193-4*   **$35.95**
by Robert Browning and Elizabeth Barrett   Biographies Pages 596

Gleanings In Genesis (volume I) *by Arthur W. Pink*   ISBN: *1-59462-130-6*   **$27.45**
Appropriately has Genesis been termed "the seed plot of the Bible" for in it we have, in germ form, almost all of the great doctrines which are afterwards fully developed in the books of Scripture which follow...   Religion Inspirational Pages 420

The Master Key *by L. W. de Laurence*   ISBN: *1-59462-001-6*   **$30.95**
In no branch of human knowledge has there been a more lively increase of the spirit of research during the past few years than in the study of Psychology, Concentration and Mental Discipline. The requests for authentic lessons in Thought Control, Mental Discipline and...   New Age Business Pages 422

The Lesser Key Of Solomon Goetia *by L. W. de Laurence*   ISBN: *1-59462-092-X*   **$9.95**
This translation of the first book of the "Lemegton" which is now for the first time made accessible to students of Talismanic Magic was done, after careful collation and edition, from numerous Ancient Manuscripts in Hebrew, Latin, and French...   New Age Occult Pages 92

Rubaiyat Of Omar Khayyam *by Edward Fitzgerald*   ISBN: *1-59462-332-5*   **$13.95**
Edward Fitzgerald, whom the world has already learned, in spite of his own efforts to remain within the shadow of anonymity, to look upon as one of the rarest poets of the century, was born at Bredfield, in Suffolk, on the 31st of March, 1809. He was the third son of John Purcell...   Music Pages 172

Ancient Law *by Henry Maine*   ISBN: *1-59462-128-4*   **$29.95**
The chief object of the following pages is to indicate some of the earliest ideas of mankind, as they are reflected in Ancient Law, and to point out the relation of those ideas to modern thought.   Religion History Pages 452

Far-Away Stories *by William J. Locke*   ISBN: *1-59462-129-2*   **$19.45**
"Good wine needs no bush, but a collection of mixed vintages does. And this book is just such a collection. Some of the stories I do not want to remain buried for ever in the museum files of dead magazine-numbers an author's not unpardonable vanity..."   Fiction Pages 272

Life of David Crockett *by David Crockett*   ISBN: *1-59462-250-7*   **$27.45**
"Colonel David Crockett was one of the most remarkable men of the times in which he lived. Born in humble life, but gifted with a strong will, an indomitable courage, and unremitting perseverance...   Biographies New Age Pages 424

Lip-Reading *by Edward Nitchie*   ISBN: *1-59462-206-X*   **$25.95**
Edward B. Nitchie, founder of the New York School for the Hard of Hearing, now the Nitchie School of Lip-Reading, Inc, wrote "LIP-READING Principles and Practice". The development and perfecting of this meritorious work on lip-reading was an undertaking...   How-to Pages 400

A Handbook of Suggestive Therapeutics, Applied Hypnotism, Psychic Science   ISBN: *1-59462-214-0*   **$24.95**
by Henry Munro   Health New Age Health Self-help Pages 376

A Doll's House: and Two Other Plays *by Henrik Ibsen*   ISBN: *1-59462-112-8*   **$19.95**
Henrik Ibsen created this classic when in revolutionary 1848 Rome. Introducing some striking concepts in playwriting for the realist genre, this play has been studied the world over.   Fiction Classics Plays 308

The Light of Asia *by sir Edwin Arnold*   ISBN: *1-59462-204-3*   **$13.95**
In this poetic masterpiece, Edwin Arnold describes the life and teachings of Buddha. The man who was to become known as Buddha to the world was born as Prince Gautama of India but he rejected the worldly riches and abandoned the reigns of power when...   Religion History Biographies Pages 170

The Complete Works of Guy de Maupassant *by Guy de Maupassant*   ISBN: *1-59462-157-8*   **$16.95**
"For days and days, nights and nights, I had dreamed of that first kiss which was to consecrate our engagement, and I knew not on what spot I should put my lips..."   Fiction Classics Pages 240

The Art of Cross-Examination *by Francis L. Wellman*   ISBN: *1-59462-309-0*   **$26.95**
Written by a renowned trial lawyer, Wellman imparts his experience and uses case studies to explain how to use psychology to extract desired information through questioning.   How-to Science Reference Pages 408

Answered or Unanswered? *by Louisa Vaughan*   ISBN: *1-59462-248-5*   **$10.95**
Miracles of Faith in China   Religion Pages 112

The Edinburgh Lectures on Mental Science (1909) *by Thomas*   ISBN: *1-59462-008-3*   **$11.95**
This book contains the substance of a course of lectures recently given by the writer in the Queen Street Hall, Edinburgh. Its purpose is to indicate the Natural Principles governing the relation between Mental Action and Material Conditions...   New Age Psychology Pages 148

Ayesha *by H. Rider Haggard*   ISBN: *1-59462-301-5*   **$24.95**
Verily and indeed it is the unexpected that happens! Probably if there was one person upon the earth from whom the Editor of this, and of a certain previous history, did not expect to hear again...   Classics Pages 380

Ayala's Angel *by Anthony Trollope*   ISBN: *1-59462-352-X*   **$29.95**
The two girls were both pretty, but Lucy who was twenty-one who supposed to be simple and comparatively unattractive, whereas Ayala was credited, as her Bombwhat romantic name might show, with poetic charm and a taste for romance. Ayala when her father died was nineteen...   Fiction Pages 484

The American Commonwealth *by James Bryce*   ISBN: *1-59462-286-8*   **$34.45**
An interpretation of American democratic political theory. It examines political mechanics and society from the perspective of Scotsman James Bryce   Politics Pages 572

Stories of the Pilgrims *by Margaret P. Pumphrey*   ISBN: *1-59462-116-0*   **$17.95**
This book explores pilgrims religious oppression in England as well as their escape to Holland and eventual crossing to America on the Mayflower, and their early days in New England...   History Pages 268

BOOK JUNGLE

Bringing Classics to Life

www.bookjungle.com *email: sales@bookjungle.com fax: 630-214-0564 mail: Book Jungle PO Box 2226 Champaign, IL 61825*

QTY

The Fasting Cure *by Sinclair Upton*   ISBN: *1-59462-222-1*   **$13.95**
In the Cosmopolitan Magazine for May, 1910, and in the Contemporary Review (London) for April, 1910, I published an article dealing with my experiences in fasting. I have written a great many magazine articles, but never one which attracted so much attention... New Age/Self Help/Health Pages 164

Hebrew Astrology *by Sepharial*   ISBN: *1-59462-308-2*   **$13.45**
In these days of advanced thinking it is a matter of common observation that we have left many of the old landmarks behind and that we are now pressing forward to greater heights and to a wider horizon than that which represented the mind-content of our progenitors... Astrology Pages 144

Thought Vibration or The Law of Attraction in the Thought World   ISBN: *1-59462-127-6*   **$12.95**
by William Walker Atkinson   *Psychology/Religion Pages 144*

Optimism *by Helen Keller*   ISBN: *1-59462-108-X*   **$15.95**
Helen Keller was blind, deaf, and mute since 19 months old, yet famously learned how to overcome these handicaps, communicate with the world, and spread her lectures promoting optimism. An inspiring read for everyone... Biographies/Inspirational Pages 84

Sara Crewe *by Frances Burnett*   ISBN: *1-59462-360-0*   **$9.45**
In the first place, Miss Minchin lived in London. Her home was a large, dull, tall one, in a large, dull square, where all the houses were alike, and all the sparrows were alike, and where all the door-knockers made the same heavy sound... Childrens Classic Pages 88

The Autobiography of Benjamin Franklin *by Benjamin Franklin*   ISBN: *1-59462-135-7*   **$24.95**
The Autobiography of Benjamin Franklin has probably been more extensively read than any other American historical work, and no other book of its kind has had such ups and downs of fortune. Franklin lived for many years in England, where he was agent... Biographies/History Pages 332

Name	
Email	
Telephone	
Address	
City, State ZIP	

☐ **Credit Card**   ☐ **Check / Money Order**

Credit Card Number	
Expiration Date	
Signature	

Please Mail to: Book Jungle
                  PO Box 2226
                  Champaign, IL 61825
or Fax to: 630-214-0564

ORDERING INFORMATION

web: *www.bookjungle.com*
email: *sales@bookjungle.com*
fax: *630-214-0564*
mail: *Book Jungle PO Box 2226 Champaign, IL 61825*
or PayPal *to sales@bookjungle.com*

Please contact us for bulk discounts

DIRECT-ORDER TERMS

20% Discount if You Order Two or More Books
Free Domestic Shipping!
Accepted: Master Card, Visa, Discover, American Express

Printed in the United Kingdom by
Lightning Source UK Ltd., Milton Keynes
141026UK00001B/72/A